THE ALCUIN CLUB, of which Dr. Walter Frere was for many years the President, exists for the object of promoting liturgical studies in general, and in particular a knowledge of the history and use of the Book of Common Prayer. Since its foundation in 1897 it has published over one hundred and twenty books and pamphlets.

The annual subscription is £3 and members of the Club are entitled to the publications of the current year *gratis.* Subscriptions and applications for membership and for the list of publications, should be sent to the Assistant Secretary.

President
The Right Reverend E.W. Kemp, D.D., Bishop of Chichester.

Committee
The Venerable G.B. Timms, M.A. (Chairman).
The Reverend A.M. Haig, B.D., A.K.C. (Honorary Secretary).
The Reverend Canon G.J. Cuming, D.D. (Editorial Secretary).
The Reverend P.F. Bradshaw, Ph.D.
The Reverend Canon J.D.C. Fisher, M.A., B.D.
The Very Reverend R.C.D. Jasper, D.D.
The Reverend C.E. Pocknee, A.K.C., D.Th., F.S.A.
The Reverend M. Tweedy, C.R.

Assistant Secretary and Treasurer
c/o St. Andrew's Vicarage, St. Andrew Street, London EC4 3AB. (Telephone 01-353-3544)

ALCUIN CLUB COLLECTIONS
No. 58

EUCHARIST AND INSTITUTION NARRATIVE

A study in the Roman and Anglican traditions
of the Consecration of the Eucharist
from the eighth to the twentieth centuries

Richard F. Buxton

Published for the Alcuin Club

MAYHEW-McCRIMMON
Great Wakering

First published in Great Britain in 1976 by
MAYHEW-McCRIMMON LTD
Great Wakering Essex England

ISBN 0-85597-101-0

Printed by the printing division of Mayhew-McCrimmon Ltd.

To
MICHAEL MORETON
and
JOHN THURMER

CONTENTS

INTRODUCTION   11

CHAPTER 1: THE THEOLOGY OF THE ROMAN
RITE OF THE EIGHTH CENTURY   15
- (i) The Canon   15
- (ii) The Secrets   23
- (iii) The Post-Communions   27
- (iv) The Ordo Romanus Primus   31
- (v) Commixture and Consecration   34

CHAPTER 2: EUCHARISTIC THEOLOGY AND
LITURGICAL PRACTICE IN THE
LATIN WEST IMMEDIATELY
PRIOR TO THE REFORMATION   41
- (i) The eucharistic theology of St Thomas
  Aquinas   41
- (ii) Changes in Liturgical Practice   45
- (iii) Provision for the correction of defects in the
  eucharistic celebration   46
- (iv) The state of eucharistic theology immediately
  prior to the Reformation   49

CHAPTER 3: CRANMER AND THE EDWARDINE
COMMUNION RITES   52
- (i) The Eucharistic Theology of the *Defence* and
  Answer   52
- (ii) The development of Cranmer's thinking about
  the eucharist   58
- (iii) The nature of Cranmer's mind   60
- (iv) The 1548 Order of Communion   61
- (v) The authorship of the 1549 Prayer Book   64
- (vi) The Great Parliamentary Debate   66
- (vii) Supplementary consecration   69
- (viii) Analysis of the 1549 Communion Rite   69
- (ix) Possible ways of interpreting the 1549 Rite   77
- (x) Reception of the 1549 Book   77
- (xi) Analysis of the 1552 Communion Rite   79
- (xii) External evidence concerning the 1552 Rite   81
- (xiii) Summary   85

CHAPTER 4: DOCTRINAL AND LITURGICAL
            DEVELOPMENTS IN THE PERIOD
            1559–1641   88
  (i)   The 1559 Prayer Book and the 39 Articles   88
  (ii)   The Johnson Case   89
  (iii) Bishop Jewel   92
  (iv)   Richard Hooker   94
  (v)   The Canons of 1604   95
  (vi)   Visitation Articles and Injunctions   100
  (vii) Irish and Scottish Canons   105
  (viii) The offertory prayer in the Coronation
         service   106

CHAPTER 5: ANGLICAN THEOLOGICAL WRITING
            ABOUT THE EUCHARIST IN THE
            PERIOD 1603–1662   110
  (i)   Sparrow's *Rationale*   110
  (ii)   L'Estrange's *Alliance of Divine Offices*   111
  (iii) Lancelot Andrewes   115
  (iv)   Thomas Morton   115
  (v)   John Bramhall   118
  (vi)   John Cosin   118
  (vii) Herbert Thorndike   121
  (viii) William Laud   124
  (ix)   Jeremy Taylor   128
  (x)   Summary   130

CHAPTER 6: THE PURITAN TRADITION OF
            EUCHARISTIC WORSHIP   133
  (i)   Knox's liturgy and subsequent developments   133
  (ii)   Cowper's draft   135
  (iii) The Westminster Directory   138
  (iv)   Baxter's Liturgy   139
  (v)   Puritan Exceptions to the Prayer Book
         Prayer of Consecration   141
  (vi)   Conclusions   142

CHAPTER 7: THE COMMUNION RITES OF 1637
            AND 1662   145
  (i)   The 1637 Rite   145
  (ii)   Suggestions for revision in England at the
         Restoration   148

(iii)	The 1662 Book	150
(iv)	Summary: The Caroline liturgical ideal	151

CHAPTER 8: DEVELOPMENTS AND THEOLOGICAL COMMENTARIES IN ENGLAND IN THE PERIOD 1662–1764 ... 153

(i)	The 1689 proposals	154
(ii)	'oblations' in the Prayer for the Church	156
(iii)	Thomas Comber	157
(iv)	William Nicholls and Thomas Bennet	158
(v)	Charles Wheatley	161
(vi)	John Johnson	169
(vii)	Robert Nelson	171
(viii)	Daniel Waterland	173

CHAPTER 9: THE RITES OF 1718 AND 1764 AND RELATED MATTERS ... 177

(i)	The 1718 Rite	178
(ii)	Thomas Brett's Commentary	183
(iii)	The 1764 Rite	188
(iv)	Concluding Comments	192

CHAPTER 10: THE LATIN RITE FROM TRENT TO THE PRESENT TIME ... 194

(i)	The Council of Trent and the Missal of 1570	194
(ii)	The Second Vatican Council and the Missal of 1970	196
(iii)	The correction of defects and supplementary consecration	200

CHAPTER 11. EUCHARISTIC CONSECRATION IN THE ANGLICAN CHURCH AFTER 1764 ... 203

(i)	Developments prior to 1960	203
(ii)	Developments since 1960	209
(iii)	Conclusions	213

CHAPTER 12: GENERAL CONCLUSIONS ... 215

APPENDIX: LITURGICAL PROVISION FOR SUPPLEMENTARY CONSECRATION ... 225

NOTES	230
BIBLIOGRAPHY	258
INDEX	271

INTRODUCTION

My interest in the subject matter of this book was first aroused when, in the course of writing a brief assessment of the English Series Two Communion rite, I noted that it made no provision for a second or supplementary consecration of any additional supply of the consecrated elements that might be needed, should that originally consecrated be insufficient to communicate all who wished to receive. A search of the literature revealed that no detailed study of supplementary consecration existed. Having undertaken such a study, the very interesting conclusion emerged that the churches of the Anglican Communion are the only churches that practise supplementary consecration, which reduces supplementary consecration itself to a matter of domestic concern to Anglicans.

Before proceeding further, it should be noted that supplementary consecration is defined as being an additional or further consecration within a single celebration of the eucharist whose purpose is to provide a fresh supply of consecrated elements for the benefit of intending communicants, and the term is used in precisely this sense and in this sense alone throughout this book. This practice is sometimes loosely referred to as 'reconsecration', but this is a misleading way of describing it, since it implies that something that has already been consecrated is being consecrated a second time, and its use is therefore to be avoided.

Nevertheless, though supplementary consecration itself is of limited interest, its study proved to be extremely illuminating of the way Anglican ideas about eucharistic consecration have developed over the centuries since the Edwardine Reformation, and of the intended consecration doctrines of the various Anglican Communion Rites. This is a subject that has not been thoroughly examined for more than thirty years, as a brief survey of the existing literature in the field will demonstrate.

The three standard text-books are F. Procter and W.H. Frere, *The Book of Common Prayer*,[1] the volume *Liturgy and Worship* edited by W.K. Lowther Clarke,[2] and G.J. Cuming's *A History of Anglican Liturgy*.[3] The volumes so far published of Horton Davies' *Worship and Theology in England*[4] are also useful. The specialised literature on Cranmer and the Edwardine Prayer Books is vast, and space forbids any general attempt to survey it here. The development of Anglican eucharistic theology in the period from 1559 onwards is very much more sparsely covered in existing published work. Of the major books in the field, C.W. Dugmore's *Eucharistic Doctrine in England from Hooker to Waterland*[5] does not relate theology to liturgical practice and use in any detail, being mainly concerned with the former, and in some respects his use of his material seems in need of re-examination. G.W.O. Addleshaw's *The High Church Tradition*[6] is concerned with every aspect of the theological and social ideals of the early seventeenth-century Caroline divines, and their life and churchmanship, which he clearly regards as the model for his own day. He regards the eighteenth-century High Churchmen as passive followers in the tradition of the men of a century earlier, whereas in fact there is the best part of a century of theological development between the two positions. Other works which attempt to cover the same field are H.R. Gummey's *The Consecration of the Eucharist*,[7] written in the early years of this century as an apologia for the American rite, and E.G.C.F. Atchley's *On the Epiclesis of the Eucharistic Liturgy and in the Consecration of the Font*,[8] which includes a brief chapter on the English divines of the sixteenth and seventeenth centuries. Although both these works note most of the important sources for the development of Anglican eucharistic theology in this period, both are dominated by the idea that it is the epiclesis that is the essential consecratory feature of the eucharistic prayer, and in consequence misunderstand the significance of their material. During the past decade, Anglicans the world over have been revising their eucharistic rites. The present moment therefore is surely a most appropriate one at which to attempt a fundamental reappraisal of Anglican eucharistic liturgical theology from its origins to the present time, and this book represents an attempt to do this.

As the title implies, I have concentrated on doctrines of

eucharistic consecration and how these relate to the liturgies and liturgical practices in question. The inter-related question of the eucharistic presence is also discussed. The further question of the eucharistic sacrifice is also mentioned, but for reasons of space much more briefly. Likewise the topic of Anglican Orders, which has considerable bearing on Anglican eucharistic theology, is not dealt with at all, having recently received definitive treatment in P.F. Bradshaw's *The Anglican Ordinal.*[9]

But of course the Anglican liturgical tradition did not arise and does not exist in a vacuum. It came into being as the English Church's response to the liturgical and theological crisis of the late Middle Ages. Therefore Anglican liturgy needs to be set in the wider context of the Western Latin Roman Rite. And indeed this latter rite, as the primary rite of Western Christendom, is a study of the first importance in itself. Therefore I have also attempted in this book to elucidate the history of how eucharistic consecration has been understood in this tradition from the classical period of its formulation in the seventh and eighth centuries right through to the present day and to set this alongside the Anglican.

Apart from a few incidental references, no attempt has been made to deal with the consecration theology of the Eastern Orthodox churches or of the churches of the continental Reformation. Both of these are major themes in themselves, and rather than include inadequate summaries of these topics, it has seemed better to omit them altogether.

Finally, I would like to express my gratitude to the many people who have helped in the preparation of this book. First to the Theology Department at Exeter University, for whom most of the original research was undertaken in the form of study for a doctorate, and in particular to the Revd Michael Moreton, my supervisor, for his constant help and encouragement during the time that I was preparing my thesis and for valuable help in the production of the book itself. Second to Canon John Thurmer, chancellor of Exeter Cathedral, sometime Lazenby chaplain to the University of Exeter, for the interest and support he gave me in it during the two years I was Assistant Chaplain. I would also like to thank the Alcuin Club for accepting it for publication, and particularly the Club's former honorary secretary, the Revd John Gunstone, for much encouragement and valuable advice. I must also thank the Revd Dr Geoffrey Willis for help received in the early stages of the work, particularly in connection with the Latin liturgy. I would also like to acknowledge Mr Roy Taperell, who first stimulated my interest in liturgical scholarship many years ago. I must also acknowledge with gratitude the help of my colleagues on the staff of Salisbury and Wells Theological College in allowing me to complete the book in the midst of the pressures of an extremely busy college life. I would like to thank Mr Jonathan Meyrick and Mr Richard Franklin, who between them checked and correlated the end-notes, Mr Keith Jones and Mrs Valerie Jones for compiling the index and checking and correcting the typescript, and Mrs JoAnn Phillips, Mrs Binnie Robson, Mrs Wendy Rusbridge, Mrs Linda Saunders, and Miss Vivien Simmonds, who between them typed the final draft of the book, also Miss Janet Sellars for invaluable help with reading the proofs. And last, but by no means least, I must express my gratitude to my longsuffering wife, who has lived with both thesis and book with patience and forbearance for far too long.

Richard F. Buxton

Salisbury, England.
December 1975.

CHAPTER ONE

The Theology of the Roman Rite of the Eighth Century

The fundamental source for this theology is the prayers of the rite, and in particular the Canon of the Mass and the variable Secret and Postcommunion prayers which always accompanied it. The ceremonial and manner in which the rite was celebrated are also important. For the former the text of the prayers in the Gelasian Sacramentary, and for the latter the *Ordo Romanus Primus* will be used in this study; though the precise natures of both of these documents are still under discussion, they may nevertheless be regarded as reliable source books for the fundamental theology of the Roman rite. Both date from the period of the seventh and eighth centuries, and it is this period that is the crucial one, for by this time the actual basic prayers of the rite were sufficiently formulated for the tradition to be considered in all essentials complete, while at the same time doctrinal developments had not begun to impose an alien theology upon it. In this period then, the prayers of the rite and the ceremonial that accompanied its celebration may speak for themselves; indeed it is only by allowing them to do this that the fundamental native theology of the Latin rite can be elucidated for what it was and is.

(i) The Canon

The Canon will be considered first of all, defined as beginning with the introductory dialogue and including the preface, as in the *Gelasianum*.[1] It consists of the following sections. Firstly, there is the introductory dialogue, just as it was later used in the 1570 missal, but without its initial greeting. Next follows the *Vere dignum* paragraph together with the *Sanctus;* the *Vere dignum* section is identical to that in the 1570 missal entitled the 'Common Preface'. The *Gelasianum* also contains a total of 55 other *Vere dignum* sections, proper to various occasions, most of which are associated with the great festivals (no fewer than eighteen belong to various occasions in Eastertide); but there are a few allocated to some saints' days, and the rest are associated with votive masses. The content of these *Vere dignum* sections is specifically concerned with the day to which they are proper. In passing it can be noted that the 'Leonine Sacramentary' (Verona 85) provides a *Vere dignum* with every mass set, whereas the 1570 missal had only eleven, so the tendency throughout history until modern times has been for proper prefaces to be reduced in number and limited to the most important occasions of the Church's year. The *Vere dignum* is followed by the *Sanctus* and *Benedictus.*

Thereafter, the various prayers of the canon follow one another in order. The *Te igitur* is basically a prayer of intercession for the whole church, with the pope and the bishop mentioned by name. But it starts as an offering prayer, praying for the acceptance and blessing of 'haec dona, haec munera, haec sancta sacrificia inlibata' (accompanied by five crossings, the only place where such occur in the Canon of the *Gelasianum)* and Jungmann considers that in the original version of the Roman Canon the *Quam oblationem* followed 'inlibata' immediately, and that it was only from the beginning of the fifth century onwards that the basically intercessory material from 'imprimis . . .' to the end of the *Hanc igit·ur* began to be inserted.[2] This view, if correct, (and even if it is not, the same is true of the language of the opening of the *Te igitur*) associates this section of the prayer with the offering of the sacrifice.

Next follows the *Memento Domine,* a prayer for the salvation of all those present at the celebration, who offer to God 'hoc sacrificium laudis', a phrase whose significance will be discussed further later on. In the *Gelasianum* it was simply a prayer for those present; the phrase 'pro quibus tibi offerimus' widens the scope of the prayer to include others than those present and for whom those present pray and offer; this is a later addition which:

made its first appearance in several manuscripts of the Gregorian Sacramentary prepared by Alcuin, and after the tenth century speedily became almost universal.[3]

It should be noted that in both these versions, the older Gelasian one and the later Gregorian one, it is the whole people − 'et omnium circumadstantium' − who pray and offer, not just the priest. This is evidence that the milieu in which the Canon evolved was one which emphasised the corporate nature of the church and its liturgical offering. Interestingly, the *Gelasianum* has preserved a proper *Memento Domine* for the 3rd Sunday in Lent, the scrutiny mass for those who were to be baptized at Easter. This includes a special phrase praying for them, and orders them to be mentioned by name.[4]

Next follows the *Communicantes,* the veneration of the Saints and invoking of God's aid through their prayers and merits. The *Gelasianum* also has proper *Communicantes* for the same six major feasts as the 1570 missal; the Maundy Thursday one simply inserts into the common form after 'Communicantes': 'et diem sacratissimum caelebrantes, quo traditus est dominus noster Jesus Christus: sed'. It is unchanged in 1570; in the *Gelasianum* it also serves for the mass for the reconciliation of a penitent on the point of death.[5] Of the other five, that for Easter is unchanged in 1570, those for Christmas and Ascension Day are very slightly different, and those for Epiphany and Pentecost rather more different.

Then follows the *Hanc igitur,* with its plea for the acceptance of the eucharistic oblation – 'oblationem servitutis nostrae' must be taken in this sense – and its prayer for safety and salvation; once again it is the offering of the whole body, the 'servitutis nostrae', that is stressed. The *Gelasianum* contains 42 proper *Hanc igitur* paragraphs apart from the common one. Of these, all are proper to votive masses, except that for Easter and Pentecost and that for Maundy Thursday; and even that for Easter and Pentecost is concerned with the newly baptized, so one can say that the proper *Hanc igitur* paragraphs are a way of directing the intention of the particular mass in question. Only those for Easter, Pentecost and Maundy Thursday survived into the 1570 missal, though the Pontifical still retained a special one for the consecration of a bishop.[6]

This is followed by the *Quam oblationem,* which prays that God will approve the sacrifice 'ut nobis corpus et sanguis fiat dilectissimi filii tui . . .'. This is followed by the institution narrative in a form which is not a direct copy of any of the biblical texts, but is a composite form with two extra-scriptural insertions peculiar to it. Next follow three clauses concerned with the offering of the sacrifice. The first, the *Unde et memores* is probably the most crucial part of the prayer in a consideration of the theology of the eucharistic sacrifice underlying the Canon; this prayer, having in mind the saving events of Christ's passion, resurrection, and ascension, continues:

offerimus praeclare maiestati tuae de tuis donis ac datis hostiam puram, hostiam sanctam, hostiam inmaculatam, panem sanctam vitae aeternae et calicem salutis perpetuae.

Once again the verb is in the plural, stressing that the offering is a corporate one of the whole church. This is followed by the *Supra quae,* which prays that God will accept this sacrifice as he did those of Abel, Abraham, and Melchisedech; and then the *Supplices te* asking that 'haec perferri', these things may be carried up to the altar on high by the hands of the holy angel, that all who partake of the body and blood of Christ at the earthly altar may receive 'omni benedictione coelesti et gratia'. There is no memorial of the dead in the text of the Canon of the *Gelasianum,* so this is followed immediately by the *Nobis quoque* which is a prayer for forgiveness and fellowship with the saints. The Canon concludes with a kind of double doxology, the first part of which is somewhat obscure in meaning but seems to imply the work of God in sanctifying, blessing, and giving life in the sacramental gifts; in this connection it should be noted that anciently the blessing of other material gifts sometimes took place at this point (for example, milk and honey in the Pentecost mass in the Leonine Sacramentary[7] and oil for anointing the sick in the Maundy Thursday chrism mass in the *Gelasianum,*[8] which latter practice was still retained in the missal of 1570). The second doxology is a doxology pure and simple, an ascription of praise to the Trinity.

It should also be noted that the Canon in the *Gelasianum* is written out without any rubrics or suggestions of ceremonial directions, except for the five crosses in the *Te igitur.*

From the doctrinal point of view of sacrifice, consecration, and presence, undoubtedly the important parts of the Canon are the beginning of the *Te igitur,* the intention of the *Hanc igitur,* and then the whole of the section from the *Quam oblationem* to the end of the *Supplices te;* from the point of view of the Canon's understanding of the eucharistic action, it is this latter long section that is crucial.

Having looked at the structure of the Canon, it is now possible to analyse its theology, and this can be done without a detailed study of the history of how it developed into the form in which it occurs in the *Gelasianum,* which is a complex and, in some respects, still unresolved problem. For it is certain that it grew and evolved and developed in the period of approximately 350-700, and thus is the genuine expression of the original native eucharistic theology of the Roman church.

To consider first the doctrine of sacrifice implicit in the Canon. The first part of the *Te igitur* refers to the eucharistic gifts as 'dona', 'munera', and 'sancta sacrificia inlibata'; that it is primarily the gifts that are referred to here, is surely indicated by the crossings. *Sacrificium* and *munus* are both words that refer to the offering of sacrifice; their precise meaning will be analysed in more detail in the discussion of the vocabulary of the Secret prayers. The use of *donum* in the canon would seem to be a specific reference to the offering of the natural gifts of bread and wine to God, which in themselves are God's gifts to us. The *Memento Domine* refers to 'hoc sacrificium laudis', and this and other very similar phrases also occur in the Secret prayers in contexts that make it quite clear that it is the eucharistic sacrifice that is being referred to, so its use in the Canon is to be seen as a reference to the whole sacrificial action of the eucharist. The *Hanc igitur* prays for the acceptance of 'oblationem servitutis nostrae' and *oblatio* is also one of the words most commonly used in the Secret prayers. Here in the *Hanc igitur* it no doubt has the same double sense of the offering of the eucharistic gifts and the eucharistic rite. The whole of the *Hanc igitur* could stand by itself quite simply as a Secret prayer, consisting as it does of an offering of the sacrifice coupled with prayer for specific ends.[9] The *Quam oblationem* (the second use of this word in the Canon) simply prays that God will make the sacrifice acceptable in every way. This emphasis on the divine action in the sacrifice is interesting and has its counterpart in the *Supplices te.* One of the points about the *Quam oblationem,* is that it makes this simple request with a rich and sonorous tautology of language; the vocabulary used is larger than strictly necessary to express the range of ideas conveyed. The second half of the *Quam oblationem* is concerned with the question of the presence, so it will be discussed later. The *Unde et memores* commences by making the memorial of Christ's passion, resurrection, and ascension, and then offers the sacrifice; the word used is *hostia,* used thrice with a different adjective each time. Here once again the tendency is to express an idea with a rich variety of language. The offering of the *hostia* is introduced with a reference to the 'tuis donis ac datis', which is a quite explicit use of *donum* in the double sense mentioned above. *Hostia* is a word whose underlying basic meaning is 'sacrificial victim'. The remaining two sections of the sacrificial section of the canon add just one idea of importance, namely the linking of the eucharistic sacrifice with the worship at the heavenly altar.

Thus in terms of vocabulary, the Canon uses a variety of words with an underlying and basic sacrificial meaning. In view of later developments and controversies it is important to note that there is no difference in range of terminology or ideas between the sacrificial language used in those sections of the Canon occurring before the institution narrative and those after it. Thus the Gelasian Canon sees the eucharist as the sacrifice that the Church offers to God through which salvation and other gifts necessary to man's well-being are mediated. The further question arises here as to how the Canon links its concept of the eucharistic sacrifice to that of Calvary. The answer to this is to be found mainly in the implications of the *Unde et memores,* the only part of the prayer actually to mention Christ's passion (apart from the introduction to the institution narrative, but the prime purpose of this is to provide the chronological setting for the account of the institution of the eucharist). Now, as described above, the *Unde et memores* starts by remembering, by commemorating the passion, resurrection, and ascension, and then, sequential to the making of this memorial, offers the eucharist.

This basic structure of 'making the memorial . . . we offer' would seem to be a common feature of all the great liturgies, as they emerged in the fourth century with roots going back earlier, as a glance at the texts collected by A. Hänggi and I. Pahl[10] will show.

In the Gelasian Canon itself, whatever the precise strength and meaning of 'memores' (and the danger of trying to analyse this too exactly would be to read a greater subtlety into it than existed in the minds of those who used the Canon in those early centuries), the meaning of the whole clause is surely reasonably clear. By, through, and because of the reconciliation of God and man at the cross, man has access to God in worship, and the eucharist is the liturgical expression of this act of reconciliation; that is, the Church offers the eucharistic sacrifice to God, and by it salvation and grace are mediated. Further, just as the eucharist was instituted by Christ in the context of his coming passion, so the Canon, by placing the institution narrative within the sacrificial paragraphs of the canon, preserves the same context liturgically. Finally, the *Supplices te* emphasises the link between the earthly worship of the eucharist and the continuing worship at the heavenly altar, and contains ideas that no doubt have some dependence on the Epistle to the Hebrews. Thus at these three points the link between Calvary and the eucharist, and the dependence of the latter upon the former, is expressed; but to ask for a more precise definition than these prayers supply in this way, is to ask for what is not to be had, for the relationship between Calvary and the eucharist was not seen as a problem in this era, and thus greater definition was not needed.

The problems of the nature of the eucharistic presence and of the view of consecration implied by the Canon can be dealt with much more shortly. References that can be taken as specifically applying to the Canon's understanding of the presence occur at three points during it. The first of these is in the *Quam oblationem,* the phrase 'ut nobis corpus et sanguis fiat . . .'. It is interesting to note that in the version of this prayer that Ambrose quotes, the equivalent phrase reads 'quod est figura corporis et sanguinis . . .,[11] which recalls the use of 'αντιτυπα in the *Liturgy of St Basil.* Probably, given the variety of linguistic usage in this matter at that time, these two Latin versions can be considered equivalent in meaning. The second phrase concerned with the presence comes in the *Supplices te:*

ut quotquot ex hac altaris participatione sacrosanctum filii tui corpus et sanguinem sumpserimus, omni benedictione caelesti et gratia repleamur: per.

This, it should be noted, assumes a real reception of the body and blood of Christ, and prays that grace might be received because of this; it does not pray for grace to receive worthily the body and blood of Christ. The third is the beautiful phrase in the *Unde et memores* 'panem sanctum

21

vitae et calicem salutis perpetuae', a phrase which has echoes in a few of the post-communion prayers, and which implies a belief in the objective holiness of the elements, while at the same time still referring to them as 'bread' and 'cup'. As with the sacrificial language, there is no change in terminology on this point after the institution narrative. Thus the Canon implies a real reception of Christ through the eucharist; that is, that it really is through the eucharistic action that Christ is present and received. Furthermore, this reception is objectively associated with the elements. Yet the emphasis is on the dynamic action of the eucharist, rather than on any kind of static definition of the presence. Thus the doctrine of the presence that the Canon implies is incapable of precise definition beyond the above considerations, because the Canon does not see the eucharist primarily in terms of presence, but as an action; and the quest for a definition of the presence should not be pressed beyond this point.

The question of consecration can be dealt with even more briefly. The concept of the eucharist in the Canon is one of the offering of sacrifice to God, and simultaneously and consequently receiving the body and blood of Christ, and grace unto salvation. The prayers of the Canon conceive of this as a single unitary action; therefore, to try and isolate from them a separate theology of consecration, let alone a moment of consecration, would be a fundamental mistake of method, for it would be to look for what is not to be found.

But at each mass, the Canon was and is accompanied by a variable secret and post-communion prayer. These prayers evolved at the same time as the Canon and are an integral part of the same liturgical tradition, and an analysis of these serves to further illuminate the theology of that tradition.

Some few years ago, Sr M.P. Ellebracht published a detailed study of the form and vocabulary of these prayers,[12] and much of what follows is based on her work.

This study is not much concerned with the literary style of these prayers, but principally with their theological meaning; and for this, two factors are of prime importance: their vocabulary, and the way this vocabulary is used in building up the meaning of the individual prayers. Nevertheless, there are a few points connected with style that it is useful to bear in mind in a study of their vocabulary and meaning. The first is that these prayers (in common with the collect that completes the mass set of celebrant's prayers in every case) originate from a long tradition of improvisation which in the course of time was formalised into a quite distinct stylistic and liturgical tradition. This means that many of them exhibit great similarity in terms of language and content. The earliest of the prayers probably date back as far as the late fourth century, the earliest period at which the Christian liturgical tradition would have felt free to adopt into its own use pagan sacral terms. From this time onwards, both vocabulary and style developed and consolidated themselves into a very stable and conservative tradition, for two reasons, the inherent conservatism of the Roman liturgical tradition, and because for educational and philological reasons there existed a continuity between the Latin of late antiquity and medieval Latin. The consequence of this is that it is usually not possible to determine from the language and style of a given prayer the date of its composition.

(ii) The Secrets

The Secret Prayers are basically offering-prayers, and all contain a noun describing and referring to the thing that is offered, and most have some kind of offering verb as well. Structurally they first offer the sacrifice, and usually follow this with a clause praying for some benefit to result from the sacrifice. Certain nouns are used again and again to describe what is offered, the commonest being *munus, oblatio, sacrificium, hostia* and *mysterium; sacramentum* also occurs, though less frequently. The function of the Secret prayers is to make articulate the offering of the bread and wine, and it is to this that these words in the first instance apply. It is worth analysing their meaning in a little more detail.

The easiest way to translate *munus* is 'gift' (it usually occurs as 'munera' i.e. 'gifts' in these prayers), though it also has the sense of 'official service, or ritual act'. In profane Latin it was originally a legal, rather than a religious, term. Thus, while the most obvious translation of this word as used in these prayers is 'gift' or 'offering', with reference to the bread and wine just placed on the altar, its etymology would also suggest that it can be taken as referring to the eucharistic action as a whole.[13]

The word *oblatio* is a late Latin formulation from *offerre*, and in the main its use is limited to eucharistic prayers. It means both the offered gifts and the ritual action.[14]

Sacrificium is a word with a somewhat broader meaning. In pagan Latin it meant any kind of sacrifice. In these prayers it means simply the eucharist as such. Nevertheless, within this, four different shades of meaning can be identified; first, a reference to the unique sacrifice of Calvary; secondly, to the gifts of bread and wine (with sometimes a link to the Christian's own sacrifice of fasting); thirdly, to the inner spiritual significance of the sacrifice; and fourthly, in post-communions, to the sacred species received in communion, though this latter usage is rare.[15]

The word *hostia* basically means a victim, and its use as applied to the eucharistic action is a constant reminder that this was seen as sacrificial. This word has a definite ritual and sacramental character, but the limitation of its meaning to the bread offered for sacrifice, or to the consecrated species of bread is a much later development.[16]

The word *mysterium* acquired a general meaning in Christian Latin as 'a revealed mystery of the faith', but in liturgical use it was specifically tied to the eucharist, where 'the whole cultic action of the eucharist is concretely included in this word', particularly when it is used in the Secrets.[17] The meaning of *sacramentum* is almost synonymous with that of *mysterium.*[18]

Thus it will be seen that all the above nouns, when used in the Secret prayers, seem to have considerable similarities in meaning; all can refer to both the eucharistic action and the eucharistic gifts. It is probably fair to draw the conclusion that both shades of meaning are usually present in most cases, and that the gifts and the action are to be seen as a unity in this liturgical tradition. The similarity in meaning between all these various terms tends to suggest that they were used more or less interchangeably in the singular or plural forms, and that the word used in any particular prayer depends as much on literary considerations as on theological ones. This impression is reinforced by the considerable number of Secrets in which more than one of these words occurs. An interesting variant from the above is the use of the phrases 'sacrificium laudis' and 'sacrificium laetantes' in prayers 1650 and 824 respectively, the first of which is from a requiem and the second from the mass for the feast of St Agnes. In both cases the reference is quite clearly to the sacrifice offered in the eucharist, which is an interesting contrast to the use Cranmer and the Reformers made of phrases like 'sacrifice of praise'.

Turning to the offering verbs, there are a much greater number of words in use, and some of the Secrets do not contain an actual offering verb at all. Four of the most commonly occurring verbs are *suscipere, offerre, deferre,* and *immolare. Suscipere* means 'to receive well, to take up', and in these prayers it is applied to God, and thus has the general sense of asking him to be pleased with the offerings.[19] *Offerre,* as noted above, is linked with *oblatio.*[20] Sometimes in the Secrets the context makes it clear that the primary connection is with the material gifts, but more usually the context is such as to make it clear that it is the whole eucharistic action that is referred to. *Deferre* has not become a technical term for the offering of sacrifice to the extent that *offerre* has[21] and though in many of the secrets it is used very similarly to *offerre,* it is not so definite in its sacrificial reference. *Immolare,* on the other hand, definitely means to offer sacrifice, and Sr Ellebracht isolates two factors as leading to its use in these prayers: firstly, in conjunction with *hostia,* its strict classical feeling of 'to immolate by slaughtering';[22] and secondly, the frequent use of Ps. 115.17 in the Latin rite.[23] Of the verbs used less frequently, some have the definite sense of performing a ritual and sacrificial action, for example *celebrare* and *gerere;* some have ideas of reconciliation and appeasement, for example *placere, complacere,* and *propitiare.* A third group ask God to look upon the sacrifice or to regard it with favour, *adsumere, accipere, respicere,* and *intendere;* and some of the others are of more general meaning and application. Thus there is a considerable variation of language and ideas behind all the various verbs by which the Secrets commend the sacrifice to God, but the whole could be summed up as many variations on a single theme which comes unmistakably through the vast majority of these prayers, namely that in the eucharist an action of sacrifice and reconciliation is being offered to God.

Having considered the vocabulary of these prayers, the wider issue of their theology may now be considered. It has already been noted that one of their characteristics is the use of a comparatively large number of words to express very much the same ideas over and over again. The same tendency is to be noted in the prayers themselves; basically similar meanings are expressed in a variety of different ways. But this variety is not great enough to obscure the very definite unity of theology that exists in them all. A secret that is both typical in its theological outlook and simple and short is 1236, which comes from *Alia Missa* 15 of *Liber Tertius:*

Haec munera, quaesumus, domine, quae oculis tuae maiestatis offeremus, salutaris nobis esse concede: per.

The sacrifice is offered, and an end, a desired result is prayed for, which can be either spiritual or material or both. It is also clear that the Secret not only makes articulate the meaning of the offertory, but embraces within its scope the whole eucharistic action. Added force is given to this latter point from the fact that the celebrant proceeds straight from the Secret into the introductory dialogue to the Canon; this is as true today as it was when the *Ordo Romanus Primus* was compiled,[24] and the Secret in a sense almost becomes part of the Canon.

In trying to summarise the overall theology of the Secrets, it may be said that they express the offering of sacrifice to God by which spiritual and temporal benefits are prayed for. This sacrifice, and thus the intention of the Secret prayers, refers to both the offering of the bread and wine (indeed this should probably be taken in an even wider sense to include gifts of money and other offerings in kind as well) and to the whole eucharistic rite, these two factors really being inseparable in their thought; this sacrifice is in fact the Church's eucharistic worship, by which God and man are reconciled together, and the needs of believers satisfied. The question arises as to what relationship was understood between the sacrifice of the eucharist and the sacrifice of Calvary, and here it must be stated that very few of the Secrets have any specific mention, or anything that can really be construed as such, of either Calvary or Christ at all. One of the few that do is prayer 1196, from *Alia Missa* 5 of *Liber Tertius.* The prayer reads as follows:

Concede nobis haec, quaesumus, domine, frequentare mysteria, quia quociens huius hostiae commemoracio caelebratur, opus nostrae redempcionis exercitur: per.

Exactly how best to express the meaning of this in English could perhaps be a matter of some argument, but Sr

Ellebracht regards the following as satisfactory:

for as often as this sacrifice of commemoration is offered, the work of our redemption is performed;[25]

that is, the prayer is to be understood as expressing the doctrine that the eucharist is a commemorative sacrifice of Calvary; but even to say this, is really to restate the problem rather than to solve it. The word 'commemoracio' was usually used of the memorial celebration of the feast of martyrs; it is only used in reference to the eucharistic sacrifice in this prayer. Perhaps one can express its meaning thus: by this memorial celebration and our part in it, Christ's redeeming work is carried out in us, a theology completely in harmony with that already seen in the Canon.

(iii) The Post-Communions

Just as the Secrets look forward to the benefits of the eucharist, so do the post-communions look back to what has been received, and some attention will next be devoted to these. In terms of vocabulary they usually contain a noun that refers to the sacramental gift received, and quite often a verb that describes the action of receiving, though many of these prayers contain no such verb. There is also a considerable number of post-communion prayers that contain no specific eucharistic reference at all.

Of the nouns that refer to what has been received, much the most common was *sacramentum,* followed by *mysterium, munus,* and *donum.* Other words such as *sacrificium* and *sancta* also occur occasionally. Phrases such as 'coelestis panis' and 'Corpus et Sanguis' also occur, but only in a very few of the prayers. Thus many of the same words occur here as do in the Secrets, though they are often used in a subtly different sense. For instance *sacramentum,* though it does not lose its sense of ritual and sacred action, does often seem to refer especially to the elements received in communion.[26] The same is true of *mysterium,* where its use with this emphasis shows that communion was seen as but one of the inseparable parts of the eucharistic action, an understanding of it that had been more or less lost completely by the time of the high Middle Ages.[27] *Munus* used here stands for nourishment, for the spiritual food received, but in the context that food so received has been eaten as part of an official public service, thus stressing the corporate nature of the liturgy, and that the gifts are received as part of this.[28] The sense of *donum* as meaning sharing or participating in the eucharist is obvious here. *Coelestis panis* and *Corpus et Sanguis* have an obvious reference to the presence of Christ in the elements received (though even here the wider sense of the eucharistic action cannot be excluded). What seems surprising is not that they are used in post-communions, but that they are used so infrequently in them. Thus analysis of the noun-vocabulary of the post-communion confirms that the eucharistic theology of the era that produced them saw the whole service as a single and indivisible action; the post-communions sum up both the effects of communion and the whole rite, because these are not really separable from one another but are both part of the same whole. The various verbs used in these prayers add little to the above discussion; for the most part they simply express the action of receiving, both the actuality of reception and the benefits thereof.

Considering these prayers as a species, one can say first of all that they assume actual reception of communion on the part of all, and clearly the general style of these prayers must date from a period well before the decline in lay communion in general and reception of the chalice in particular; though it is to be noted that this literary style continued to be used in prayers composed in later times when congregational communion was rare. The post-communions are mainly prayers for benefits of one sort or another, and all pre-suppose that real spiritual food does come by reception. They also suggest that reception of communion availed for both spiritual and temporal needs, and here there is a parallel with the Secrets which offered the sacrifice for both. Most of these prayers have a very simple structure; a brief phrase describing the reception of the gifts is followed by a single petition asking for some blessing consequent thereupon. A typical example is 1212 (from *Alia Missa* 9 of *Liber Tertius*), which prays that the sacraments may advance us towards our eternal redemption:

Sumptis, domine, caelestibus sacramentis ad redemptionis aeternae, quaesumus, proficiat augmentum: per.

The use of the plural is interesting here; it doubtless reflects the existence of the eucharistic gifts under two species, though certainly not a belief that the eucharist was two separate sacraments. The language of these prayers is literary and devotional, not that of precise definition.

These prayers assume that the liturgical action and the spiritual reality are one and the same; it is by the first that the second comes to be. All the prayers witness to this belief, but 1093 (from *Orationes in Natale Plutrimorum Sanctorum*) expresses it particularly clearly:

... ut quae temporali caelebramus accione, perpetua salvacione capiamus: per.

That which is ritually performed in time is to be received to eternal salvation. These prayers suppose that the spiritual and temporal benefits really are the consequence of the ritual action of the eucharist.

That much is clear: what is much less clear is the doctrine they teach about the presence of Christ in the eucharist. A prayer that perhaps has some bearing on this question is 1051, which comes from a set of prayers headed *In XII Lecciones Die Sabbati.* This reads as follows:

Perficiant in nobis ... tua sacramenta quod continent, ut quae nunc specie gerimus, rerum veritate capiamus: per.

This prayer at least points to some kind of reality present in the eucharistic action and received, but it would probably be unwise to attempt to analyse its meaning much further than this. The rarity of references to the Body and Blood and of phrases such as 'coelestis panis' has already been noted; and this in itself is a further indication that the emphasis of these prayers is on the dynamic action of the eucharist rather than any static ideas about the presence of Christ in it. But a few prayers do contain such phrases, for example 112, which comes from the Monday of the first week in Lent:

Quaesumus, omnipotens deus, ut inter eius numeremur membra, cuius corpore communicamus et sanguinem: per.

This prayer certainly witnesses to a belief in a real reception of the body and blood of Christ, but beyond this it could be used with a good conscience by people holding to a wide variety of opinions on this subject. A post-communion containing references to the heavenly bread is 166, from *Secunda Dominica in Quadragesima:*

Refecti, domine, panae caelesti, ad vitam, quaesumus, nutriamur aeternam: per.

Here the emphasis of the prayer is on the spiritual effect of the communion, not on the nature of the presence. Another is prayer 1330 (from *Alia Missa* 27 of *Liber Tertius*):

Spiritum nobis, domine, tuae caritatis infunde, ut quos uno caelesti pane satiasti, una facias pietate concordes: per.

Here the desired spiritual effect is paralleled with being satisfied with the heavenly bread, and once again the emphasis would seem to be on the action rather than the presence. Thus the conclusion of this study has to be that these prayers witness to no particular definition or understanding of the nature of the eucharistic presence; most of them never even refer to it. Rather, the whole stress of these prayers is on the reality of the eucharistic action and of the benefits received therefrom.

An overall summary of the theology of the prayers of this eucharistic tradition can now be given. They see the eucharist as an action, as a sacrifice, as the sacrifice by which the reconciliation of God and man is expressed; the gifts, the offering, the whole of the action and communion are seen as an inseparable unity, and the liturgical action and the inner spiritual reality are seen as one and the same. It is the whole of this, in which all are seen as fully involved and fully part, that avails for the spiritual and temporal needs of the believers (and by extension to requiems, for the departed). Though the vocabulary used is basically small, it is still larger than strictly necessary to express the range of ideas, and in some respects a rich variety of language is used to express the underlying themes. But the question of how the eucharistic sacrifice is related to Calvary is left largely undefined and is seldom even referred to; the same is true of the question of the nature of the eucharistic presence, possibly in this latter case partly because the whole ethos of these prayers seems to stress activity, divine and human, and thus to think in static terms of a presence is irrelevant to their general sense and intention. Nevertheless, it would seem fair to say that these two issues, on which so much discussion and controversy was to centre later, simply do not seem to have been raised as controversial matters in the centuries during which the Romano-Gallican liturgical tradition was developing and forming. One must conclude that the men of that era just did not think about the eucharist in such a way as to raise these issues as points of controversy, but that the way they did think about the eucharist is illustrated and defined by the prayers they wrote and used. Thus the Secrets and the post-communion are fully in harmony with the Canon they accompany, and constitute a faithful and illuminating commentary upon it.

(iv) The 'Ordo Romanus Primus'

The theology of the Roman liturgical tradition, as derived from its prayers, has been set out above. The liturgical setting *par excellence* of these prayers is that of the papal stational masses of this period, whose ritual and shape (which the *Ordo Romanus Primus* describes) no doubt provided the basis of all the other eucharistic liturgical life of Rome and its environs during this time.

What may be noted as the salient characteristics of this liturgy? Firstly, that it was an intensely corporate affair; its performance demanded the presence of a very large number of people, each of whom had his own part to play. Secondly, though it was highly ceremonious, it was neither over-elaborate nor fussy; there is an absence of merely decorative additions or elaborate ceremonial intrusions. Given the large number of people taking part, and the obvious grandeur of such occasions and their settings, the essentials of the eucharistic action are performed with some directness and simplicity. Thirdly, it is reasonably clear that the whole of the service is said aloud, and 'understood of the people'; this includes the Canon, as Jungmann demonstrates.[29] Latin was still sufficiently the vernacular for all those present to be able to follow the whole of the service and thus participate fully in the rite itself. Lastly, the number of communicants was large; it would seem that most people present communicated, and doubtless all had the opportunity to do so if they wished.

Bearing later doctrinal and liturgical developments in mind, it is to be noted that there were no elevations or genuflections at the institution narrative, though there was an elevation at the very end of the Canon, at the doxology.[30]

There are in particular a few points of importance that

should be noted concerning theologies of consecration and of the eucharistic presence. Firstly, the eucharistic breads are called 'oblationes' before and after the Canon, which tends to suggest that the eucharistic action was seen as a whole, and that no attempt was made to isolate a 'Moment of Consecration' within it. Secondly, the point concerning the sacrament reserved from a previous celebration: this was shown to the pontiff on entering the church, and he venerated it, 'Tunc inclinato capite pontifex vel diaconus salutat sancta',[31] a practice which seems to indicate belief in an objective holiness of the elements. Thirdly, there is the question of the pouring of some of the wine from the pope's chalice in the *scyphus* held by the acolyte, and the communion of the people from this latter vessel. Whether or not this commixture was held to constitute the consecration of the wine in the *scyphus* is a question of some complexity, needing careful consideration.

The *Ordo* describes the procedure followed with the wine in some detail. At the offertory all bring up their own bread and wine. The archdeacon receives the flasks of wine, pours their contents into the 'calix maior', which is being held by the regionary sub-deacon.[32] When this vessel is full, its contents are poured into the *scyphus*, which in its turn is being held by an acolyte; the reason for this double transfer of wine from one vessel to another is not apparent, and seems redundant, for there seems to be no reason why this wine should not have been poured directly into the *scyphus* by the archdeacon. A few sentences later, another deacon, who is following the archdeacon, is described as receiving some further flasks of wine, and he does pour their contents directly into the *scyphus*. By this time the *scyphus* must have contained a considerable quantity of wine and have been quite heavy. The *scyphus* is not mentioned again until the description of the preparations made for the giving of communion, and so the question arises as to what was done with it during the recitation of the Canon. In the absence of any direct reference, and from the fact that at the offertory it was being held by an acolyte, the most probable assumption would seem to be that he continued to stand near the altar holding it throughout this period, for it is difficult to see where else he could have gone with it or what else he could have done during this time. Also, the description in the *Ordo* of the offertory and what is done by those concerned with all the bread and wine is quite detailed, and so if something else had been done with the *scyphus,* it would presumably have been mentioned. So the above assumption would seem to be a fair one to make, but it is only an assumption, none-the-less. A few paragraphs further on, the *Ordo* describes the archdeacon preparing the papal chalice,[33] which he fills with wine offered by the pope, and on festal days by high dignitaries as well; and this chalice is placed on the altar, the only one to be so. The next mention of the *scyphus* comes at the beginning of the communion, when the archdeacon pours a small quantity of wine from the papal chalice into it – 'parum de calice in sciffo inter manus acolyti', a phrase which perhaps can be taken as a further indication that he has been standing there with it all the time. Then the pontiff and certain dignitaries are communicated from the pope's chalice, and then the archdeacon pours the rest of its contents into the *scyphus.* The empty chalice is taken to the sacristy, and the rest of the congregation are communicated from the *scyphus.*[34]

The question is usually asked whether this double commixture constitutes consecration of the wine in the *scyphus,* but this is surely to ask the question with the wrong emphasis. One of the characteristics of this Latin liturgical tradition was that it saw the eucharistic action as a unity, and all the wine in the *scyphus* had been included in the offertory, and thus had become part of the eucharistic action. Therefore it seems probable that when this ceremonial was evolved, no difference was seen in terms of 'consecration' between the wine in the pope's chalice on the altar and the wine in the *scyphus;* both had been offered, the Canon had been said within the 'hearing' of both as it were, and both were used for giving communion. Having said this it can now be asked why both chalice and *scyphus* were not placed on the altar. The answer to this would seem to be that the Roman liturgical tradition seemed to regard it as improper to have more than one cup actually on the altar, because Christ only used one cup at the Last Supper, witness a letter written in 726 by pope Gregory II to Boniface.[35] But if this be the case, why the double commixture? Perhaps the first should be seen as a gesture of fellowship, a physical symbol whose purpose was to demonstrate the oneness of the sacrament received from the pope's chalice and the people's *scyphus,* and thus the unity of all sharing in the eucharistic action and communion. And perhaps the second should be seen as purely utilitarian: no more people were to be communicated from the pope's chalice, so what could be more logical than simply to pour its remaining contents into the vessel that was to be used for communicating the rest of the congregation?

Two modern scholarly comments on this provide an interesting contrast. Duchesne interpreted the commixture here simply as a gesture of fellowship, and thus seems to have regarded all the wine as consecrated[36]. Jungmann, on the other hand, argued that the contents of the *scyphus* were not consecrated at all, either by the eucharistic prayer, or by the commixture. But Jungmann regarded the communion of the people from a chalice containing 'unconsecrated' wine (in his view), to which a few drops of 'consecrated' had been added, as a device adopted to lessen the danger of irreverence to the consecrated species[37]. This is surely to read back into this era the pre-suppositions and outlook of a much later age, which would seem to have led him to a false interpretation of this commixture.

This brief description of the ethos of the *Ordo Romanus Primus* demonstrates its harmony with the theology of the prayers themselves. Both the ceremonial and the verbal parts of this liturgical tradition constitute a unity, and together provide a commentary on how the Latin Roman liturgical tradition should be understood. This then is the basis against which all later Western eucharistic theology and liturgical practice is to be judged.

(v) Commixture and Consecration

To conclude this chapter, some space will now be devoted to a discussion of the topic of Commixture and Consecration, not ieast because of the relevance it has to later developments in theories of consecration, particularly to some Anglican proposals for supplementary consecration.

However the ceremonial of *Ordo I* in this respect was originally interpreted, there are a substantial number of instances of liturgical practices and commentaries from the eighth century onwards that do witness to a belief in 'consecration by contact', and no doubt the practice of *Ordo I* was interpreted as such by some. M. Andrieu did a detailed study on this topic in a series of articles published in Paris in the early 1920s, entitled 'Immixtio et Consecratio';[38] and it is these that provide the sources of information for much of the following discussion. These practices are concerned with three basic instances; firstly, those concerned with the normal celebration of the eucharist, as in *Ordo I;* secondly, the question of reservation from Maundy Thursday and the Mass of the pre-sanctified on Good Friday; and thirdly, *viaticum* and communion of the sick.

One of the important references to this commixture in a normal eucharist occurs in *Ordo VI,* an *ordo* describing a papal mass in very similar terms to *Ordo I.* The archdeacon is described as pouring a little wine from the pope's chalice into the other vessel held by the acolyte, and to this description this explanation has been added: 'quia vinum etiam non consecratum, sed sanguine domini commixtum sanctificatur per omnem modum'.[39] Thus here is exactly the same liturgical practice as in *Ordo I,* but now a theological explanation has been added. The wine in the *scyphus* or large chalice held by the acolyte is not consecrated by the recitation of the Canon, in spite of its having been included in the offertory; but it is consecrated by the commixture *(consecrare* and *sanctificare* being synonymous in meaning at this period, as Andrieu demonstrated with many examples from the third to the thirteenth centuries).[40] That an explanation should be added in this way, is witness to a tendency to analyse the eucharistic action into its various parts, and to attach a different theological significance to each part. This tendency is evidence of a fundamental change of approach to the eucharist, from the corporate dynamic approach of the prayers of the sacramentaries to something more static and analytical. Andrieu says *Ordo VI* is based on *Ordo I,* and compiled by someone unfamiliar with the ceremonial of the Roman stational masses at first hand. He is unable to date it precisely, but regards it as later than Amalarius (see below), because of its theology of consecration at the commixture.[41]

The sort of liturgical practice described by *Ordines I* and *VI* seems to have continued for almost as long as communion in both kinds remained common. Since this went on for longer in the religious orders than elsewhere, so too did commixture in the chalice, in some cases as late as the fifteenth century. Sometimes in these examples the chalice is replenished with fresh wine by the sub-deacon as communion proceeds, as in the *Constitutiones Hirsangienses* of William, abbot of Hirschau (1068-1091),[42] and this is the nearest any of these practices come to being supplementary consecration in the Anglican sense. But as time goes on, the theological explanation of such practices changes, with an increasing tendency to say that the commixture does not consecrate; Innocent III, Alexander of Hales, and Bonaventure all said this.[43]

The second group of references concerns the Good Friday liturgy, and the commentaries upon this of Amalarius of Metz (780-850), a liturgical scholar and pupil of Alcuin, most of whose life was spent working in Carolingian France. He was the author of the extremely important liturgical treatise *De ecclesiasticis officiis*. This great work first appeared about 820, and afterwards in a revised version. About 832 he went to Rome and, in the light of what he had learned there, revised his work again. Thus Amalarius is a witness to liturgical practice and thought in both Rome and Gaul in the early ninth century, and no doubt was influenced by both, and contributed to the development of both, liturgically and theologically.[44]

The mass of the pre-sanctified began in the East, was introduced to Rome, and spread from there to other Western churches. Originally, both kinds were reserved on Maundy Thursday and used for communion on Good Friday, and there was no commixture. This is the practice described in the *Gelasianum*,[45] and also in the Gelasians of the eighth century, for example Angoulême and Gellone,[46] as well as *Ordines XVI*[47] and *XVII*.[48] However by the ninth century it had become the custom to reserve the species of bread alone. In *Ordo XXIV* the priest goes to the sacristy on Good Friday to collect 'corpus domini quod pridie remansit', and places it on a paten. When the arrangements are complete,

subdiaconus teneat ante ipsos calicem cum vina non consecrato et alter subdiaconus patenam cum corpore domini,

a statement which makes quite explicit the consecratory status of both elements at this point. After the *Libera nos* the pontiff 'sumit de sancta et ponit in calicem nihil dicens', and communion follows.[49] The *Ordo* is quite explicit that this commixture is performed in silence, and so if the wine was regarded as consecrated, it could only be so because of the commixture. This practice of reserving in one kind and placing some of the reserved consecrated bread in a chalice of unconsecrated wine became the liturgical norm in the West, and it was this practice on which Amalarius commented.[50] He notes that the 'corpus domini' is placed on the altar together with a chalice of unconsecrated wine. Then the Lord's Prayer is said and a portion of the 'sanctum corpus' placed in the chalice in silence. Amalarius explains what he understands to be the theological significance of this: 'sanctificatur enim vinum non consecratum per sanctificatum panem'; since *sanctificare* and *consecrare* were synonymous in meaning at this period, Amalarius quite clearly regarded the commixture as effecting the consecration of the wine. This is what he wrote in his original version which contained only the first three books. When he added book 4, he had come to believe that the Lord's Prayer had consecratory power, and that because of this, reservation from Maundy Thursday to Good Friday was unnecessary. All that one needed to do was to recite the Lord's Prayer over unconsecrated bread and wine on Good Friday. However, he seems to have abandoned this idea after his visit to Rome, for it does not appear in the later editions of his work. During his visit to Rome he was told that the Pope and his assistants did not communicate after the Veneration of the Cross, there being no celebration of the sacrament on the two penitential days. From the way in which this is worded:

Qui iuxta ordinem libelli per commixtionem panis et vini consecrat vinum, non observat traditionem ecclesiae, de qua dicit Innocentius isto biduo sacramenta penitus non celebrari,

it is quite clear that for Amalarius there is no difference between normal consecration and consecration by commixture.

What is of importance for this study is Amalarius' principle 'sanctificatur enim vinum non consecratum per sanctificationem panem'. He was the first to express this viewpoint explicitly, though since he was commenting on an existing if recent liturgical practice, he was no doubt making explicit what was implicitly in men's minds at the time. His theory held undisputed sway for the next four centuries or so, until the rise of the scholastic theology of the thirteenth century. Many liturgical books from the ninth century onwards make it quite clear that they regard the Good Friday rite as achieving consecration of the wine by commixture, some saying explicitly 'Hic consecratum vinum per corpus domini'; for example many French books, and the English books of Hereford, Sarum, and Exeter[51] witness to the same belief. Some books are neutral, mentioning this commixture, without assigning theological significance to it. On the other hand some books reject the idea that this commixture causes consecration of the wine, and these are all twelfth century or later, the time when the new scholastic theories about consecration began to make headway. But the old liturgical practice of the commixture continued for some time after this, and so a new gloss or explanation had to be found for it. Some of the books, in providing for this commixture, forbid the wine to be referred to as the Blood of the Lord, or for prayers that include such a reference to be said, 'quia non est ibi sanguis domini'. It is at this point that a distinction in meaning begins to appear between *consecrare* and *sanctificare,* the latter word acquiring the sense of being made holy but not consecrated — phrases such as 'sanctificatur, id est ex tactu sacrae rei reverendum officitur', or 'sanctificatur autem vinum in calice per corpus dominicum sed non consecratur' make this quite explicit.[52] Thus Amalarius' phrase would now have been understood in a sense different from the one he intended when he originally wrote it. In addition to this, the omission of the prayer 'Haec commixtio et consecratio . . .' is often given as a reason for the fact that the wine in the chalice on Good Friday was in this period no longer regarded as consecrated. Thus the wine was regarded as holy or venerable but no longer consecrated. But it was during this period that communion in one kind became the norm, together with the accompanying scholastic doctrine of concomitance, and thus the need to provide a chalice for general communion on Good Friday disappeared, though interestingly enough the practice of this commixture was retained in the 1570 missal, the celebrant alone drinking the wine with the consecrated particle from the chalice. The decline in general communion from the intincted chalice on Good Friday occurred in much the same period as people ceased in general to believe this wine to be consecrated. Whether this is more than coincidence is hard to say, but certainly the juxtaposition is interesting, and must be related to the phenomenon of communicants ceasing to receive from the chalice in any case.

The question of commixture, *viaticum,* and the

communion of the sick can be dealt with in a sentence. The liturgical practices followed, and the explanations concerning them, are exactly parallel and similar to those in the Maundy Thursday Good Friday rite, and develop similarly with the passage of time.[53]

The interrelated practices of commixture throw considerable light on the development of thought about the eucharist from the ninth to the thirteenth century. *Ordo I* sees the eucharist as an organic whole, and dates from, and reflects the thought of, an era that did not isolate a specific doctrine of consecration as such from the rest of the eucharistic action. But by the time the later *ordines* such as *VI* came to be written, thought about the eucharist had begun to express itself in terms of specific doctrines such as consecration, and thus the consecratory status of the wine that had been offered and put into the *scyphus,* as opposed to the pontiff's chalice, had become a matter requiring definition. And the view that evolved was that physical contact and mixing of consecrated with unconsecrated consecrates the unconsecrated. Such commixture was of course only possible for consecrating wine, but the consecratory agent could be either consecrated bread or wine. Perhaps the doctrine arose in connection with practices of an *Ordo I* type and was then adopted and reapplied to the mass of the pre-sanctified, once wine was no longer reserved in the latter; this would have been an extremely simple and obvious adaptation of the doctrine to make. This all suggests that a considerable number of different liturgical practices were regarded as consecratory at the time when the idea of a doctrine of consecration as such first evolved and for several centuries thereafter. The consecration was variously located in different verbal formulae, principally the Canon or parts of it. But Amalarius believed, at least for a time, that the Our Father could consecrate, and the prayer at the commixture 'Haec commixtio et consecratio . . .' may well have been similarly regarded by some, as its wording might suggest. And it was also held that wine could be consecrated by its commixture with the consecrated eucharistic species, either bread or wine. This was the state of affairs until the scholastic doctrine that consecration was achieved only by the recitation of the dominical words in the institution narrative became the dominant one. Thus the fluid and flexible doctrines of consecration of an earlier period had narrowed down into one precise inflexible doctrine of consecration. Naturally, when this happened, commixture was no longer regarded as consecratory, but by this time communion in one kind was becoming the norm, and so the matter had ceased to have much practical importance.

When comparing this with later developments in Anglican liturgy and theology, two main points seem to emerge. Firstly, that all the above commixture practices were normal to the rites in question, the usual and regular way by which wine in each case was consecrated. They are not supplementary consecration in the Anglican sense, that is, they are not subsidiary consecrations to remedy accidental and unexpected shortages. Secondly, they seem to have had no influence at all on Anglican thinking about supplementary consecration in the period 1548-1764, and indeed no one seems to show any knowledge of or interest in them. The trial of Robert Johnson in 1573 revolved around the necessity for supplementary consecration in itself,[54] and neither side seems even to have thought about commixture as a possible solution; Johnson considered no consecration necessary, and his judges insisted on a verbal formula. And where supplementary consecration is brought in by Anglicans during this period, it is always by verbal formula.

CHAPTER TWO

Eucharistic Theology and Liturgical Practice in the Latin West immediately prior to the Reformation

All Reformed eucharistic rites, including the Anglican, were produced in response to the prevailing liturgical situation in the West in the late Middle Ages. What this latter was will now be briefly analysed in order to contrast it both with Anglican rites and with the original theology and ethos of the Latin rite as described in the previous chapter.

(i) The eucharistic theology of St Thomas Aquinas

A convenient point with which to start is the eucharistic theology and liturgical practice of St Thomas Aquinas, which may be taken as the high peak of medieval scholasticism in this respect. This may be dealt with under the three basic headings of the eucharistic sacrifice, his doctrine of consecration, and the eucharistic presence. One general point may first be mentioned. Thomas held that the eucharist was accomplished in the consecration of the matter, whereas with the other sacraments this was only the case with the due use of the matter.[1]

Thomas gives two reasons for saying that the mass is a sacrifice. First, that it is the image or representation of Christ's sacrifice on the cross; that is, it is not that sacrifice itself but a picture of it.[2] The second reason is that the mass mediates the merits of the passion of Christ, hence one may say that Christ is sacrificed *(immolatur)* in its celebration.[3] It is quite clear that by this last phrase he means no more than that the merits of Christ's sacrifice are mediated through the celebration of the eucharist. This is true in spite of the fact that the word he used for 'sacrifice', *'immolare'*, has the strict classical meaning of ritual slaughter; he is using it in a metaphorical sense, and in this respect his usage is in

41

accordance with that of the sacramentaries.

That this interpretation of Thomas' doctrine of the eucharistic sacrifice is the correct one is demonstrated by his discussion of the question as to whether Christ would have died in the sacrament, had this been reserved in a pyx or consecrated by one of the Apostles at that precise moment in time when he died upon the cross. Since Thomas held Christ to exist in the sacrament in the same form as he exists in himself, he concludes that Christ would have died in the sacrament at the moment of his death on the cross, because that was what was happening to him at that particular moment in time.[4] The corollary to this is abundantly clear, though Thomas does not specifically state it as such, namely that at no other point in time can Christ die in the sacrament. Since he is now in glory with the Father, it is his glorious resurrection body that is present in the sacramental species; thus any kind of idea of a 'slaying' of Christ in the mass, or any kind of identification between Calvary and the mass is obviously ruled out. In Thomas' eucharistic theology the uniqueness and all-sufficiency of Calvary is adequately safeguarded, even though what he says has to be read as a whole and with care, if this is to become absolutely clear to modern ears.

Thomas' doctrine of consecration is quite simply that the sole and essential form for the consecration of the bread is 'Hoc est corpus meum', and that for the wine is 'Hic est calix sanguinis mei . . . remissionem peccatorum'.[5] He says the rest of the Canon is not necessary for the consecration, though a priest who omitted it would sin gravely in that he would not be observing the rite of the church.[6] So rigid is his definition of the form that he even regards the nonscriptural 'enim' in the institution narrative of the Roman Canon as not part of it.

Thomas further states that the transubstantiation takes place in the last instant of the words of the form being spoken. He also maintains that the consecration of the bread takes effect immediately the form for the bread is spoken,[7] though he admits that some earlier theologians had thought that the change did not occur in the bread until the form for the wine had been spoken as well. He solves the problem of the incompleteness of the sacrament that such a view of the consecration might be held to pose by his doctrine of concomitance.

Nevertheless, the separate consecration of the bread and wine is not without its importance for Thomas. The separate consecration of the wine symbolises Christ's passion, for in Christ's death the blood was separated from the body.[8]

Yet though Thomas believed that the bread and wine are consecrated separately by their respective and different forms, he also held that one must not be consecrated without the other, because the sacrament was ordained by Christ in both kinds; hence, without consecration in both kinds it would not be a complete sacrament.[9]

One further point in connection with Thomas' doctrine of consecration is important. He held that to mix unconsecrated wine with the already consecrated would corrupt the sacrament, and that the blood of Christ would no longer be there.[10] It is thus apparent that he rejected any idea of consecration by commixture.

He also comments on the Canon of the Mass as such, and some interesting points emerge. It is clear from his comments on the post-institution narrative section, that he sees the mass as a priestly action on the people's behalf, rather than the priest's role being the articulation of the offering of the whole church.

Yet he does retain an understanding of the eucharist as the corporate action of the whole faithful, for he defends the inclusion of intercessions in the rite on the grounds that the eucharist is the sacrament of unity of the whole church. Again, in reply to the objection that the priest as minister of the sacrament ought not to share the service with other ministers and a choir, he shows himself familiar with the concept that the eucharist is the offering of worship by the entire Christian church, all of whose various members, priest, other ministers, choir, and people, have their own roles to fulfil.[11] He also retains the concept of the necessary unity of the rite as a whole. This is demonstrated by his insistence that there must be a communion in both kinds as well as a consecration in both kinds for the celebration to be complete. It is however sufficient that the priest communicate in both kinds,[12] since he offers and consumes on behalf of the people. The people, he says, receive in one kind, and then only of necessity at the time prescribed by the precepts of the church.[13] Here may be seen in Thomas' discussion two overlapping theologies, that of the later Middle Ages with its excessive concentration on the function and status of the priest, and that of an earlier period when the overall corporate nature of the church and its worship and the unity of the eucharistic rite were better understood.

Thomas believed that Christ is truly and bodily present in the sacrament, made present by the special and unique miracle of transubstantiation, wrought by the infinite divine power, whereby the substances of the bread and wine are changed into the body and blood of Christ. But all the accidents of bread and wine remain,[14] which means that they still possess every property, and are capable of every action, exactly as before the transubstantiation took place.[15]

He discusses the question of the fraction, acknowledging that this was a matter about which many opinions had been held in previous times. He says that it is only the accidents, the sacramental species, that are actually broken, but not the substantially present body of Christ, because this is incorruptible and impassible, and is in any case entire both in the unbroken host and in each part of the host after it has been broken. There is an interesting parallel here with the rubric in the 1549 rite which reaches a very similar doctrine. It is thus a logical impossibility to postulate an actual breaking of the substantial body of Christ at the fraction.[16]

He also defines how he understood the two species to be related to each other. The whole Christ is under each species: the body of Christ is present in the species of bread by the power of the sacrament, and the blood by real concomitance, and *vice versa* with the wine.[17] This principle enables him to justify the practice of receiving communion in one kind only.[18]

The essence of Thomas' doctrine of the presence is that the substance, the inner reality, the essential being, is changed, while the accidents, the outward appearance and properties remain as they were before. And this is something that makes sense within the terms of the scholastic philosophy, the 'science' (if one may use the term), that provided the framework within which it was evolved. But what does it mean in terms of modern ways of thinking? Surely one has to say something like that, by a miracle of the divine power, the spiritual presence of the risen and glorified Christ indwells the bread and wine as a permanent effect of consecration, and ignore the difficulties posed by his belief that the substances of bread and wine cease to be present.

(ii) Changes in liturgical practice

Between the eighth century and the sixteenth the central prayers of the eucharistic rite discussed in chapter I continued to be used more or less unchanged, though much of a secondary and superficial nature was added. What did change was the ceremonial and the spiritual and devotional ethos that accompanied the celebration of the rite. These changes were vast, and they may best be summarised by listing some of the more obvious contrasts.

The liturgy of the *Ordo Romanus Primus* was a truly vernacular rite, understood of the people, who thus participated corporately in the worship of the liturgy itself. By the sixteenth century this was no longer remotely true for the average worshipper, who had become a passive spectator at a rite performed by others. This was accentuated by the fact that the offertory was no longer corporate in any real sense, and that lay reception of the sacrament was exceedingly rare, and then only in one kind. The view held about the mass gradually changed from the corporate offering of the whole people into a mysterious ritual performed by the priest on behalf of others; this viewpoint was emphasised and gained strength from the fact that it became the custom to recite the Canon silently. Hence the emphasis on the elevations (and that of the host was always more important than that of the chalice) during the institution narrative, and the accompanying devotion of genuflection, both thirteenth century innovations. The other major change of practical importance in the late Middle Ages was the vast inflation in the number of masses said and of priests ordained to say them. Though High Mass remained the theoretical liturgical norm, the great majority of these masses of necessity were said as low masses; most of them were votive masses, often requiems, offered with a particular intention, and probably paid for with a mass stipend or chantry endowment. There also grew up the cultus of extra-liturgical devotions to the blessed sacrament; and seeing and adoring thus became the substitute for actually receiving. Thus between the eighth and the fifteenth centuries the corporate community mass in which all participated changed into an atomised multitude of individual low masses, at which all but priest and assistant were really passive spectators.

(iii) Provision for the correction of defects in the eucharistic celebration

The Middle Ages saw the origin of detailed treatments of how to deal with possible defects and mistakes that might arise during the celebration of mass, as well as elaborate and extremely scrupulous provisions for dealing with accidental loss or spillage of the consecrated elements; these were codified and developed during the later part of the period.

This is something that Aquinas comments on in some detail, and from his discussion a number of interesting points emerge. First, that if for any reason the mass is not completed by the celebrant and the break occurs before the consecration, it is to be left unfinished; but if during or after the consecration, another priest must finish it.[19] The second point he makes is that, if the priest during the celebration realises that there is some impediment to his celebrating, such as a lack of fasting, he must continue, for to fail to complete the sacrifice is the far graver sin; nevertheless, if he becomes aware of the impediment before the consecration, he had better stop, unless grave scandal will be caused by this.[20] He next deals with the question of a defiled or poisoned chalice; if this is discovered before the consecration, the defiled or poisoned wine is to be poured away, fresh taken, and the service resumed. If it is not discovered until after the consecration, the defiled wine is to be placed in a suitable vessel in the reliquary and, in order to complete the sacrament and the sacrifice, fresh wine is to be placed in the chalice and the mass resumed from the consecration of the chalice.[21] He discusses at some length what the priest is to do if he discovers the chalice to be empty, or either the wine or the water to be missing. If, before consecrating the chalice and after consecrating the host, he notices either wine or water to be missing, they are to be added and the consecration continued. If he notices the absence of water after having consecrated the chalice, he is to proceed without interruption because the presence of water is not essential to the sacrament. On no account is he to add water to the already consecrated wine because this would corrupt the sacrament in part. If he notice the absence of wine after the consecration but before he receives the host, then he puts wine and water into the chalice and resumes the Canon from the appropriate point. But if he does not notice it until he has received the host, then he is to take fresh bread and wine, and say the forms for the whole of the consecration again and continue from there to the end of the Canon once more. For if he consecrated just wine in the absence of a consecrated host, the sacrifice would neither be complete nor in order. Then he is to consume the newly consecrated bread and wine, even if he has already broken his fast by drinking any water that may have been in the chalice, because completion of the sacrament is much more important than fasting communion.[22]

The next question Thomas deals with is that of forgetfulness on the part of the priest leading to the omission of part of the service. No attempt is to be made to rectify this unless anything absolutely necessary for the sacrament has been left out, that is, only the form of the consecration. If this is omitted, the celebrant should begin again at this point and continue again to the end of the Canon in order to preserve the correct order of the sacrifice.[23] He does not regard the omission of either fraction or commixture as vital defects to the integrity of the rite, and so no repetition is called for in these particular cases.[24] His final section here is concerned with the problem of accidental spillage, which he demands should be dealt with with great rigour and scrupulosity.[25]

Thus it will be seen that his provisions for dealing with defect of matter or form during the celebration of mass do involve a second consecration in some instances, but it is to be remembered that the only purpose of this is to remedy defects. A second consecration for the benefit of intending communicants is not covered by what Thomas says here; and such a practice would seen to be as foreign to his ideas about the liturgy as it is to the whole of the Western Latin liturgical tradition, of which it has never been a part. And the important underlying principle behind his provisions for the remedying of defects is that the rite should always be complete, with consecration in both kinds in the right order. Indeed, consecration in one kind only he specifically excludes; a defect of the chalice may not be corrected by a further consecration except in the presence of a consecrated host.

It became the custom in liturgical books from about 1200 onwards to include instructions concerned with the correction of defects in the celebration of mass and other provisions concerning the conduct of the rite in a section called the 'cautels'. Maskell reprinted a set from the Sarum use.[26] The Roman Missal of 1474 also contained some, and these are for the most part identical with the Sarum ones with the insertion of some additional material.[27]

The provision most commonly made to correct defects is that fresh elements be taken, and the appropriate part of the institution narrative be repeated. Since the cautels are mainly the product of the scholastic era, this is to be expected. There are however some interesting variants to be found in some instances. The Sarum cautels direct that if the priest find there is no wine in the chalice after he has received the bread, he ought to take fresh bread and wine and repeat the whole of the institution narrative; but if he thinks the delay caused by such a procedure would cause scandal, he may rectify the defect by the consecration of wine only. This provision is contained in some other early sixteenth century missals.[28]

Two other examples from a somewhat earlier period may be noted as providing an interesting contrast.[29] A council meeting at Münster in 1279 ordered the commonest method for correcting a defect of the chalice, namely fresh wine and repetition of the institution narrative from 'Simili modo . . .',[30] whereas a synod meeting at Clermont in 1268 orders a priest who finds the chalice to be empty to put the host already consecrated aside, take fresh bread and wine and begin the Canon again from 'Te igitur . . .'. The first host is to be consumed before the celebrant drinks the wine.[31] Considerably later in time, a somewhat similar provision is to be found in a set of introductory instructions prefixed to a Roman missal printed in Venice in 1493, which requires important defects in the contents of the chalice to be made good by taking fresh bread and wine, the host already consecrated to be reverently put on one side and consumed later, and the Canon repeated again, starting from 'Hanc igitur oblationem'.[32] J. Wickham Legg thought that this tract was probably of French origin, of unknown authorship, and listed some thirteen missals published between 1493 and 1532 which contain it, most of which were in the British Museum or the Bodleian Library when he wrote.[33]

Thus it can be seen that late medieval practice with regard to a second consecration was solely concerned with remedying defects in a celebration, and that a variety of forms were used to achieve this, some of which clearly date from before the period when the scholastic doctrine that consecration was achieved solely by the institution narrative was universally accepted.

(iv) The state of eucharistic theology immediately prior to the Reformation

Those who celebrated the eucharist according to the ceremonial of the *Ordo Romanus Primus* regarded the eucharistic action as a single indivisible unity. As time passed, the tendency increased to analyse how the mass worked in detail, and specific doctrines of consecration, the eucharistic presence, and the eucharistic sacrifice were developed and elaborated.

When doctrines of consecration as such first arose, a considerable variety of opinions co-existed as to what could and did consecrate. By the time of the Lateran definition of 1215 these had all condensed into one inflexible doctrine of consecration, namely, that it was the institution narrative alone that consecrated. This was elucidated in detail by Aquinas, and it did not change significantly between his time and the Reformation. Likewise with the doctrine of transubstantiation, which became the exclusive doctrine of the eucharistic presence in this period. This did not change in substance after 1215, though in popular belief it was often expressed in far cruder and more materialistic terms than the skilful and refined manner expounded by Aquinas.

It was with the doctrine of the sacrifice of the mass that a significant change occurred between the time of Aquinas and the eve of the Reformation. This had two facets. On a theoretical level theologians such as Biel drew the conclusion that had always been possible since the isolation of a moment of consecration at the institution narrative; namely, they interpreted the eucharistic action as the production of the body and blood of Christ at the consecration in order then to offer them to the Father as a ritual sacrificial oblation, thus in effect making the mass into a separate sacrifice apart from Calvary. Liturgically, to interpret the *Unde et memores* in this way was quite to misunderstand the nature of the Latin Canon. The second facet of this development was the more practical one of explaining and justifying the vast number of masses said. There seems no doubt that the popular view was that each mass said applied a finite and distinct amount of grace to its intention, and that thus two masses were worth twice as much as one. Since most masses were paid for, one may perhaps style this 'cash-register theology'. The theologians of the day, such as Biel, were faced with the task of justifying this, and though they may have succeeded in defending it against conviction as formally heretical, it cannot be said that they did more than this. Indeed, for the most part they were content simply to elaborate it, and it seems that most of their elaborations were simply an exposition of thoroughly bad liturgical practice that they felt no need to criticise.

Probably nominalist philosophy helped to produce this state of affairs, for under its influence the concepts of memorial and representation had lost their strong sense and become weakened into meaning a purely psychological remembering. When this state of affairs is coupled with the traditional belief in the mass as the Christian sacrifice by which grace is mediated, it was perhaps easy to arrive at the development of considering the mass as a second, subsidiary, and additional sacrifice. It would seem too that the prevailing thoroughly unhealthy mass-system and this bad theology supported one another in a kind of vicious circle, probably with practice providing the spur and keeping the initiative. No wonder, then, when the Reformers read the New Testament intelligently, they weighed the prevailing mass-system in the balance and found it wanting, for it was alien to the New Testament. Tragically, what they did not realise (in the circumstances, how could they?) was that it was also wholly alien to the essential basic prayers and structure of the Latin rite as such. When Cranmer identified the doctrines of transubstantiation and the propitiatory sacrifice of the mass as the two root causes of all the trouble he had made an accurate diagnosis;[34] it was the ideas that the bread and wine were first transubstantiated and then ritually offered that both arose in response to the late medieval mass-system and justified it. Where he went wrong was in assuming that the Latin rite in itself contained these errors.[35] The evidence of this chapter and the previous one is put forward in part to demonstrate that the later medieval mass-system and its theology was as alien to the spirit of the Latin rite as it was to the New Testament. Nevertheless it was this system and theology that provided the circumstances in which the Reformers in general and Cranmer in particular had to work, and with this in mind we must now turn to an elucidation of

Cranmer's eucharistic theology, and the doctrines he intended his eucharistic rites to express.

Before leaving the study of the late medieval period, one additional point ought to be made concerning the people's devotional approach at mass. Unable to participate in the rite itself, their part was limited to private devotions during mass that were independent of the liturgy itself. Many such devotional exercises survive from this period, for example Langforde's *Meditations*,[36] the Corpus Christi sermon in Mirk's *Festial*[37] and the *Lay-Folk's Mass Book*.[38] By and large, these were not commentaries on the liturgy at all, but highly allegorical works, one of whose major purposes was to stimulate the people to meditate on the passion of Christ while mass was being said, so that their devotion to Him might be increased. Thus the people's part at mass had already become a subjective devotional remembering of Christ's passion. (Is this to be seen as the devotional counterpart to the nominalist tendencies that led to the memorial of Christ on the cross and the offering of sacrifice in the mass being seen as theologically separate?) The Reformers inherited the medieval concentration on the passion of Christ. Is it therefore surprising that what had been the people's devotional response to the mass tended to become the actual substance and content of Reformed rites?

CHAPTER THREE

Cranmer and the Edwardine Communion Rites

The problems that arise in a discussion of this topic are the interrelated ones of archbishop Cranmer's final state of mind on the eucharist, the point in time at which he reached it, and the relationship that both these topics have to the doctrinal intentions of 1548, 1549 and 1552. Lesser but still important problems associated with these are those related to the history of the composition of these rites. It is undisputed that Cranmer was responsible for most of their contents. The question is, therefore, to what extent have the political and theological pressures in England at the time modified the content of these rites away from what Cranmer would have wished to say at the points in time at which they were respectively published.

(i) The Eucharistic Theology of the Defence and Answer

The first and fundamental problem in this inter-related series of problems is that of Cranmer's final state of mind on the eucharist. This he set out in his *Defence of the true and Catholic doctrine . . .* and in his *Answer* to Gardiner's attack on his *Defence.* It is these works that are mainly to be used in an attempt to elucidate what he thought. He only refers to the 1549 rite once in the *Defence,* and that at the very end where he says:[1]

But, thanks be to the eternal God, the manner of the Holy Communion which is now set forth within this realm, is agreeable with the institution of Christ, with St Paul and the old primitive and apostolic Church, with the right faith of the sacrifice of Christ upon the cross for our redemption, and with the true doctrine of our salvation, justification, and remission of all our sins by that only sacrifice. Now resteth nothing but that all faithful subjects will gladly receive and embrace the same, being sorry for their former ignorance . . .

This establishes quite clearly that Cranmer regarded the eucharistic doctrine of 1549 to be that which he expressed in the *Defence.* Furthermore he rigorously defended and maintained this point of view in his controversy with Gardiner.

This also tends to suggest that, whatever were the processes of composition that led to 1549, Cranmer was its principal architect, and thus there is already a good case for interpreting the 1549 rite in the light of the *Defence.*

The above quotation also makes it clear that·Cranmer thought his beliefs were those of Scripture and the Fathers. Indeed, he goes further than this, maintaining that the true doctrine prevailed for the first thousand years, whereafter the bishops of Rome started progressively to corrupt it.[2]

It is easier to describe what Cranmer denies than what he affirms about the eucharist, and therefore his denials will be taken as a starting point.

Firstly, he denies that the eucharist is in any sense a propitiatory sacrifice, that it is one that remits sins. This he makes quite clear in Book V of the *Defence,* chapter 1 of which sums it up:

> The greatest blasphemy and injury that can be against Christ, and yet universally used through the popish kingdom, is this, that the priests make their mass a sacrifice propitiatory, to remit the sins as well of themselves as of other, both quick and dead, to whom they list to apply the same. Thus, under the pretence of holiness, the papistical priests have taken upon them to be Christ's successors, and to make such an oblation and sacrifice as never creature made but Christ alone, neither he made the same any more times than once, and that was by his death upon the cross. [3]

He amplifies this a little later saying that there are two kinds of sacrifice; one is called 'propitiatory', which pacifies God's

> wrath and indignation, obtains mercy and forgiveness for sins, and is the ransom for redemption from everlasting damnation.[4]

There is only one such sacrifice, namely the death of Christ upon the cross.

The second kind of sacrifice is the thankful response of the already reconciled, and is therefore called a sacrifice of praise and thanksgiving.[5] The eucharist is this second kind of sacrifice: it can never be the first, because this would be to commit the wicked blasphemy of slaying Christ again. [6]

Cranmer accused the papists of turning the mass into a propitiatory sacrifice, which he regards as manifest wickedness and idolatry:

> all such popish masses are to be clearly taken away out of Christian Churches, and the true use of the Lord's Supper is to be restored again,

wherein godly people assembled together may receive the sacrament every man for himself, to declare that he remembereth what benefit he hath received by the death of Christ, and to testify that he is a member of Christ's body, fed with his flesh, and drinking his blood spiritually.[7]

The similarity between this and the 1549 post-communion prayer is obvious.

Thus, when Cranmer refers to the eucharist as a sacrifice, he means a sacrifice of laud, praise, and thanksgiving as he defines it, and he interprets the references of the Fathers to the eucharist as a sacrifice in this sense.

The second point that he is concerned to disprove is the doctrine of transubstantiation which, together with the current Roman doctrine of sacrifice in the mass, he regards as the root of medieval error and superstition, as he states in the Preface to the *Defence.*[8]

His arguments against transubstantiation rest partly on arguments from scripture and the Fathers, and partly on the absurd conclusions that the doctrine gives rise to when discussed in the philosophical terms that gave rise to it. These are set out at some length in Chapter 14 of Book II of the *Defence.*

In his discussion both about the sacrifice and about transubstantiation, it is quite clear that Cranmer is reacting to and rejecting medieval distortions of earlier eucharistic doctrine. It was against this background of medieval eucharistic doctrine that his positive ideas about the eucharist were worked out.

One other negative conclusion must be stated, namely that, for Cranmer, the bread and wine were in no sense the body and blood of Christ themselves, nor did they have any holiness in themselves. Christ's body and blood are communicated 'to the faithful receiver, and not to the dumb creatures of bread and wine.'[9] Also 'we say, that Christ is not there, neither corporally nor spiritually', referring to the bread and wine.[10] And in a discussion of the meaning of consecration he says:

Not that the bread and wine have or can have any holiness in them, but that they be used to an holy work, and represent holy and godly things.[11]

Having established what Cranmer denied, it is now possible to try and state what he did believe the eucharist to be, which may be deduced from the first, third, and fourth books of the *Defence,* where he discusses respectively 'The true and catholic doctrine and use of the sacrament of the body and blood of our Saviour Christ', 'The manner how Christ is present in his supper' and 'the eating and drinking of the body and blood of our saviour Christ'. Cranmer says that he derived his doctrine from the scriptural accounts, and no-one is to be required to believe anything beyond this.

One of the points that he comes back to again and again is a comparison of the effects of the eucharist with those of baptism. In chapter 12 of Book I after saying

so that the washing in water of baptism is, as it were, a showing of Christ before our eyes, and a sensible touching, feeling and groping of him, to the confirmation of the inward faith which we have in him,

he goes on to say about the eucharist:

And in like manner Christ ordained the sacrament of his body and blood in bread and wine, to preach unto us, that as our bodies be fed, nourished, and preserved with meat and drink, so (as touching our spiritual life towards God) we be fed, nourished, and preserved by the body and blood of our Saviour Christ . . . And for this cause Christ ordained this sacrament in bread and wine, (which we eat and drink, and be chief nutriments of our body,) to the intent that as surely as we see the bread and wine with our eyes, smell them with our noses, touch them with our hands, and taste them with our mouths; so assuredly ought we to believe, that Christ is our spiritual life and sustenance of our bodies . . . Thus our saviour Christ knowing us to be in this world, as it were, but babes and weaklings in faith, hath ordained sensible signs and tokens, whereby to allure and draw us to more strength and more constant faith in him. So that the eating and drinking of this sacramental bread and wine is, as it were, a showing of Christ before our eyes, a smelling of him with our noses, a feeling and groping of him with our hands, and an eating, chewing, digesting, and feeding upon him to our spiritual strength and perfection.[12]

This long passage is a good example of his central ideas. The sacrament is ordained to preach to us that our souls be nourished with the body and blood of Christ. As we eat the bread and wine, so we are to believe. Thus we do not receive Christ in the bread and wine, but the bread and wine remind us that we receive Christ in faith. Elsewhere, he makes much of the point that as the Holy Ghost is not 'inaquate' in baptism, so Christ is not 'impanate' in the eucharist.[13] He also says that the change in the bread and wine in the eucharist is a change in use, and is exactly similar to the change in the use in the water of baptism.[14]

In the third book of the *Defence* he sets out to explain how he understands the presence. The dominical words are not to be taken literally:

Wherefore in these words must needs be sought out another sense and meaning than the words of themselves do bear.[15]

After some intervening argument involving patristic quotations, he says:

Now this being fully proved, it must needs follow consequently, that this manner of speaking is a figurative speech: for in plain and proper speech it is not true to say, that bread is Christ's body, or wine his blood.[16]

Again:

These speeches . . . be speeches not taken in the proper signification of every word, but by translation of these words 'eating' and 'drinking' from the signification of a corporal thing to signify a spiritual thing.[17]

Again, he says it is

not to be understood, that we shall eat Christ with our teeth grossly and carnally, but that we shall spiritually and ghostly with our faith eat him, being carnally absent from us in heaven; and in such wise as Abraham and other holy fathers did eat him, many years before he was incarnated and born.[18]

The phrases 'This is my body', 'This is my blood' are for Cranmer symbolic, and symbols of something that is absent:

In the New Testament, the bread and wine be not Christ's very body and blood, but they be figures, which by Christ's institution be unto the godly receivers thereof sacraments, tokens, significations, and representations of his very flesh and blood: instructing their faith, that as the bread and wine feed them corporally, and continue this temporal life; so the very flesh and blood of Christ feedeth them spiritually, and giveth them everlasting life.[19]

The key ideas seem to be: signs, instructing faith; as one eats corporally, so one feeds spiritually.

Yet he can also express himself positively, for he warns against coming to the Holy Table unworthily:

wherein is not only represented, but also spiritually given unto us, very Christ himself.[20]

When discussing St Ambrose, Cranmer sets down what he means by consecration, which he defines as:

the separation of any thing from a profane and worldly use unto a spiritual and godly use.[21]

And he compares the water consecrated for use in the font in baptism with the bread and wine consecrated in Holy Communion. They are separated for *use*, not for what they become themselves, which indeed is not changed.

The whole sense of Cranmer's positive doctrine seems to be that as we eat the bread and wine, so we are reminded that it is Christ's body and blood that feeds our souls; and, if we worthily receive, we are so spiritually fed by Christ's body and blood at that time, and continue to be while we dwell in him. He says:

For the sacramental bread and wine be not bare and naked figures, but so pithy and effectuous, that whosoever worthily eateth them, eateth spiritually Christ's flesh and blood, and hath by them everlasting life.[22]

He develops this further in Book 4 of the *Defence,* the main purpose of which is to demonstrate that the wicked do not eat the body and blood of Christ in any sense in the eucharist. At the same time he furnishes additional evidence as to how he believes the faithful receive Christ.

And every good and faithful Christian man feeleth in himself how he feedeth of Christ, eating his flesh and drinking his blood. For he putteth the whole hope and trust of his redemption and salvation in that only sacrifice, which Christ made upon the cross, having his body there broken, and his blood there shed for the remission of his sins. And this great benefit of Christ the faithful man earnestly considereth in his mind, cheweth and digesteth it with the stomach of his heart, spiritually receiving Christ wholly unto him, and giving again himself wholly unto Christ. And this is the eating of Christ's flesh and drinking of his blood, the feeling whereof is to every man the feeling how he eateth and drinketh Christ, which none evil man nor member of the Devil can do. For as Christ is a spiritual meat, so he is spiritually eaten and digested with the spiritual part of us.[23]

The final part of Book IV is a condemnation of reservation. Christ is to be worshipped in heaven and dwelling in the believer, not in the bread.[24]

Thus, to attempt a summary of his views in a sentence, the action of the eucharist consists only in that by its performance the worthy believer is enabled to make an act of spiritual communion. Everything else, a relationship between the eucharist and the propitiatory sacrifice of Christ, any kind of objective presence of Christ in the rite or in the sacramental species, is denied.

Certainly this is how Gardiner understood him:

For by the effect of this author's doctrine the sacrament is but a visible preaching by the tokens and signs of bread and wine; that in believing and remembering Christ's benefits, with revolving them in our mind, we should in faith feed upon Christ spiritually, believing that, as the bread and wine feedeth and nourisheth our bodies, so Christ feedeth and nourisheth our souls.[25]

And although Cranmer vigorously denies that the tokens and signs are bare tokens and signs, and maintains that Christ is present in his sacraments and does work in them, when what he says is analysed in detail, it is difficult to avoid the conclusion that Gardiner's understanding of Cranmer is substantially the correct one. The ministration of the sacrament stimulates the faith of the worthy receiver, and thus enables him to feed on Christ spiritually, and that is all.

(ii) The development of Cranmer's thinking about the eucharist

In seeking to relate Cranmer's doctrine of the eucharist to his liturgical work, it is this final state of mind that is the most important factor to be considered. There is, however, some uncertainty as to the exact date at which he reached it, and this may well have a bearing on some of the actual content of the rites of 1548 and 1549.

The point from which the development of his eucharistic theology started is clear[26], namely the received catholic Western standpoint of the church in which he grew up. His final state of mind is not in doubt either, even if elucidation of it has caused great controversy, and by it he stood to the end; witness the last theological affirmation he made before his martyrdom. It is the transition between the two that causes problems.

The dating and pace of this change of mind has to be conjectured from the comparatively few pieces of useful contemporary evidence that have come down to us. These are as follows:[27]

1. Sir John Cheke in a preface to the Latin edition of the *Defence* published in Emden in 1557 gives the date as 1546.

2. About the middle of 1548 Cranmer published in translation the catechism of Justus Jonas, a Lutheran document, an action that may have helped to give rise to the belief that at one stage Cranmer was definitely Lutheran in his views. But, as P.N. Brooks has pointed out, Cranmer altered the sense in his translation. The original said:

Ideo credere debemus, quod vere corpus et sanguis ejus sit;[28]

which Cranmer rendered as:

Wherefore we ought to believe, that in the sacrament we receive truly the body and blood of Christ.[29]

There can be no doubt that this shift in meaning from the original is deliberate and intentional, though Brooks argues that

the modification was probably a shrewd attempt both to defy Roman doctrine and to modify the Lutheran position without giving undue cause for offence.[30]

Brooks regards the eucharistic doctrine of the catechism as of a markedly conservative nature. Having said this, it must be noted that Cranmer defended its doctrine in the *Defence* as being wholly consistent with what he was therein setting forth, complaining that it had been misunderstood,[31] and reaffirming this to Gardiner.[32] This raises the same sort of questions as have to be posed about the 1549 rite, namely whether he is really giving a true explanation of the doctrine he meant the catechism to set forth, or interpreting something ambiguous in the light of later convictions. This is a question to which it is impossible to give a completely precise answer; all that can be said with certainty is that using the words to mean what Cranmer later defines them to mean, that which he says in the *Defence* and *Answer* cannot be contradicted.

3. It is worth quoting his statement in *The Answer to Smith's Preface:*

But this I confess of myself, that not long before I wrote the said catechism, I was in error of the real presence, as I was many years past in divers other errors: as of transubstantiation, of the sacrifice propitiatory of the priests in the mass . . . [33]

4. The records of the great parliamentary debate on the Lord's Supper held in December 1548 show that by that time he had come to hold a fully reformed position, to which position he adhered to the end.[34]

Thus it would seem that his mind was finally made up in matters of eucharistic doctrine at the very latest by the end of 1548. Does this contradict Sir John Cheke's evidence, quoted above, about the date as 1546? Not if one supposes that Ridley started Cranmer off on a process of thought that crystallised some two years later. But because of the time-scale involved, this would not help to settle in any more detail the original theological intention of 1549 (with which the earlier Order is to a lesser extent tied up).

(iii) The nature of Cranmer's mind

Beyond this point, it is necessary to look at the way Cranmer's mind worked and how he made up his mind about things. Cranmer was an academic, a professional scholar, who had spent virtually the whole of his adult life at Cambridge University until Henry VIII made him archbishop of Canterbury. Further, his reputation as a scholar must have been considerable in the 1520s, because Wolsey wanted to appoint him as a don at Cardinal College. Again, he possessed a very considerable library, and from the large number of marginal comments with which his books are annotated, it is clear that he read widely, in depth and in detail, and that he must have had a very considerable knowledge of all branches of the theology of his day.[35]

Two quotations from Cranmer himself are important indications of the way his scholarly mind worked:

I have come to the conclusion that the writings of every man must be read with discrimination;[36]

and

We must turn every stone, as the proverb saith, to seek out the truth, but specially when godly matters be propounded.[37]

These two quotations seem typical of a man who considered all the evidence and all the different opinions about a certain matter, and then made up his own mind and reached his own independent conclusions.[38] To picture Cranmer as being 'blown about by every wind of strange doctrine' seems to be fundamentally false in the light of his scholarly care and precision. It also surely means that Cranmer could and did use sources and materials for his liturgical compositions without necessarily accepting all the theological ideas in or behind these sources. To give a specific example: to argue from Cranmer's use of Lutheran liturgical materials that he necessarily held Lutheran ideas seems to be a false piece of reasoning.

Because of this independent mind and scholarly nature, what can, it seems, be said with certainty is that his liturgical composition always reflected and expressed his completely worked-out theological convictions at whatever stage these had reached when he was working, and do not reflect whatever theological pressure or influence was impinging at any given moment on an unstable mind, because he simply did not have that sort of mind. Whether his rites reflect political pressure, is another question.

Cranmer's mature views on the eucharist as expressed in the *Defence* and *Answer* are in great contrast to the 'Catholic' belief that the eucharist constitutes a real action of Christ in his church. But because Cranmer had used positive traditional language to express his views, no doubt feeling that he was using this language correctly, many have found his views difficult to understand. He needs to be read as a whole; quotation of isolated sentences can be very misleading. In order to simplify the problem of terminology here, the term 'virtual receptionist' is used to describe Cranmer's mature theology, the position he had adopted by 1548 and adhered to to the end. Whether in getting there he went through a phase in which his views about the nature of the eucharistic presence could be described as approximating to Lutheranism, and whether this has left any trace in 1548 or 1549 still remains a question to which neither the time-scale of his theological development, nor the 'virtual receptionist' doctrine he professed from 1548 onwards, provide a decisive answer.

This leads directly to a consideration of the 1548 *Order of the Communion* and the Edwardine Prayer Book Orders of 1549 and 1552. The extent to which people other than Cranmer influenced their content and structure, and the precise eucharistic doctrine they were intended to express, prove to be extremely complicated questions, and very hard to obtain precise answers to, because of the vagueness of the few contemporary records upon which historical reconstruction has to be based.

(iv) The 1548 Order of the Communion

The first stage of the Edwardine liturgical reconstruction was the publication of the 1548 Order and the steps that led up to it. Parliament passed an act in November 1547 which combined legislation against ungodly disputes with provision for communion in both kinds.[39] Most of this act is concerned with proceedings to be taken against revilers, and is careful to describe the institution of the eucharist in general scriptural terms. The last three paragraphs only concern communion in both kinds. The first of these enact that the Blessed Sacrament be ministered in both kinds (specifically referred to as bread and wine) except necessity require otherwise, remarking that this was the practice for the first five hundred years after the Ascension, and commending that the people should receive, though it does not require this. The second paragraph commends the priest to exhort the people 'at least one day before' to receive prepared. The third says that the sacrament is to be denied to no person that devoutly and humbly desires it; it also refuses to condemn the usage of foreign churches. There is no reference to the provision of liturgical material for this enactment. This act was supplemented by a 'proclamation concerning the irreverent talkers of the sacrament', designed to stop endless disruptive speculation. Its interest lies in its positive doctrinal statements, which are as follows:

with obedient faith to accept in the said sacrament according to the saying of St. Paul, the bread is the communion or partaking of the Body of the Lord; the wine, likewise, the partaking of the blood of Christ, by the words instituted and taught of Christ, and that the body and blood of Jesus Christ is there; which is our comfort, thanksgiving, love-token of Christ's love towards us, and of ours as his members within ourselves.

And also:

In the meanwhile the king's highness pleasure is, by the advice aforesaid, that every his loving subjects shall devoutly and reverently affirm and take that holy bread to be Christ's body, and that cup to be the cup of his holy blood, according to the purpose and effect of the holy scriptures, contained in the act before expressed, and accommodate themselves rather to take the same sacrament worthily, than rashly to enter into the discussion of the high mystery thereof.[40]

This carefully confines itself to scriptural terminology, and seems to express a real presence in the elements, though the manner of the presence is carefully left undefined. This proclamation was put forth by the King in council, and presumably represents their views.[41] It would be very interesting to know how much of a hand Cranmer had in its composition, but no details as to who actually wrote it seem to be recorded.

At the same time that Parliament passed the act providing for communion in both kinds, the Convocation gave its assent in principle to this practice. At the session at which this took place:

the prolocutor showed and caused to be publicly read the form of a certain ordinance delivered to him, as he asserts, by the archbishop of Canterbury, for the taking of the Body of Our Lord under both kinds of bread and also of wine.[42]

This was then subscribed by a minority of those present, and at a later session a further general verbal assent was given. Gasquet and Bishop argue that this document was not a ritual form, but only a proposal setting out the general principle of communion in both kinds. However the phrase 'a certain ordinance' could presumably mean either of these possibilities, and it is not possible to decide conclusively which it was. They do seem to be on surer ground in regarding the procedure by which the consent of Convocation was given to this as evidence that the consent was an unwilling one.

The proclamation affixed to the 1548 *Ordo* says it was put out with the authority of the Council, but does not comment at all on authorship. The letter of the Council commending its use to the bishops, dated 13 March 1547/8, says it was the work of:

sundry of his Majesty's most grave and well learned prelates and other learned men in the scripture . . . who, after long conference together with deliberate advice, finally agreed upon a form.[43]

There seems to be no evidence as to who these people were, or indeed, evidence that the statement is in itself true.[44] Assuming that Cranmer wrote most of it, we do not know if it represents his real state of mind around the turn of the years 1547/48 (modern chronology), or whether it is influenced by a need for theological compromise. Internally, it can be said that the language of the exhortation is compatible with that of the *Defence,* whereas other provisions in it, of which the provision for the supplementary consecration of the chalice is much the most important, seem to suggest an undefined real presence theology; this is perhaps significant if compared with the December proclamation. To go beyond this would be speculation, but it does look perhaps as though official doctrine was going through some kind of undefined real presence phase at this time.

The form of the method of supplementary consecration adopted, though not the use to which it was put, had the precedent of the medieval cautels. It is consonant with the medieval belief that the institution narrative is the essential consecratory part of the rite, but not with the earlier belief that the eucharistic action is a unity that may only be performed in its entirety or not at all, which demonstrates that this latter theological outlook had been largely lost sight of in this period.

(v) The authorship of the 1549 Prayer Book

The first Act of Uniformity was passed by Parliament on 21 January 1548/9, and says concerning the authorship of the book:

His highness by the most prudent advice has appointed the archbishop of Canterbury, and certain of the most learned and discreet bishops, and other learned men of this realm . . . should draw and make one convenient and meet order, rite, and fashion of common and open prayer and administration of the sacraments to be had, and used in his majesty's realm.[45]

Cranmer alone is mentioned by name; who the rest were, has to be inferred from such scattered pieces of information as have come down to us.

F. Procter and W. H. Frere,[46] F. Gasquet and E. Bishop,[47] and W. Page in an article published in 1924,[48] all discuss this point in some detail, with reference to such original sources as have survived. Their general conclusion is that it would appear that a group of people of mixed views gathered in September 1548 at Chertsey, that they debated work already completed and put before them, and that there was disagreement about some of it; and further, that they had some dealings with the court at Windsor during that month.

The only piece of contemporary evidence to mention actual names is the entry in Cranmer's register of Farrar's consecration to be bishop of St David's. This took place at Chertsey on 9 September 1548. This register shows as present on this occasion, besides Cranmer, bishops Holbeach of Lincoln, Ridley of Rochester, Goodrich of Ely, and Thirlby of Westminster, together with William May, dean of St Paul's, Simon Haynes, dean of Exeter, Thomas Robertson, and John Redman. These people, then, we know to have been at Chertsey at the appropriate time.[49] There seem to be sufficient contemporary references surviving to be able to take it as certain that such a body of people met, and that they discussed some of what later became the 1549 Prayer Book. Nor is any great difficulty raised by the two place names Windsor and Chertsey: both lie on the Thames, only a few miles apart, which would have been a comparatively easy journey by sixteenth century standards.

It is only when we get to the middle of the seventeenth century that a full list of names appears, given for the first time by Fuller in his Church History, published in 1655. To the nine names mentioned above he adds four more, bishops Skip of Hereford and Day of Chichester together with Drs Cox and Taylor.[50] He quotes no authority for this, and whether he was using other records now lost, or just guessing, would seem to be a matter not susceptible of proof one way or the other. Most subsequent writers, including Anthony Sparrow, seem to have simply copied this list, and to have attributed the production of 1548 to the same group. For this latter assertion there is no evidence at all. There would seem to be no evidence of any kind to corroborate the statement in the Council's letter to the bishops; Page examined the patent rolls for 1548 with care, and found no entry for any such commission relating to either the 1548 *Ordo* or the 1549 book.[51]

On the other hand Fuller's list has a certain probability about it; nine of the persons in it are named in Cranmer's register as being present at Farrar's consecration. In addition Somerset in the Lords' debate mentions Day of Chichester as having refused to subscribe, so presumably he was there too. Also, the composition of Fuller's committee is intrinsically probable. It consists of six bishops and six other divines under Cranmer's chairmanship, a committee of this composition being specifically mentioned in the act of 1550 authorising the composition of the Ordinal.[52] Again, Fuller's list is a fairly representative sample of the variety of opinions current in 1549, and in this sense it would have been a fair commission to have appointed.

What the commission actually did, is another question. No minutes or even brief description of their proceedings exist, so this is another matter that has to be conjectured as far as possible from such small amount of indirect evidence as there is. Two factors in particular lead to the supposition that they did not compose anything, but considered material already before them. The first of these is that there is some contemporary evidence for the use of English in the main services of the church in official circles before September 1548.[53] The second is that it is quite clear from the records of the December 1548 Parliamentary debate about the sacrament that the commission had disagreed about the doctrinal content of the proposals before them. In the final vote in the Lords, Skip, Thirlby, and Day voted against the book;[54] all men who, according to Fuller and his successors, had helped to draw it up! With such scanty evidence available it is not really possible to say what the Windsor Commission did, but it does seem fair to conjecture that they cannot be considered the originators of the 1549 rite or of its doctrinal content.

(vi) The 'Great Parliamentary Debate'

The record of the 'Great Parliamentary Debate' is one of the most important pieces of contemporary evidence to survive, and considerable use has been made of it since the end of the last century in attempting to solve the problem of the development of English eucharistic theology in this vital period. One of the most important points to arise out of it is the assessment of Thirlby's contributions. Gasquet and Bishop[55] deduced that he had accused the Government of tampering with the book after the Windsor Commission's meetings, an interpretation tentatively supported by Procter and Frere[56] and, much more recently, definitely and without discussion, by G.J. Cuming.[57] This interpretation was rejected by J.T. Tomlinson.[58] It is therefore worth examining the evidence of the report of the debate at first hand to assess this and other conclusions that have been drawn from it.

Both Gasquet and Bishop and Tomlinson[59] print verbatim the surviving manuscript of the report of this debate, which Tomlinson comments is probably the earliest known specimen of parliamentary reporting. Tomlinson reprints it complete with all the ancient irregular spelling, and makes two particular criticisms of Gasquet's transcription and handling of the text; in fact Tomlinson's pamphlet seems to have been published as something of a reply to Gasquet, whose interpretation of the document he challenges in several respects. In this context perhaps it ought to be noted that he was a man of decidedly protestant views.[60]

There are two critical points in dispute between Gasquet

and Tomlinson about the debate. The first of these is whether the book read in the House was the 1549 rite itself, as Gasquet argued, or whether Tomlinson was right in maintaining that it was only a statement of summarised doctrinal agreement. On balance it would seem that Gasquet and Bishop were right in their interpretation.[61]

With regard to the second vexed question, namely whether or not Thirlby's reference to the omission of oblation was an accusation that the book had been altered after the Windsor meetings or that it had not been there in the first place, the evidence seems to suggest that the balance of probability lies with the second interpretation,[62] though the nature of the record of the parliamentary debate is not such that it is possible to be at all certain about this. This provides yet one more illustration of the host of difficulties and uncertainties that surround the production of the 1549 book, and thus of its intentions.

This is further illustrated by Day's rejection of the phrase 'that it may be unto us'; he would have preferred 'be made unto us'. It is, however, to be doubted if the imprecise and poetic Latin of the Gelasian Canon will bear this distinction in meaning. Indeed, it would seem that Cranmer would have regarded the two phrases as equivalent in meaning; for him the 'unto us' were the important words.[64] Likewise twentieth century Roman Catholic translations of the 1570 Missal have used a similar variety of phrase at this point.[65]

One other point that emerges from the debate is that Cranmer quite clearly takes his fully mature and fully reformed standpoint. This can be quite simply illustrated by a few quotations from the speeches he made in the debate. In his first major speech on the first day he says:

They be two things, to eat the sacrament and to eat the body of Christ. The eating of the body is to dwell in Christ, and this may be though a man never tastes of the sacrament.

He denies that the wicked receive the body in any sense, and goes on to say:

Our faith is not to believe him to be in bread and wine, but that he is in heaven; this is proved by Scripture and doctors ... Then no man drinketh Christ or eateth him, except he dwell in Christ and Christ in him.[66]

Again, on the second day:

I believe that Christ is eaten with the heart. The eating with our mouth cannot give us life.[67]

And again:

Scripture and doctors prove that *Hic calix* is figurative which he often used and *significabat vinum.*[68]

And yet again towards the end of the debate on the fourth day:

the bread and wine are not changed outwardly but inwardly, as we are changed to be new men and yet we are men still. Thou art made God's son, and Christ dwelleth in thy mind. The change is inward, not in the bread but in the receiver. To have Christ really present here, when I may receive him in faith, is not available to do me good.[69]

These quotations show that the doctrinal position Cranmer adopted during this debate is that which he later expounded at length in his *Defence* and *Answer.* Though he does not directly mention the liturgy, the theological position he adopted shows that this is how he must have understood the 1549 rite at this time, a position which he later maintained in the *Defence.* Cranmer's standpoint in this debate is perhaps a further piece of conjectural evidence that the original theological intention of 1549 really was that later made clear in 1552.

This impression is strengthened by the position the conservatives, such as Bonner, Day, Heath and Thirlby took in the debate. It is clear throughout that they regarded the catholic faith as they understood it to be under attack, and that the rite they were discussing represented a denial of it. Thirlby objects to the omission of the elevation, adoration, and oblation.[70] Bonner regarded the book as heretical – 'There is heresy because it is called bread'.[71] For the rest the conservatives defended their understanding of the catholic faith in general terms but, within the context of this debate, their attitude to the rite before them is clear. This is further evidence for its original protestant intentions. Tunstal, Bonner, Heath, Rugg, Aldrich, Skip, Thirlby, and Day all voted against the Act of Uniformity.[72]

Thus the examination in detail of the account of this debate increases the strength of the conclusion that the 'Windsor Commission' cannot really be said to be the author of the 1549 Prayer Book, but that they discussed services already compiled beforehand. Indeed one receives the impression that the 'Windsor Commission' was something of a public relations exercise, whose purpose was to try to persuade a cross-section of opinion to accept liturgical (and thus doctrinal) changes already agreed upon, perhaps in the hope that the rest of the country might follow their lead. The record of the parliamentary debate shows this attempt at agreement (if that is what it was) to have been a failure; but the government pressed ahead in spite of conservative opposition, which then took every advantage of the conservative shape and outward appearance of the 1549 rite, together with what could be read into its wording (e.g. Gardiner's comments), to minimise the effect of the changes.

In general it may be concluded that the record of the great parliamentary debate strengthens the weight of evidence in favour of the conclusion that the 1549 eucharist is an attempt at expressing a fully reformed eucharistic theology using the shape, structure, and many of the ceremonial accompaniments of the Western rite, but as always the evidence stops short of proof.

(vii) Supplementary consecration

Thus such historical reconstruction as appears to be possible cannot be used to settle definitely the questions either as to the development of Cranmer's mind during 1548,[73] or of the precise doctrine 1549 was meant to express when it was written and published. Nor does it answer the question as to how much influence people apart from Cranmer have had on it, except the guess that the effect of the 'Windsor Commission' was slight. Thus the significance of the omission of the provision for supplementary consecration in 1549 has to be weighed in a partial vacuum. But if the suggestion made above about the official doctrinal position at the turn of the years 1547/48 is correct, this omission would seem to be significant both for the development of archbishop Cranmer's mind and for the theological intentions of 1549, and a powerful piece of supporting evidence that the doctrinal intention of 1549 when published was a fully reformed one.

(viii) Analysis of the 1549 Communion rite

In this analysis it will be useful to compare the 1549 rite with the Sarum-Roman rite it was designed to supersede, as well as with Cranmer's eucharistic theology. From the point of view of the rite's theology of sacrifice, consecration, and presence, it is the section from the offertory onwards that is important; but it is worth noting that the language of the two long exhortations following the creed seems most easily interpreted in the light of Cranmer's fully mature virtual receptionist theology. Most of the offertory sentences provided are about money or christian duty or generosity of one kind or another, and it is quite clear from the rubrics that the word 'offertory' in this rite is intended to mean collection and payment of money, and no more. After the rubric separating communicants from non-communicants, there follows the rubric directing:

Then shall the minister take so much bread and wine, as shall suffice for the persons appointed to receive holy communion,[74]

and place them upon the altar; the mixed chalice is ordered. There are no offertory prayers of any description; the Secret has gone. Doubtless this is all part of the plan to show that the eucharist is not a sacrifice in the currently accepted sense of the term. It could be asked whether this rubric is to be taken as a deliberate command to avoid the problem of supplementary consecration; but because the 1548 Order contained a similar rubrical direction, this seems unlikely.[75]

Immediately after this follows the Canon, starting with salutation, *Sursum corda* and preface. After Sanctus and Benedictus, comes the rite's greatest innovation, the new Canon in substitution for the Latin Canon. To what extent it is legitimate to compare the structure and content of these Canons is perhaps debatable. Certainly 1549 is not to be regarded as a revised vernacular Latin Canon. It is a new composition, designed to take the place of the old. But they do both occupy the same fundamental position in their respective eucharistic rites, and thus a comparison of their contents is very important and revealing for the understanding of the fundamental theologies of both rites.

The 1549 Canon starts with a long intercession which later, somewhat modified, became the 'prayer for the Church militant'. Though there is no verbal resemblance between it and the Latin Canon, in terms of content it can be said to be approximately equivalent to the *Te igitur, Memento Domine, Communicantes, Hanc igitur* and *Memento etiam* paragraphs, with all trace of any idea of offering of the elements for those prayed for cut out; theology as well as tidiness doubtless influenced the placing of the prayer for the dead here.

Next follows the paragraph which contains the institution

narrative. This starts with an introduction mentioning Christ's death upon the cross:

to suffer death upon the cross for our redemption, who made there (by his one oblation, once offered) a full, perfect, and sufficient sacrifice, oblation, and satisfaction for the sins of the whole world, and did institute, and in his holy gospel command us to celebrate, a perpetual memory of that his precious death . . .[76]

In the light of the theological debates of the time, this represents an extreme contrast with the language of the Latin Canon, and heavily underlines the total rejection of any idea of propitiatory or objective sacrifice in the eucharist, and is entirely in line with what Cranmer thought about the eucharistic sacrifice.

This exordium is followed immediately by the so-called 'epiclesis':

Hear us (O merciful Father) we beseech thee; and with thy holy spirit and word vouchsafe to bless and sanctify these thy gifts and creatures of bread and wine, that they may be unto us the body and blood of thy most dearly beloved son Jesus Christ.

Cranmer, in his discussion with Gardiner on this point, heavily stressed the 'unto us';[77] but, before taking this as firm evidence of its protestant intention, it must be noted that the *Quam oblationem,* which is this paragraph's equivalent, reads 'ut *nobis* corpus et sanguis fiat dilectissimi filii tui Domini Nostri Jesu Christi', which the English could be held to translate exactly.[78] Thus the first part of this paragraph has substituted a prayer for the blessing of the elements by spirit and word for one explicitly praying for the acceptance of the oblation; once again all notion of sacrifice in the traditional sense has been cut out. So much is clear, but the reason for and intended sense of the so-called 'epiclesis' is much more of a problem. It has been suggested that there is an Eastern influence here, and certainly some Eastern liturgical texts were printed in the West before this time.[79] Cranmer only once mentions Eastern liturgies in his writings on the sacrament, in a brief reference 'to the liturgy ascribed unto St Basil';[80] he cites it in Book III of the *Defence* as supporting the viewpoints he is expressing, but gives no clue as to what in that rite he is referring. There are two limited verbal similarities between the rite of St Basil and 1549 at the epiclesis: firstly, that both rites refer to the elements at this point as 'gifts' (Basil: $\delta\omega\rho\alpha$); and secondly, perhaps of more significance, 1549 asks the holy spirit and word to 'bless and sanctify', which is to be compared with εὐλογῆσαι καὶ ἁγιάσαι καὶ ἀναδεῖξαι of St Basil.[81] The phrase εὐλογῆσαι καὶ ἁγιάσαι occurs nowhere in the Septuagint, so this phrase cannot have been independently borrowed by Basil and Cranmer from this source.[82] Also a few words earlier, St Basil refers to the elements as ἀντίτυπα, which may have appealed to Cranmer if he had understood this word to mean sign or figure in his sense. On the other hand St Basil is much˙ longer, it is much more positively a direct prayer for conversion, and it prays for the descent of the Spirit upon us and the gifts, and not that the gifts 'may be . . . unto us'. Furthermore in 1549 the epiclesis comes before the institution narrative, whereas in St Basil it comes afterwards. Also 1549 couples holy Spirit and word (which in this context almost certainly is a reference to the words of Christ at the last supper, and not the λόγος), whereas St Basil has no mention of 'word' at this point or anything like it. From a direct comparison of the two rites this is all that can be said on the subject of Cranmer's possible indebtedness to the Byzantine rite at this point.

J. Dowden has drawn attention to a partial similarity of wording and structure between the 1549 rite at his point and the Pfalz-Neuburg Order of 1543, though he is not confident that this order can be shown to have directly influenced the Prayer Book.[83] Another possibliity is that Cranmer could have made up his epiclesis purely from his own ideas about the Spirit and the word of God, and of how they operate in the sacraments, his only indebtedness to sources being to Western ones, as Ratcliff maintained,[84] and also Brightman in his later years.[85]

The problem of the sources Cranmer drew on in composing the 1549 'epiclesis' is one that is probably incapable of final solution. But if Eastern rites did suggest its wording to him, it seems certain that this is not evidence that he believed in an 'Eastern' theology of consecration when he composed it, for he almost certainly would not have understood what that was. It will be argued later that Anglicans did not really understand Eastern consecration theology until the early eighteenth century.[86] Thus Cranmer's use of Eastern liturgical material (if he did use it) is at most evidence that he regarded the Eastern prayers as early support for his own eucharistic theology.

Then follows an institution narrative that has been simplified and its terminology reduced to forms found in scripture, with the elevation strictly prohibited, surely a very significant indication of the intended theology of the rite. No fraction is ordered at the institution narrative, but it has been suggested that one might have been intended because this was the current custom, and the compilers of 1549 expected and intended this custom to continue. The rubrics of the Sarum Missal do not command such a practice, but the Sarum Manual of 1554 mentions such a practice as an abuse and condemns it[87] . The 1554 Manual dates from the Counter-Reformation under Mary, but no doubt reflected continuity with liturgical practice prior to the Edwardine prayer books, which were only in use for a maximum of four years. The 1543 *Rationale of Ceremonial* describes the consecration of the bread at the institution narrative, without a fraction or prohibition of a fraction. Later the fraction is described in its proper place.[88] John de Burgo in his *Pupilla Oculi* also says that no symbolic breaking should take place at the institution narrative.[89] Thus though the performance of such a fraction was not unknown, and may have been common in Sarum usage,[90] official educated Sarum liturgical practice regarded it as an abuse. This the compilers of 1549 must have known; had they wished to convert what was formerly an abuse into a precept, they would surely have commanded it. Silence therefore leads to the supposition that it was not intended. This is reinforced by three further considerations: first, that everybody was to be communicated with a broken host (thus 1549 made its fraction a matter of utility – its primitive origin? But would Cranmer have known this?); second, that the ceremonial of 1549 everywhere represents a simplification of Sarum; third, that all manual acts disappeared in 1552.

The 1549 rite then continues with a paragraph making the memorial in the gifts,[91] which is to be compared with the *Unde et memores* and following. Here, the references to specific offering of the elements are removed, and the sacrifice is made one of praise and thanksgiving; this is Cranmer's language. In this prayer, we pray that by Christ's death and our faith in his blood we may obtain the benefits of his passion, that whoever may partake of this communion, may worthily receive the most precious body and blood. It is this Cranmer believed to be the memorial that Christ commanded us to make in the gifts. All reference to the sacrificial offering of the Old Testament worthies is omitted, and it is 'our prayers' that are to be brought up, replacing *'haec perferri,'* to 'thy holy Tabernacle' (note too the change from altar to tabernacle). *'Perferri'* means 'to be carried' with the sense of 'brought to a person or place';[92] *'haec'* is neuter plural, and in the Roman rite could be held to refer to the eucharistic gifts themselves or to the prayers of the rite, but in 1549 the reference is unambiguous, and thus there is a weakening of doctrine here. This whole section from 'Wherefore . . .' to the doxology exactly expresses Cranmer's doctrine of the eucharistic sacrifice, and he surely must have written it; the only possible exception to this conclusion is that the phrase 'with these thy holy gifts' could be held to express a more positive theology than Cranmer's.

Then follows the Lord's Prayer (without *Libera nos*), the peace without fraction or commixture,[93] and a new paragraph about Christ our paschal lamb offered 'once for all when he bare our sins upon his body upon the cross'; once again the uniqueness and all-sufficiency of Christ's sacrifice upon the cross is emphasised. Then follows Invitation, Confession, Absolution, Comfortable Words, and Prayer of Humble Access, all without significant alteration from 1548; the Prayer of Humble Access is unchanged. This prays:

> Grant unto us so to eat the flesh . . . and drink his blood in these holy mysteries, that we may continually dwell . . . [94]

This can be seen as a prayer for worthy reception and benefits of communion in the Cranmerian manner, even if it is possible to interpret it differently, as did Gardiner.

The formulae of administration are perfectly consonant with the theology of the *Defence,* if one takes all the words and phrases to mean what Cranmer uses them to mean in the *Defence.* The rubric refers to 'the sacrament of the body of Christ . . . the sacrament of the blood of Christ . . .', that is, the sign or figure of what is to be spiritually received, and the words of administration are a prayer that by right reception the communicant will receive the desired ends. It is of course very easy to understand them in a much more literal sense. The forms themselves come from 1548, slightly altered by the coupling together of 'body and soul' in both of them,[95] and are a combination of Sarum (from the order for the visitation of the sick) with the Lutheran addition 'which was given for you'.[96]

The rubric concerned with assistants at the administration has in fact been strengthened in a catholic direction in 1549 from the original 1548 version. This latter simply referred to 'bread' and 'wine' whereas in 1549 the reference is to 'sacrament of the body' and 'sacrament of the blood',[97] in conformity with the preceding rubric introducing the words of administration, thus eliminating an inconsistency of terminology in the 1548 *Ordo*. This may have been the only motive for the change, but it is nevertheless odd in that it appears to represent a move against the flow of doctrinal and liturgical development.

The singing of the *Agnus Dei*, a traditional part of the Roman rite, was no doubt intended by Cranmer to be here a devotion to Christ sitting at the right hand of God the Father, and possibly to him spiritually present in those receiving communion, but not to any objective presence of Christ in the sacrament. The post-communion sentences, all of which come from the gospels or epistles, could all be classed under the heading of general points about the christian life; none are in any sense specifically sacramental, and significantly none are from John 6. [98]

The post-communion prayer thanks God for feeding

us in these holy mysteries, with the spiritual food of the most precious body and blood . . . and hast assured us (duly receiving the same) . . . [99]

which again expresses Cranmer's theology exactly, if spiritual food is interpreted in the way he does, though again it would be possible to interpret it in a more positive sense.

Of the rubrics at the end of the rite, the first two are concerned to ensure that there is no celebration without communicants, and the third orders the use of unleavened bread:

that is to say, unleavened and round, as it was afore, but without all manner of print, and something more larger and thicker than it was, so that it may be aptly divided in divers pieces; and every one shall be divided in two pieces, at the least, or more, by the discretion of the minister, and so distributed. And men must not think less to be received in part than in whole, but in each of them the whole body of our saviour Jesu Christ.[100]

This comes from 1548, but the provision that the bread be larger and 'without all manner of print' is new. In connection with the argument Gardiner and Cranmer had on this point, it should perhaps be noted that it refers to 'reception in each' rather than 'presence in each'. To take it this way comes nearer to Cranmer's belief, even if it still seems possible to interpret it quite differently.

The rite makes no rubrical provision for consumption of any 'consecrated' bread and wine that remain after communion or for ablution of the communion vessels, in contrast to the elaborate provisions of the Sarum Missal. Though it could be argued that a proper ablution is assumed and implied, in fact the evidence would seem to be against such an assumption; the rite lacks no other essential rubrical direction. This omission and the extremely important omission of the 1548 provision for supplementary consecration both seem highly significant indications of the Protestant intentions of the rite.

It must also be remembered that the overall structure of the rite is significant in itself; in particular, the fact that the Canon is separated from reception of communion by the lengthy communion devotions. These communion devotions give expression to Cranmer's understanding of the doctrine of justification by faith, and are designed to elicit the right response of faith from the believer before reception of communion; the exercise of such faith being for Cranmer the essential feature of the eucharistic action, In this respect the shape of the 1549 rite provides additional evidence for its doctrinal intention being in accordance with Cranmer's ideas.

There is also the evidence of the final rubric in the order for the 'Communion of the Sick'. This says that if any man for any reason does not actually receive

the sacrament of Christ's body and blood; then the curate shall instruct him, if he do truly repent him of his sins, and steadfastly believe that Jesus Christ hath suffered death upon the cross for him, and shed his blood for his redemption, earnestly remembering the benefits he hath thereby, and giving him hearty thanks therefore; he doth eat and drink spiritually the body and blood of our saviour Christ, profitably to his soul's health, although he do not receive the sacrament with his mouth. [101]

This exactly sums up Cranmer's eucharistic doctrine, with its assertion that it is through right faith that the benefits of communion are received and that actual reception of the elements is unnecessary for this. This rubric then would seem to be evidence both for Cranmerian authorship and for the eucharistic doctrinal intention of the 1549 book being that of the *Defence*. [102]

To sum up: there is no doubt that the 1549 rite totally rejects the received view of the eucharistic sacrifice, and substitutes for it the sacrifice of praise and thanksgiving, exactly as Cranmer understood it, in his language and terminology. It is much easier to see ambiguities in it when it comes to the mode of the presence of Christ in the eucharist. It can all be interpreted in the light of the theology of the *Defence,* and there are a number of indications that point powerfully to this conclusion, but it is also possible to interpret it as teaching some kind of objective real presence. Gardiner did this, maintaining that the rite was Lutheran in its doctrine,[103] that the epiclesis,[104] the prayer of humble access,[105] and the rubric about all communicating from broken bread[106] all witness to a real presence doctrine, and further that the intercessions in the Canon indicate a sacrificial doctrine of the eucharist.[107] He hints at the same time that Cranmer in the *Defence* was theologically more advanced and not consistent with 1549.[108] In the heat of the debate Cranmer vehemently denies this, but sometimes in abusive general terms instead of dealing with the individual criticisms, and the doubts remain.

(ix) Possible ways of interpreting the 1549 rite

Thus there are several possible ways of interpreting the 1549 rite:

1. That Cranmer is right, and 1549 represented the theology of the *Defence,* as he maintained in his *Answer* to Gardiner. Here the last paragraph but one of the *Defence* must surely be given its appropriate weight; this is after all what Cranmer said.

2. That it represents in places an intermediate phase in Cranmer's thinking as regards the presence (he rejected the sacrifice, it would seem, before the presence).

3. That it represents a compromise between what Cranmer really wanted to say, and what the realities of the situation forced him to say.

As will already be appreciated, deciding between them is no easy task.

(x) Reception of the 1549 book

The next series of events to be considered is the reception

of the 1549 Prayer Book and the steps that led up to the production of 1552. Far from it producing peace and quiet, dissension and strife continued apace, with conservatives using it as a vernacular equivalent to the Latin Mass, and the Protestants going far beyond what it ordered; Ridley in London was guilty of this.[109] Comparatively few, it would seem, used it in the sense that Cranmer later defended. Opinion expressed about it ranged from the claim that it was universally popular[110] to refusal to use it.[111] In between these two extremes there are a fair number of moderate comments that combine relative approval with some criticism, and often include the suggestion that the 1549 rite is to be seen as an interim measure. Most of these are comments contained in letters to people written abroad. They were collected together during the last century and published in the Parker Society volumes of *Original Letters*.[112] They should be seen as the comments of interested and sympathetic bystanders, but it must be remembered that most of the people who wrote them were advocates of a fully reformed churchmanship. Also, being largely bystanders, they may well not have known as much as they thought they did. Therefore the evidence of these letters needs to be used with a considerable degree of caution. And in considering the suggestion contained in some of these letters that 1549 was an interim measure, it must be remembered that Cranmer himself never admitted any such thing, or that it represented anything in the nature of a political compromise, but always defended it as exactly expressing his later beliefs.

The 1549 rite was an attempt at a radical doctrinal reformation within a conservative liturgical framework. As such it failed, as perhaps it was bound to. Composed by a scholar, it needs a scholarly approach and knowledge of liturgy to appreciate. Yet it was easy for traditionalists, lettered and unlettered, to use a vernacular equivalent of the Sarum rite. So it was replaced by 1552.

Amidst all the conflicting opinions and events of these years, it is once again very difficult to assess who actually wrote the 1552 book, and the influences and interests it represents; this is the next problem that must be discussed. There was no doubt a great deal of pressure for further change in a Protestant direction; the question as far as Cranmer is concerned is, does the 1552 book go further than he himself would have wanted?

From the point of view of internal evidence, a comparison of the 1552 rite with that of 1549, noting the changes that have been made in the latter, and with the *Defence* and *Answer,* will serve to throw some light on this question.

(xi) Analysis of the 1552 Communion rite

The first significant change is the removal of the intercession from the Canon and letting it stand on its own after the offertory (money only). The omission of all reference to the saints and departed is not significant from the point of view of fundamental eucharistic theology (1549 may have prayed for the dead; it did not offer the eucharist for them).

Next follow three long exhortations, the first of which is a new composition to be read when people neglect to come, exhorting people to stay and communicate and firmly discouraging non-communicating attendance. Its theology is wholly in accordance with the mind of the *Defence.* The second exhortation of 1552 is a shortened version of the second of 1549, containing similar material. The third is a reprint of the first of 1549, with 'holy sacrament' substituted for 'blessed bread' and the phrase which qualifies 'holy mysteries': 'his own blessed body and precious blood, for us to feed on spiritually' omitted.[113] These changes do not alter its theology if it is understood in the light of the *Defence* in the first place; they do make it impossible to understand in any other sense.

Then follows Invitation, Confession, Absolution, Comfortable Words, *Sursum corda* and Prefaces; the shape of the Western rite retained in 1549 has now been dispensed with. The Prayer of Humble Access, which follows next, eliminates the phrase 'in these holy mysteries', and now no longer comes immediately before communion; again, changes that do not alter its theology when understood by the theology of the *Defence,* but make it impossible to understand otherwise.[114]

Then follows the prayer now known as 'the Prayer of Consecration', though it was not given this name until 1662. It consists of a thanksgiving for the sacrifice of the cross, exactly the same as 1549 except that 'celebrate' is altered to 'continue' in the reference to 'perpetual memory'; the 'epiclesis section' has been reduced to a prayer that those who receive the creatures of bread and wine may be partakers of the blessed body and blood (exactly Cranmer's ideas), followed by a recital of the institution narrative. In the sense that this prayer can be regarded as setting aside the bread and wine for the holy and godly use of communion, Cranmer might have been happy with the title 'prayer of consecration'.[115] There is no reference to placing the bread and wine on the table at any point.

Next follows the administration. The rubrics refer to the 'bread' and the 'cup'; the change from 'sacrament of the body', 'sacrament of the blood' is a 'more plain and manifest explanation' of what Cranmer would have understood by the rubric of 1549.[116] And the words of administration:

Take and eat this in remembrance that Christ died for thee, and feed on him in thy heart by faith, with thanksgiving,[117]

and similarly with the cup, exactly sum up what Cranmer understood the eucharistic action to be, and again explain the language of the 1549 formulae understood in a Cranmerian sense.

1552 has two post-communion prayers, the first a slightly reduced version of the 'Wherefore . . .' section of the 1549 canon, and the second the post-communion of 1549, again slightly altered.[118] These two prayers, now placed as alternatives, exactly duplicate one another in meaning, and both express the theology of the eucharist as set forth in the *Defence*.

The rubrics at the end of the service are quite different from those of 1549; of these, two are of theological importance, one of which orders the use of:

the best and purest wheat bread that conveniently may be gotten,

and which finishes with the sentence:

And if any bread or wine remain, the curate shall have it to his own use,[119]

which seems quite clearly to refer to that which has been used in the celebration. Since for Cranmer the bread and wine had no holiness in themselves, but only in use, presumably once the use was over, he would have been quite happy for the celebrant to remove all that was left over and take it home to use in the normal course of events. Extremely Protestant though this rubric is, it does not seem out of accord with what Cranmer believed about the eucharist.

The second rubric of importance is the so-called 'black

80

rubric',[120] about which there is controversy as to whether it was legally part of the book or not, an irrelevant controversy from the point of view of theology. The wording of this rubric is in every sense in accordance with Cranmer's views of the eucharist.

The rubric in 'The Communion of the Sick' adds 'or for lack of company to receive with him' to the reasons for the sick man not actually receiving communion, and omits 'spiritually. after 'eat and drink'[121]. Since Cranmer believed that 'spiritually' was the only way in which the believer received anyway, once again 1552 has made 'plain' the meaning of 1549. Thus this rubric in both rites emphasises Cranmer's belief that actually receiving communion was not necessary to feeding on Christ — helpful and desirable, but not necessary.

Thus the conclusion of this short study of the 1552 rite is that it everywhere expresses the theology of the *Defence* and *Answer,* and that, at every point where 1549 has been altered, the corresponding 1552 wording and structure need not be represented as a change in theology, but the making of a plain and direct expression of the same theology. Thus, on the basis of the internal evidence, it does not appear to be more radical than Cranmer would have wished it to be, and the most obvious conclusion is that the 1549 and 1552 rites are theologically equivalent.

(xii) External evidence concerning the 1552 rite

Turning from the internal evidence to the external, it is to be noted that the 1552 Act of Uniformity adopts this viewpoint, demonstrating it to be the official government one. This act describes 1549 as a 'very Godly order . . . agreeable to the word of God' and later describes why it is being replaced:

And because there hath arisen in the use and exercise of the aforesaid common service in the church heretofore set forth, divers doubts for the fashion and manner of the ministration of the same, rather by the curiosity of the minister and mistakers, than of any other worthy cause: therefore as well for the more plain and manifest explanation thereof, as for the more perfection of the said order of common service, in some places where it is necessary to make the same prayer and fashion of service more earnest and fit to stir christian people to the true honouring of Almighty God . . .[122]

and goes on to legislate for the new book. This Act gives no information about authorship of the book. However, it would seem fair to state that whoever was consulted, the conservative bishops were not; these had mostly been deprived, imprisoned, or otherwise restricted. Again, it would seem in character that Cranmer should have consulted widely and then made up his own mind about the changes suggested to him; if he adopted someone else's idea about something, it would be because he really thought it a good idea. Thus to argue, for example, because some aspect of 1552 represents a known view of Hooper, that Cranmer had given in to theological pressure, seems to conclude something that is not proven. Again, this does not settle the argument about political pressures, though it is to be noted that he was quite prepared to, and did, resist political pressure put upon him; witness the letter to the Council about the black rubric.[123]

There also exist two letters that Peter Martyr wrote to Bucer in early 1551 that throw valuable light on proceedings at this stage and the part Martyr played in them. The first of these was written on 10 January 1550/1,[124] and the second a few weeks later, in early February.[125] It is clear that his knowledge of the 1549 book does not appear to have been very accurate, for he objects to the 1548 provision for supplementary consecration of the chalice. The questions that arise from this are: were some people still doing this when necessary, and had Martyr seen it done? Or was he working from an imperfect set of translations (a difficulty that Martyr specifically mentions in connection with the work he was doing for Cranmer on the 1549 Book) and simply muddled? He says he had submitted criticisms of 1549 to Cranmer at the latter's request. (Does not this fact argue that Cranmer asked other people to make suggestions for him to consider, rather than submit to pressure applied by others?) On the actual business of the revision he comments in his first letter that the archbishop had told him that many things were to be changed, but not what they were. Martyr also says that he had been told by Cheke that, if the bishops would not make the necessary changes, the king would do it himself by the imposition of his royal authority in Parliament.[126] In the second letter Martyr says he had seen the agreed corrections, but knowing no English could not understand them. He was of the opinion that not all of his and Bucer's suggestions had been adopted. He says that he had urged the archbishop that complete simplicity and purity be achieved, to obviate the necessity for any further change. He says that he was convinced that, had the revision been left to Cranmer alone, this would have been done, but Cranmer was prevented from achieving this by the resolute opposition of his colleagues.[127]

These letters show that, up to the beginning of 1551 at least, Martyr was not a member of the inner circle who actually did the revision, and, partly because he did not understand English, his knowledge of these matters was far from accurate. They suggest that some kind of episcopal committee was considering the matter, and the second also contains the intriguing suggestion that Cranmer was prevented from going as far as he would have liked to go in a Protestant direction in preparing the 1552 book by conservative pressure; this is the very opposite to what has so often been conjectured about Cranmer's relation to the 1552 book. However, it must be remembered that the date of these letters is more than a year earlier than the passage of the 1552 book by Parliament.

On the question of consecration itself, we know that Martyr and Bucer both held that the words of institution were read for the benefit of the congregation and not for the elements:

Since I (Martyr) agree with you in thinking that the words of the Supper belong more to men than to bread and wine.[128]

The context of this remark is his dislike of the 1549 provision for reservation for the sick, and the 1548 provision for supplementary consecration.

So once again it has to be said that no definite evidence of the processes of revision exist; it is a matter of conjecture from such few pieces of contemporary evidence as do exist. So the assessment of external pressures is therefore a task of some difficulty. In considering these, it must be remembered that Cranmer could be regarded to a considerable extent as responsible for encouraging them. He did after all exhort and invite many of the foreign Protestant divines to come to England in the first place, and was no doubt in large part responsible for the influential positions that some of them held (e.g. the Regius Professorships held by Bucer and Martyr).

Some facts concerning external influences can however be deduced from contemporary sources. For example, about half the suggestions contained in Bucer's *Censura* were adopted into the 1552 Book.[129] The influence of Hooper, one of the leading radicals, may also be considered. Hooper regarded the ten commandments as being of the greatest importance,[130] wished all references to the saints and the departed to be cut out[131] (but so did Bucer), wished for the utmost simplicity in the externals of worship,[132] and disliked the practice of giving communion into the mouth;[133] and in all these respects the 1552 rite is in accordance with his thinking. On the other hand, Hooper wanted chancels to be shut up,[134] thought the fraction very important,[135] and wished people to sit to receive communion.[136] None of these points were followed in 1552, and Cranmer took a very firm stand on the issue of kneeling reception. This may suggest that the compilers of 1552 adopted some of Hooper's ideas after free and critical consideration; it certainly does not indicate that he was in any position to pressurise them into altering the book against their will. Ab Ulmis also suggests that Cranmer and Ridley were in fundamental agreement with Hooper about the issue of ecclesiastical vesture, but thought it wrong to anticipate the law in this respect.[137] This information should, however, be treated with the same reserve as the other viewpoints expressed in the *Original Letters*.

J.I. Packer maintains that the difference between Cranmer and Hooper was not fundamental, but one of mental method.[138] Hooper too denies that the sacramental species are just bare signs and tokens,[139] and his more positive utterances are very like those of Cranmer.[140] The differences between them seem to have been very largely about matters of ceremonial, and not about doctrinal issues.

Cranmer's letter to the Council about kneeling is interesting for the grounds on which Cranmer rested his defence of the 1552 book as it stood. He argued that:

1. To alter without the consent of Parliament what Parliament has already passed is to set a dangerous precedent.

2. Kneeling to receive was reverent within the context of this service: to kneel for the prayers and after communion but to sit for the communion itself would not be reverent.

3. To object to kneeling on the grounds that it is unscriptural is to go the same way as the Anabaptists; one might as well not have a prayer book at all. He also points out that reclining was the posture that would have been adopted at the Last Supper. Cranmer also subtly hints that to give way to the

clamour of 'glorious and unquiet spirits' at that point would only be to encourage fresh demands for innovations on the part of people who would never be satisfied, even though the book were made every year anew.[141] It is also to be noted that Cranmer did not oppose the 'black rubric' as such; indeed he may have helped to compose it, for it certainly expresses his ideas. What he did oppose was extra-parliamentary tampering with legislation already passed by Parliament.

The final point of interest in this discussion of the 1552 rite is the suggestion that a third prayer book, even more radical than 1552, was being planned towards the end of the reign of Edward VI, but that the king's death prevented this project coming to fruition. George Withers, a puritan divine, maintained that this was the case. The source of this is a letter that he wrote to the Prince Elector Palatine. It is undated, but internal evidence suggests that it was written soon after the issue of Parker's *Advertisements* of 1564.[142] Robert Horne is also reported in the *Troubles at Frankfort* to have been of the same opinion.[143] Horne,[144] a strict puritan, was dean of Durham during the latter part of the reign of Edward VI, and so may have been in a position to know something. These two pieces of evidence, together with Martyr's suggestion that 1552 was more conservative than Cranmer would have liked, amount to no more than insubstantial rumour, but they do at least lend some weight to the conclusion that the 1552 rite was not more radical than Cranmer wished it to be. On the other hand, none of Horne's correspondence in the *Zurich Letters* contain any such reference,[145] and this includes the letter he sent to Bullinger containing a description of the 1552 book.[146]

(xiii) Summary

In attempting to draw a general conclusion from this discussion of the Edwardine Communion rites, it must be repeated that it is extremely difficult to say with certainty and precision who was really responsible for the various stages of the Edwardine liturgical revolution. But the internal evidence shows that the whole of the 1549 and 1552 Communion rites can be regarded as compatible with the theology of the *Defence* and *Answer*, and the external evidence, on a balance of probabilities, would seem to show that there was no major theological point at which Cranmer's wishes and beliefs were contradicted or over-ruled. The received opinion that these rites are his work is thus confirmed. Thus the declared aim of 1552, as expressed in the Act of Uniformity, that its purpose was to make plain the meaning of 1549, would seem to have been an honest one. The viewpoint that the 1549 and 1552 rites are to be regarded as different liturgical expressions of the same theology is thus upheld. When the results of this discussion are referred back to those about the 1549 rite and the development of archbishop Cranmer's mind on the eucharist, the following conclusions may also be stated:

1. When Parliament passed the first Act of Uniformity, the understood doctrinal intention of the 1549 rite was a fully reformed one, that is, that later expressed and 'made plain' by 1552.

2. Cranmer's arriving at his final state of mind can perhaps be fairly accurately located in the late spring or early summer of 1548, by which time much of the 1549 rite may have existed in draft and was perhaps being used in the King's chapel and elsewhere. Perhaps, then, some of the 1549 rite was originally composed by Cranmer when he still held to some kind of undefined real presence theology; but when he had finally abandoned this position, he still used this material in a fully reformed sense and defended it as such. Perhaps the ambiguous *appearance* of some of the 1549 rite is to be accounted for in this way.

3. The evidence of the *Original Letters* gives some support to the view that the 1549 Book was intended as an interim stage in a continuing process of reformation, and this for reasons of political compromise; and that this is particularly so in matters of ceremonial and outward appearance. Yet it must be remembered that these letters were all written by men of a fully reformed standpoint, and that the evidence they offer is not wholly consistent. These letters were written by men on the periphery of the 'corridors of power', who may have thought they were better informed than they actually were, and who because of their views, would have been subject to temptation, probably unconsciously, to exaggerate progress in a fully reformed direction.

4. Again, in terms of outward appearance and ceremonial, the progress of the Edwardine Reformation looks like a progress from Henrician Catholicism to a kind of 'Lutheranism' in the first Prayer Book through to the fully reformed position of the second. But insofar as this reflects the doctrinal process of development, this process was complete *before* the final drafting, enactment, and publication of the first Prayer Book.

CHAPTER FOUR

Doctrinal and Liturgical Developments
in the period 1559-1641

(i) The 1559 Prayer Book and the 39 Articles

On her accession to the throne in 1558, queen Elizabeth I and her advisers were faced with the immense task of reconstructing English religious life after the theological and liturgical revolution and counter-revolution of the previous two reigns. It is this reconstruction that can be said to be the foundation of Anglicanism as a specific christian tradition. It was undertaken using as source materials the legacy of the Edwardine Reformation. It is the way that these source materials were used that is important and significant. One important point needs to be made at this stage, namely that political considerations and pressures dictated the following of a moderate course in order to commend acceptance to as wide a range of different viewpoints as possible. This does not mean that the Elizabethan religious settlement did not represent the religious convictions of its authors; but it does mean that their freedom of expression was severely limited and restricted. Throughout Elizabeth's reign, a great deal of government energy was absorbed in keeping the Church of England on the *via media* prescribed for it in 1559.

The 1559 Prayer Book was imposed by Act of Uniformity and ordered to be used from St John the Baptist's Day, 1559. It consisted of the 1552 book with a few alterations in a Catholic direction. Of these only three affect the Communion service, namely the alteration of the vestments rubric, the joining together of the formulae of administration of communion from both the Edwardine prayer books, and the omission of the black rubric. It could be argued on legal grounds that the omission of the black rubric was not a change in the 1552 prayer book, since it had been inserted in this latter book without the authority of Parliament: archbishop Parker does not mention it in a letter he wrote to lord Burghley on the subject.[1] The change in the ornaments rubric, which moved from the position of the 1552 book to the position as it had been in the second year of Edward VI, was doubtless intended as a measure of comprehension, but it does perhaps have doctrinal overtones in a catholic direction. By far the most important change is that concerned with the formulae of administration; in themselves they may not signify very much (Cranmer had maintained the whole 1549 rite was an expression of the doctrine of the *Defence* and *Answer*), but this change probably does represent a desire on the part of the government to make the book at least compatible with belief in some kind of real presence doctrine. Historically, it would seem that the Queen would have liked to return to 1549, whereas most of the returned protestant exiles would have liked 1552 changed still further in a protestant direction. In fact 1559 is 1552 slightly altered in a Catholic sense, and thus represents a compromise.[2]

The same would seem to be true of the 39 Articles, which represent the Elizabethan church's revision of the 42 Articles, the final doctrinal heritage of the Edwardian Reformation. Detailed comparison of the changes made, both in general and with particular reference to sacramental and eucharistic doctrine, suggest not so much a change of doctrine as a move towards a more positive, comprehensive, and irenic expression of the same doctrine. The one possible exception to this is the condemnation of the *ex opere operato* theory of the sacraments eliminated from article 26 of the 42 when it became article 25 of the 39.[3]

(ii) The Johnson Case

The next event of real importance is the trial of Robert Johnson in 1573. He had run out of wine during the administration of communion, and, sending for more, had delivered this to the communicants without repeating the relevant portion of the institution narrative. For this he was tried before the Queen's Commissioners, who included the bishop of London and the dean of Westminster, on 20 February 1573. Johnson admitted that such was his practice, and defended himself on the grounds that firstly, there was nothing in the Prayer Book that prescribed supplementary consecration, and secondly, that his procedure was justified on theological grounds. E.C. Ratcliff prints out a substantial proportion of Johnson's own account of the proccedings.[4] From this several things emerge concerning the official Elizabethan church standpoint in this matter. The first of these is that, since the newly brought wine had not had the words of institution spoken over it, 'it was no sacrament, and so the people were mocked'. Secondly and consequently, that the words of institution were necessary to make the sacrament, and the words of institution were spoken for the bread and wine and for the benefit of the people, and thus must be spoken over all bread and wine used for giving communion. Thirdly, that this was regarded as the meaning and directive of the 1559 rite. Johnson was duly convicted, in spite of his shrewd assertion that his views were in accordance with those of Cranmer, which is in itself evidence as to how Cranmer was understood near his own time. Thus the Elizabethan church returned in this respect to the position of the 1548 *Ordo,* and thus apparently decisively commited itself in liturgical practice to a belief in some kind of consecration of the elements themselves, thus by implication rejecting Cranmer's eucharistic theology. In terms of theological statements the Elizabethan church may often seem as Protestant as Cranmer; in terms of liturgical usage they had theoretically returned towards something arguably similar to and possibly derived from Western Catholic practice, a fact of seemingly the greatest significance. But that it did so by means of a judicial decision, rather than by an acknowledged legislative process, is strange, and gives rise to the question as to how widely known (and hence conformed to) it was at the time.

Ratcliff in his discussion of this topic commented as follows:

The sharp sentence passed upon Johnson was evidence of the gravity with which Elizabethan ecclesiastical authority viewed the matter, and of the Commissioner's resolve to secure compliance with the official instruction.[5]

Granted the truth of this with regard to the sentence passed upon Johnson, it is surely odd therefore that the Elizabethan ecclesiastical authorities seem to have made no attempt to publicise or enforce this decision either at the time, or later on in Elizabeth's reign. None of the embryonic attempts at making canon law refer to it,[6] nor do such sets of visitation articles as have survived. Indeed, it raises the question as to why the prosecution against Johnson was ever brought at all.

W.H. Frere[7] and W.M. Kennedy[8] between them printed no fewer than 139 sets of visitation articles and injunctions from the reign of Elizabeth I, none of which contain any reference to the subject of supplementary consecration.[9] (Of these 67 date from before 1573, and 72 in or after that year.) It is true that a number of these sets of articles, particularly those from the earlier part of the reign, are of quite minor importance, being addressed to a single institution such as a cathedral or college, and are almost wholly concerned with personal disciplinary problems, such as non-residence, and matters of property. But the majority are full sets of visitation articles addressed to a diocese or cathedral corporation, and concern themselves with every facet of ecclesiastical life.

Even those sets of articles issued by people connected with the Johnson case, or by people who might have been expected to have some knowledge of it, make no mention of the matter. Sandys, who as bishop of London had taken part in Johnson's trial, does not mention the subject in the articles he issued as archbishop of York in 1578,[10] nor did Aylmer, Sandys' successor as bishop of London, in his articles for London in 1577[11] and 1586[12].

Most of the full sets of articles do contain general queries as to whether the sacraments be administered according to the laws of the realm or the Book of Common Prayer; a typical example occurs in the articles Bancroft issued for London in 1601:

Whether doth your parson use the forms and prayers prescribed in the Communion Book, without omitting or altering any part of them, and without any of his own additions.[13]

No doubt a lawyer could argue that after the decision in the Johnson case such a general query covered the requirement for supplementary consecration. But in the circumstances of the time very few people would have known about the Johnson case decision; and, therefore, in the absence of specific mention of the subject, it must be concluded that the Elizabethan Church made no attempt to ensure that supplementary consecration where needed became the general practice.[14] This had to wait until the next reign. Thus while the Johnson case is of the greatest theological importance, its actual influence on Elizabethan ecclesiastical practice would seem to have been fairly minimal.

Another pointer that this was probably the case lies in the fact that our principal account of the proceedings at Johnson's trial comes not from an official Anglican source, but from Johnson's own account of it published in a puritan tract some 20 years later.[15] In view of all the above facts, or lack of them, perhaps it is fair to say that Ratcliff has rather overestimated the practical effect of the Johnson case on the liturgical practice of the Elizabethan church.

While considering the question of Elizabethan ecclesiastical practice, it may be noted that many of these sets of articles show the Elizabethan bishops, after seeking to ensure that the law of public worship was obeyed, to have been far more concerned about the elimination of remaining traces of pre-Reformation liturgical practices than they were to ensure a decent minimum of 'Catholic' observance. In 1583 Middleton, bishop of St David's, even went so far as to forbid any kind of manual acts during the recitation of the institution narrative, ordering the bread and wine to lie upon the table until the distribution, then the bread to be broken, both kinds received by the minister, and then distributed.[16] This he directed for the avoidance of popery and superstition, which he regarded as rife in his diocese, an interesting comment coming as it does a full generation or so after the date of the Elizabethan Settlement. Middleton represents in an extreme form what seems to have been the typical state of mind of many of the Elizabethan bishops.

(iii) Bishop Jewel

It now remains to investigate something of how the Elizabethan church in the person of its leading divines explained its understanding of the eucharist. Of the Elizabethan divines, John Jewel and Richard Hooker were pre-eminent in theological defence and apologetic, the former in defence against the Roman attack in the early part of the reign, witness his *An Apology of the Church of England* and his long controversy with Harding, while the latter's *Ecclesiastical Policy* published in the 1590s was mainly directed against the puritan onslaught.

Jewel's doctrine of consecration can best be succinctly illustrated by two quotations, taken from his controversy with Harding:

We pronounce the same words of consecration that Christ pronounced: we do the same thing that Christ bid us do: we proclaim the death of the Lord: we speak openly in a known tongue; and the people understandeth us; we consecrate for the congregation and not only for ourself: we have the element: we join God's word to it; and so it is made a sacrament.[17]

And:

We ought to do the thing that Christ both did himself, and also commanded us to do . . . he said thus: 'Do ye this': that is, take ye bread: bless it: break it: give it 'in my remembrance'.[18]

These two quotations can be coupled with one that illustrates his understanding of how the eucharist is efficacious:

We affirm that bread and wine are holy and heavenly mysteries of the body and blood of Christ, and that by them Christ himself, being the true bread of eternal life, is so presently given unto us that by faith we verily receive his body and blood.[19]

A detailed study of their writings shows that both Cranmer and Jewel held to very similar doctrines of the eucharist in many respects. However, Jewel parts company from Cranmer in the two words 'by them' — 'and that *by them* Christ himself is so presently given unto us . . .' This is precisely what Cranmer did not believe, and thus for Jewel the bread and wine are a necessary part of the eucharistic action in themselves. The above quotation also shows that Jewel held a proper liturgical setting-aside, or consecration, to be necessary that they might be this, thus demonstrating that he has returned back in a Catholic direction over that fine but distinctive dividing line between those who do regard the elements as an essential part of the eucharistic action and those who do not. Anglican liturgical practice returned with him, for Jewel's work was regarded as an official apologia for the Church of England.

The essence of the consecration as such he would seem to understand as both word and performance of the eucharistic action, a repetition of the words and actions of the New

Testament accounts of the institution, which is not dissimilar from contemporary Western Latin ideas on the subject.

(iv) Richard Hooker

Richard Hooker was born in 1554, and thus belongs to the first generation that grew up in the church of the Elizabethan Settlement, having known no other, and in his work there is a sense of detachment from the immediate and violent Reformation controversies. In his writing about the eucharist he tries to be as irenic and positive as possible,, concentrating on the benefits of communion, where he sees a large measure of agreement between all contending parties. The controversy between Reformed, Lutheran, and Papist about the nature of the eucharistic presence he regards as largely futile, an attitude that is a measure of his detachment from the immediate Reformation period

The sacraments in general, and the eucharist in particular, he regards as real means of grace which effect what they signify, while the substances of their matter remain unchanged.[20]

Chapter 67 of Book 5 contains his discussion of eucharistic doctrine, and the first section ends with the assertion:

through faith we perceive in the body and blood sacramentally presented the very taste of eternal life.[21]

In the next section he asserts that the elements are

made for ever the instruments of life by virtue of his divine benediction,

spoken at the Last Supper when the disciples saw Jesus

first bless and consecrate for the endless good of all generations till the world's end the chosen elements of bread and wine.

The fruits of this were applied not only to the disciples at the Last Supper, but also to

whomsoever they and their successors after this did duly administer the same.[22]

He interprets the dominical words, using the teaching of St Paul:

The bread and the cup are his body and blood because they are the causes instrumental upon the receipt whereof the *participation* of his body and blood ensueth.[23]

From this he concludes:

The real presence of Christ's most blessed body and blood is not therefore to be sought for in the sacrament, but in the worthy receiver of the sacrament.

This he demonstrates from the gospel narratives, showing that Christ said 'take and eat' before 'this is my body', and likewise with the cup:

The fruit of the Eucharist is the participation in the body and blood of Christ . . . our participation of Christ in this sacrament dependeth on the co-operation of his omnipotent power which maketh it his body and blood to us, whether with change or without alteration of the elements such as they imagine we need not greatly to care nor inquire.[24]

Thus:

Let it therefore be sufficient for me presenting myself at the Lord's table to know what there I receive from him, without searching or inquiring of the manner how Christ performeth his promise.

It is sufficient to believe that

this bread hath in it more than the substance which our eyes behold, this cup hallowed with solemn benediction availeth . . . what these elements are in themselves it skilleth not, it is enough that to me which take them they are the body and blood of Christ, his promise in witness hereof sufficeth, his word he knoweth which way to accomplish.[25]

In summary it may be said that for Hooker the elements were an essential part of the eucharistic action; they are the means by which the fruits of communion are received, and not simply stimuli to faith by which the fruits of communion are received, as Cranmer would have maintained. They become this through the celebration of the liturgical action, the 'hallowing with solemn benediction', which is very much a key phrase in his thought. Hooker may therefore be classed as a 'real receptionist' in his eucharistic doctrine, a position that may be seen as a logical development from that advocated by Jewel some 30 years earlier.

(v) The Canons of 1604

Within ten years of the publication of Book Five of the *Ecclesiastical Polity,* the Church of England had formally incorporated into its canon law the Elizabethan ecclesiastical case-law decision with regard to supplementary consecration, in canon 21 of 1604. It has already been noticed that no apparent attempt was made by the Elizabethan Church to publicise or enforce the decision made in the Johnson case, and so the question arises here as to why this particular liturgical principle with its very important theological implications was embodied in the canon law at this particular point in time. To answer this question one must look at the general ecclesiastical situation prevailing at the time, and specifically at the genesis of the 1604 canons themselves.

The accession of James I to the English throne in March 1603 provided the opportunity for a reappraisal of the Elizabethan settlement on the part of the Church at large, and the production of the canons of 1604 was one of the results of the renewal and reform of the Church undertaken at this time. It would seem that the leading personality in this from the Anglican side was Richard Bancroft, bishop of London when James I succeeded to the throne, and thereafter Whitgift's successor at Canterbury. He was Whitgift's protégé and a noted anti-puritan. He continued to guide the church through the first seven years of the new king's reign.

With this background in mind the events of the Hampton Court Conference and the promulgation of the new canons can now be discussed. Chronologically, the Hampton Court Conference met before the process of canon law revision was undertaken. The Hampton Court Conference was the result of James' acceding to puritan requests that their grievances concerning the Prayer Book might be considered. In the main it took the form of a debate between puritans and Anglicans under James' chairmanship. The outcome was very small changes in the Prayer Book, made in concession to the puritans, none of which affected the eucharistic rite.[26] Opportunity was however taken to add the section on the sacraments to the catechism. This stresses remembrance, benefits of communion, and the need for worthy reception in general uncontroversial terms, but contains no specific ideas about how consecration is effected as such. It does however express a belief in the real reception of the body and blood of Christ in the eucharist, and thus witnesses to the position that Anglicanism was adopting about the turn of the seventeenth century. These questions and answers were repeated verbatim in the books of 1637 and 1662. Because this section of the catechism was a product of the Hampton

Court Conference, perhaps one may also conclude that the doctrine contained in it would also have been acceptable to moderate puritan opinion at the time; this is a subject that will be discussed later. It is interesting to note that one of the puritan requests was for a revision of the canon law, so that they might know what they had to obey.[27] Thus revision of the canon law as such was not something the puritans would have been opposed to at that time.

After discussing them for some two months, convocation passed the canons on 25 June 1604, and they were given royal approval on 6 September.[28] It is to be noted that they were English canons, that only had authority in England. James' letter of assent with its specific references to the provinces of Canterbury and York[29] makes this quite clear; thus they did not have and were not meant to have any authority in Scotland or Ireland. Indeed they were not regarded as valid in the northern province until the Convocation of York too had passed them,[30] further evidence that they were only regarded as authoritative in England.

On the question of who actually drafted their text in the form that we have it, S. B. Babbage says:

Little is known about the authorship of the canons themselves, though Usher surmises that three ecclesiastical lawyers John Cowell, Sir Thomas Ridley, and Sir Edward Stanhope were Bancroft's assistants. There is a rough list of 21 articles extant in the British Museum endorsed 'Artickells agreed one by ye convocations House, 1604', clearly an early draft.[31]

The 1947 report categorically states that these three lawyers were responsible for the actual codification working 'under the leadership and supervision of Richard Bancroft'[32] but it gives no source or authority for this; Usher's work is however listed in the bibliography.[33] Thus once again the conclusion is that the precise authorship of a vital document in the development of Anglican eucharistic theology is a matter of some doubt. But there can be little doubt that Bancroft was the principal architect in the construction of the canons, and that he must thus be held responsible for the decision to introduce a supplementary consecration provision into them.

The questions therefore arise as to why he did this, why he arranged for it to be inserted in the canons rather than in the revised Prayer Book of 1604, and what was his theological rationale of it. To the third of these questions no definite answer can be given, since he does not seem to have left on record his own theology of consecration. The second of these questions does perhaps admit of a slightly easier answer. All the alterations made in the Prayer Book at this time were made in response to points the puritans had brought up at the Hampton Court Conference. This point had not been raised there, and so the opportunity to so insert it was lacking. Doubtless Bancroft could have manufactured the opportunity had he wished, but he no doubt judged it easier and more expedient to use the process of canon law revision instead. Some light is perhaps shed on the first of those questions by the general intention and content of the canons themselves.

The canons of 1604 were to a large extent a codification and re-enactment of the large number and variety of regulations, visitation articles, and injunctions that had been produced during the reign of Elizabeth I, the *ad hoc* measures that had been needed to make the Elizabethan Settlement work. No fewer than 97 of the 141 canons have some kind of legislative precedent of this sort, mostly Elizabethan, but some dating from the *Injunctions* of Edward VI.[34] Usher concludes that no fewer than 47 of the canons were anti-puritan, and he lists canon 21 as one of these.[35]

In order to set the supplementary consecration provision of canon 21 in its context, it will be useful to examine all the canons in the code that are concerned with the conduct of the Communion service, together with their precedents. There are four of these, 20, 21, 24, and 27; only the first sentence of 27 is strictly relevant to the conduct of the service as such. Canon 20 concerns the provision of bread and wine for the communion, and puts into canonical form the requirement of the penultimate rubric of the 1559 communion rite.[36] Canon 24 concerns the administration of the sacrament in cathedrals, and orders the wearing of the cope, thus re-enacting the provision of Parker's *Advertisements.*[37] The first sentence of canon 27 forbids the minister to communicate anyone who does not kneel to receive, following the precedent of the *Advertisements,* and also one of the provisions of the rubric at the end of the prayer containing the institution narrative.[38] Canon 21 itself contains four provisions. The first requires the communion to be administered sufficiently often for every parishioner to be able to communicate three times a year, of which Easter is to be one. Usher gives as precedent for this Grindal's visitation articles of 1576,[39] the 52nd of which simply enquires of the incumbent whether there are any of his parishioners who have not received the statutory minimum of three times a year, of which Easter is to be one.[40] One can also note that Whitgift in the visitation articles he issued for Salisbury in 1588 enquired if all of convenient age attended church on Sundays and holy days, and received communion thrice yearly.[41] However, the important precedent for this provision is the final rubric of the Communion rite which orders parishioners to fulfil their minimum communion obligations;[42] the purpose of this section of the canon is to ensure that this is possible for them. The second requirement of the Canon is that the minister himself communicates every time he celebrates. This seeks to enforce another of the provisions of the rubric at the end of the prayer containing the institution narrative.[43] The third requirement is the supplementary consecration provision. This has no previous precedent in either Prayer Book or legislative or administrative enactment. The fourth requirement is that the minister shall deliver the bread and wine to each communicant individually, which clarifies and seeks to enforce another of the provisions of the rubric at the end of the prayer containing the institution narrative.[44] Thus of all the provisions governing the conduct of the Communion service in the canons of 1604, the supplementary consecration provision is the only one that has no previous precedent.

All the canonical provisions here enacted with regard to the conduct of the Communion Service were designed to ensure that the service was celebrated in an orderly and seemly manner in accordance with the traditions of the Prayer Book, and a number of them were definitely aimed against the puritans, for example the requirement on kneeling and the command that the minister is to communicate each person individually. In fact it is probably fair to conclude that the whole of these enactments about the Communion service are anti-puritan in tone, and that therefore the supplementary consecration provision has this general intention too. From this one may conclude that at this date puritans would not have used it, and might not have liked the idea very much, though whether their reaction would have been one of violent dislike or mild distaste or anything in between, it is not possible to say.

The questions also arise as to why the provision was introduced at this particular time, and what was the positive theology behind it. As to the first, in 1604 the threat to the Anglican establishment was far stronger from the puritans than it was from the papists, a reversal of the situation that had prevailed during the earlier part of Elizabeth's reign; hence the increasing stress on anti-puritan measures at this period. This perhaps provides a partial answer to a question to which there is no complete answer. Second, its positive rationale is even more difficult to assess. The text of the preliminary draft noted by Babbage read as follows:

That no bread and wine be used at the communion but such as by the minister hath been blessed by reading the word of institution and therefore if there want of either any new which was not on the table at the beginning of the administration be brought in by the Churchwardens the minister shall not deliver it before he hath again read over the words of institution.[45]

This version at least implies that the blessing of the elements was achieved by the reading of the institution narrative, and thus argues for a doctrine of consecration being held apparently similar to the Roman one. But such similarity would seem to be far more apparent than real, for the Roman church would almost certainly not have accepted the validity of such a practice, and in any case an early seventeenth century Anglican understanding of consecration was very different from what an early seventeenth century papist would have meant by it; this topic will be discussed later. In canon 21 as published, this draft was shortened and simplified, merely requiring the rehearsal of the words of institution over the newly brought bread and wine on the communion table, a form of expression that appears to be as simple and theologically neutral as possible. From it can be concluded no more than that it was held that something had to be said over all the bread and wine used in giving communion before it was so given, in order to ensure validity, and that the scriptural account of Christ instituting the sacrament was the most logical and proper thing to read. The evidence does not exist to go further than this.

(vi) Visitation Articles and Injunctions

Once the supplementary consecration provision was part

of the canon law of the Church, it became part of the administrative task of the bishops and others to see that it was obeyed, hence the frequent appearance of queries concerning it in the visitation articles and injunctions issued in the period between the passage of the canons in 1604 and the effective ceasing of episcopal government in the early 1640s. The 1868 Ritual report[46] printed and collated no fewer than 66 such sets of articles from the period 1604-1641 inclusive; after 1641 no more were issued until after the Restoration. Though doubtless this sample is far from being a complete record of all visitations carried out in this period, it does include the metropolitical visitation articles put out by the three archbishops of Canterbury concerned, and can surely be taken as a statistically representative sample of all those issued during this time. Of these 66 sets of articles and injunctions, no fewer than 46 specifically enquire about obedience to the supplementary consecration provision of Canon 21. Of the 20 sets that do not, two, those issued by bishop Chaderton of Lincoln[47] and bishop Bridges of Oxford,[48] both in 1604, were put out after the enactment of the canons but before the publication of Bancroft's metropolitical visitation articles of 1605,[49] the first set of articles in which the specific query appears. This latter point is in itself another piece of evidence for Bancroft's personal responsibility in this matter. A further eight sets of articles ask whether the incumbent possesses and/or reads the book of canons in public on occasion, a query that surely contains within itself an implicit reminder of what the Church required in the matter of supplementary consecration. A further ten sets do not mention the matter directly or by implication by reference to the book of canons; of these, one alone is of particular interest, namely that set issued by bishop Williams of Lincoln in 1641, shortly before his translation to York.

These articles are an amended version of his 1635 articles. which did contain the supplementary consecration query. A comparison between his 1635 articles and the 1641 set derived from them[50] shows that in the latter, references to the canons have been very largely omitted, as have other sections to which the puritans might have particularly objected. In addition to this a further article has been added to the 1641 set concerning various Laudian practices such as bowing to the holy table and kneeling at the communion rail for communion; it describes these things as 'offensive rites and ceremonies . . . not established by the laws of the land'. The purpose of this article is clearly in reference to and in rejection of the canons of 1640,[51] and is yet another indication that these articles were an attempt at a reconciliation with moderate puritans. The 1641 articles are concluded with the addition of two parliamentary orders of early 1641, the first ordering that divine service be ministered in accordance with the appropriate Acts of Parliament, and the second concerning the communion table, that it

do stand decently in the ancient place where it ought to do by the law, and as it hath done for the greater part of these three-score years last past.

Thus Williams was here making a deliberate attempt to reconcile moderate Anglican and moderate Puritan, applying in his own diocese a policy he was seeking to promote nationally; at this time he was leading a moderate reconciling party in the House of Lords.[52] The fact that in pursuing this policy he omitted the provision for supplementary consecration is fairly firm evidence that some puritans did not like and did not follow the practice. Perhaps in the public mind it had come to be associated with Laudian high churchmanship and anti-puritanism; its enforcement was not a Laudian innovation, though no doubt Laud approved of it and was happy to continue to enforce it.

The figures quoted above show that throughout the period 1604-1641 the majority of visitation articles do contain a query about supplementary consecration; but since visitation articles have as their primary function the enforcement of ecclesiastical law, of which supplementary consecration was now part, this is hardly surprising, and this fact alone sheds very little extra light on the development of Anglican ideas of consecration in this period. The form of wording in which the query was put might, however, do this. Of these 46 sets of articles mentioning supplementary consecration, 42 use language copied direct from canon 21, simply referring to the using of the words of institution, thus perpetuating the theologically neutral words of the canon itself, and they include those issued by Laud. To this category may be added the 1631 Articles of Davenant, archdeacon of Berkshire, who simply asks if the canon is obeyed.[53] So from the wording in these cases nothing specific can be concluded about the theology of those who issued them, apart from the fact that they wished to see the standard of worship implied by the canons upheld. Only in three cases is different wording employed, in the injunctions Wren issued in 1636 as bishop of Norwich, in the visitation articles Duppa issued for Chichester in 1638, and in the visitation articles Montague issued for Norwich also in 1638. All three bishops were well-known Laudians, and it is worth examining what they asked in a little more detail.

Wren issued his *Injunctions* as an appendix to his set of visitation articles in 1636. The articles contain the usual query in the standard wording, but in the *Injunctions* he requires

that the breads be brought in a clean cloth or napkin, and that the words of consecration be audibly repeated again if any bread or wine be used which was not at the first consecrated.[54]

That he uses two different forms of words in close conjunction one to another indicates that he did not differentiate in meaning between them. Presumably also he regarded the reciting of the institution narrative over the bread and wine as being in some sense essentially consecratory, though this does not of itself tell one what Wren understood consecration in the eucharist to mean. And the fact that he had been one of those consulted during the production of the 1637 rite, and presumably approved of it, must be borne in mind here.[55]

Duppa's articles indicate a high doctrine of the eucharist:

Is it administered in that reverent and decent manner as becomes so high a mystery? Are the words of consecration solemnly pronounced? The elements reverently touched and handled?

The reference to supplementary consecration comes a little further on:

Is the bread and wine of the best sort, is a sufficient quantity of each provided? or if either fails, are the words of consecration renewed over them before they be distributed?[56]

Here once again the inference is that it is the reciting of the institution narrative that he regards as essentially consecratory, though, as before, this does not show in itself what he understood the meaning of consecration to be.

Montague in his primary visitation articles issued for Norwich in 1638[57] attempts to make them more devotional in content, by the occasional use of scripture and by some exhortation, as opposed to a simply and strictly legal enquiry, and a reading of his articles gives a good impression of the high Laudian ideal of churchmanship. About consecration in the eucharist he says specifically:

Doth he first receive himself in both kinds . . . upon his knees having consecrated the bread and wine by the solemn and powerful words of our Saviour, and none other?[58]

and on the matter of supplementary consecration:

If the consecrated wine fail, or sufficeth not, doth your minister, before he give it to the communicants, consecrate that also which is newly supplied, as the former? or doth he give it as it cometh from the tavern, without benediction? For there is no sacrament, until the words of institution be pronounced upon it. This is my blood, etc.[59]

Two points can be noticed here: first, the definite emphasis that all the wine used in giving communion must receive specific consecration; and second, that he seems to regard the reading of the institution narrative as that which essentially consecrates. The equation in terminology between 'the words of institution' and 'consecration' can also be noted again; though once more it is to be borne in mind that this linguistic usage does not in itself illuminate what Montague understood by consecration, but merely illustrates what he regarded as being the essential in performing it. That Montague talks about the institution narrative as consecratory, is not to be taken as meaning that he held to something approaching a contemporary Roman view of the matter, or in some way anticipated what a nineteenth century high-church Anglican would have thought about it; what he meant has to be worked out within the context of his own time.

Cosin, in the articles he issued in 1627 as archdeacon for the East Riding of Yorkshire, asked:[60]

When the bread and wine is renewed, doth he again use the words of consecration upon them, having always a care to bless no more than shall suffice the number of communicants? And after the communion ended, doth he send away or take home to his private use, any bread and wine from the Holy table, but that which was left unblessed and unconsecrated, the rest being reverently taken by some of the communicants, before they depart from their devotions?

Here Cosin refers to the institution narrative as 'words of

consecration'; interesting too is the interpretation he applies to the rubric concerning the remains. He has in fact glossed this in a sense directly opposite to its probable original meaning and grammatically most obvious sense.

The general conclusion of this study of the visitation articles and injunctions issued in the period 1604-1641 is that most of those that refer to supplementary consecration carefully use the theologically neutral language of canon 21, but that a few of the more advanced high-churchmen add or substitute 'consecration' to or for 'words of institution', often in a way that implies that they saw little or no difference in meaning between the two forms. Further, it would seem fair to conclude that, while these articles form a very interesting and valuable record of ecclesiastical administrative practice in the period, they do not give any very clear idea about early seventeenth century theologies of consecration or theological rationales of the form of supplementary consecration they order; this must be looked for in other sources, in the theological writings of the period.

(vii) Irish and Scottish Canons

Some events connected with the Churches in Ireland and Scotland may now be briefly noted. In 1615 the Irish Church adopted a set of 104 articles[61] which, though based on the 39 to a considerable extent, were substantially more Calvinistic. Comparing those articles in both sets that concern the eucharist, it may be said that, despite their more rigidly Protestant tone, the Irish probably only make more explicit what would have been regarded at that time as the doctrinal import of the equivalent English articles. In 1634 the Irish Convocation adopted the 39 articles; whether in addition to or in substitution for the earlier Irish set, seems to have been a matter of some doubt. At the same time a set of canons was enacted, based on the English ones of 1604 but modified to take account of the puritan susceptibilities of the Irish Church. The supplementary consecration provision of the English canons was incorporated without significant change into the Irish.[62]

The Scottish canons of 1636,[63] intended as a 'companion' volume to the Prayer Book of 1637, are quite different from the English ones of 1604, and are clearly in no sense dependent upon them. They contain little detailed instruction about the conduct of the communion service, no doubt because this was regarded as adequately covered by the rubrics of the 1637 rite. In particular, they contain no reference to supplementary consecration, for this was now in the Prayer Book itself. Kneeling to receive is commanded, with the remark that both profanity and superstition are to be avoided.[64] Any of the consecrated elements remaining at the end of the celebration are to be distributed to poor communicants for them to eat and drink before they leave the church,[65] presumably for their physical nourishment, an interesting combination of sacramental observance and charitable provision for the poor.

(viii) The offertory prayer in the Coronation service

One of the aspects of the Western liturgical tradition completely eliminated by Cranmer from the Anglican, and not restored by any of the English revisions, is that of the so-called Secret prayer, or *oratio super oblata;* no doubt he eliminated it because he associated it with what he regarded as a false view of the eucharistic sacrifice. It is therefore all the more interesting to note that it survived in the coronation eucharist. The first English king to be crowned in English was James I, both Edward VI and Elizabeth I having had Latin coronation services.[66] This latter, at first sight perhaps surprising, is really only to be expected, since they were both crowned very early in their reigns[67] when the Latin rite was the only legal English liturgy. But it is for the coronation of Charles I that the fullest records seem to exist, and great care and consideration appear to have been taken in drawing it up, Laud, then prebendary of Westminster and bishop of St David's, having had a considerable hand in the matter.[65] It is worth describing fairly fully the section of Charles I's coronation service that comes after the creed. First the archbishop is directed to read the first of the offertory sentences in the Prayer Book, 'Let your light so shine . . .' The organ is to play and the choir is to sing:

Let my prayer come up into thy presence as the Incense, and the lifting up of my hands be as an evening sacrifice.

This is certainly not one of the offertory sentences from the Prayer Book, and its choice is all the more interesting because of its implication of the offering of sacrificial worship. Its use seems to have been an innovation for the coronation of Charles I, for no special anthem or sentence was specified at the coronation of James I, though it appears that one was sung.[70] This sentence was sung at the offertory at the coronation of William III and Mary II,[71] and at all subsequent coronations up to and including that of George III.[72] While this sentence is being sung, the king descends from his throne and, going to the altar, there offers bread and wine for the communion, upon which the archbishop is directed to say the following prayer, here quoted in full:

Bless, O Lord, we beseech thee, these thy gifts, and sanctify them unto this holy use, that by them we may be (made) partakers of the Body and Blood of thine only-begotten Son Jesus Christ: and thy servant King Charles may be fed unto everlasting life of soul and body, and enabled to the discharge of this great place, and Office whereunto thou hast called him, Of thy great goodness. Grant this, O Lord, for the honour of Jesus Christ his sake, our only Mediator and Advocate. Amen.

The same prayer was used at the coronation of James I,[74] and, with the name of the sovereign transferred to follow the phrase 'may be fed unto everlasting life of soul and body', at that of William III and Mary II.[75] In this latter form it has been used in this place at the coronations of all subsequent sovereigns up to and including that of the present monarch.[76] This prayer is a rather free translation of one of the two Secrets used at the coronation of the kings of medieval England, the use of which goes well back into Saxon times. The Latin text still appeared in the *Missa pro Rege* among the *orationes diversae* of the 1570 Roman Missal,[77] a votive mass which goes back to the supplementary material added by Alcuin to the Hadrianum; the prayer itself may very well be older than this. As such, it is part of the general Western liturgical tradition of such prayers, as discussed in Chapter I above.

Wickham Legg gives the latin text of this prayer in his reprint of an Anglo-Saxon coronation order:

Munera domine quaesumus oblata sanctifica. ut et nobis unigeniti tui corpus et sanguis salutare fiat. et ill. regi et optinendam anime corporisque salutem. et peragendum iniunctum officium te largiente usquequoque proficiat. per christum.

He points out in his introduction that the word 'salutare'

has been interpolated into this prayer, and the verbs 'fiat' and 'proficiat' changed from the plural into the singular; ordinarily this prayer is without these alterations.[79] He rightly says that at this period these two forms of the prayer were different expressions of the same basic doctrinal outlook.

The English version of this prayer is arguably a perfectly fair and correct translation of the original Latin of the uninterpolated version of the prayer; and even if translation of 'Munera oblata' as 'these thy gifts' seems to slightly weaken the sacrificial sense of the prayer, it cannot really be said to alter its sense or object at all. Again 'that by them we may be made partakers . . .' expresses exactly the same meaning as 'ut et nobis unigeniti tui corpus et sanguis fiant', even if wording reminiscent of the 'prayer of consecration' (not of course called by this name in 1603 or 1626) has been preferred to a more literal rendering of the Latin. In this context it should be noted that the English coronation Secret contains the vital words 'by them' lacking in the 'consecration prayer', and thus is evidence for a stronger doctrine of the eucharistic presence than the 'consecration prayer' itself. Thus the conclusion is that in every important respect the English redactors of this prayer produced an exact and fair rendering of the sense of the Latin original. Who these redactors were is not known, records for James I's coronation not being explicit on this point, but presumably it at least had the approval of Whitgift or Bancroft. And there is nothing in it that Hooker, for example, would have been unhappy with.

Yet the question remains why the compilers of the first two English coronation services reintroduced this feature into this special eucharist, a feature of which it is the only example in official post-Reformation English liturgy. To this there can be no definite answer, but perhaps it would not be too far from the truth to say that they included it because they wished to produce a coronation service that was as faithful as possible to the Latin originals that they were working from; thus they included it because they viewed it as part of the coronation rite rather than a new addition to the communion service. Certainly from the careful way in which they translated it, it seems fair to conclude that they regarded a prayer of such content in this position as being in harmony with Anglican eucharistic theology as understood in 1603 and 1626. Once included in the English coronation rite, the force of tradition was sufficiently strong to ensure its retention there from that day to this.

This prayer is interesting and unique, as being the only surviving post-Reformation Secret in the Church of England. It does seem fair to conclude that it is further evidence that it had become the standard and official Anglican belief by the beginning of the seventeenth century that the gifts of the body and blood were really conveyed to the believer through reception of the elements, and not simply by faith for which reception of the elements was merely a catalyst; the coronation service is of course used by and overseen by the most important clerics in the land. To conclude more than this would be to conclude too much; the prayer never seems to have been referred to by any of those who wrote about the Prayer Book and Anglican eucharistic theology in this period. Nor is this surprising, considering the extreme rarity with which this prayer has been used, namely a total of four times in the seventeenth century (there was no communion at James II's coronation) and four times in the eighteenth. Moreover in those days coronations were more or less private affairs, limited to those who took part in them. Very few people other than those present would have known anything about the services themselves at all, and only a minute proportion of those present would have had sufficient knowledge to appreciate the theological significance of the prayer when they heard it. For the record, it may be noted that the prayer was said a further three times in the nineteenth century and a further four times in this century, making a total of only fifteen times in the entire history of the post-Reformation Church of England.

CHAPTER FIVE

Anglican Theological Writing about the Eucharist in the period 1603-1662

The first half of the seventeenth century was a period in which a great deal of theological literature was produced by Anglican divines, and not least about the eucharist. From this literature may be derived their views about consecration in the eucharist and the nature of the eucharistic presence (that is, how Christ is present in the eucharistic action and received by the faithful); these are interrelated issues that cannot be separated from one another. In the previous century, at least until the time of Hooker, the government had been content to preserve intact the compromise of the Elizabethan Settlement. Now from the foundations of this settlement there developed a positive theology in its own right, and the attempt will now be made to demonstrate what this theology was in regard to these aspects of the eucharist.

It will be convenient to start by considering the two complete and detailed commentaries on the Prayer Book published during the period, even though they were both published towards its end, in the 1650s. These are Sparrow's *Rationale* and L'Estrange's *Alliance of Divine Offices.*

(i) Sparrow's 'Rationale'

In the second half of the 1650s[1] Anthony Sparrow, who later became bishop of Exeter, published his *Rationale,* which was a devotional commentary on the whole Prayer Book as well as a defence and commendation of it; it is of course the book as revised in 1604 on which he is commenting. Sparrow obviously knew the Fathers very well, and it is by his understanding of the Fathers and of the Catholic tradition of the undivided Church that he interprets the Prayer Book. He devotes considerable space to discussing the communion rite. His comments on the offertory are solely concerned with alms,[2] as of course was the offertory in the 1604 book. His doctrine of consecration is that it is effected by recital of the institution narrative, and this he establishes and expounds almost entirely by a series of quotations and references from Chrysostom, Cyril, Cyprian, Ambrose, and Augustine. He also clearly believes in a real presence at the very least associated with reception of the consecrated elements, and further understands and expounds the Prayer Book as teaching this doctrine. In communion Christ is really received in and through the elements.

He interprets the rubrics concerned with the remains as meaning that the curate may only take home that which was unconsecrated. He does not discuss the issue of supplementary consecration. He further argues that the 1549 practice of reservation for the sick was still allowable and usable, and defends the use of the terms 'altar' and 'priest'.

(ii) L'Estrange's 'Alliance of Divine Offices'

L'Estrange's *Alliance of Divine Offices* was first published in 1659,[3] on the eve of the Restoration, and in it he comments on the whole of Anglican liturgy published up to the time at which he was writing. In his introduction L'Estrange said it was reading the Whitgift—Cartwright controversy and the works of Hooker that gave him his belief in the virtue of the Prayer Book liturgy,[4] and that his studies of the Fathers confirmed and deepened this. He maintained that there was a harmony between the Prayer Book and the Fathers that they simply did not have with the popish mass; he denies that the Prayer Book was derived from the Mass-book.[5] In a very brief historical sketch of the Edwardine Reformation, he mentions the first book as 'being compiled by the most judicious bishops and others of the time', and appears to regard the second as explaining and expressing the meaning of the first, the first not being free enough from superstition. On the question of authorship, he says the command to produce the second book was committed 'probably to the same persons, or so many of them as then were living.'[6] As a source of genuine information about the origins of the Edwardine Prayer Books, what L'Estrange has to say is of little value, and he presents the whole of the Henrician and Edwardine Reformations as a continuous movement from darkness into light, carried out throughout by men of goodwill.

But the real interest of L'Estrange lies in his own views on eucharistic sacrifice, presence, and consecration. On the first point he regards the whole eucharistic rite as sacrificial in character, and he specifies four points in particular.[7] Firstly, the offering of the bread and wine linked with almsgiving; and the association of the latter with the former he clearly regards as very important. Since he is commenting on the Scottish as well as the English rite, this fits what he is commenting on, and one is led to wonder whether some of the English clergy were already inserting an offertory of bread and wine into the English rite before the Prayer for the Church militant. The second sacrificial element is the consecration itself; the third is 'sacrifices of prayers and praises unto God'; and the fourth, the eucharist as a pleading or commemoration of the sacrifice of Christ, comes in his comments on the *Gloria in excelsis.*

In passing, it is of interest to note that he knows of the 'Clementine' liturgy of *Apostolic Constitutions* VIII, and clearly regards it as an authoritative source to cite;[8] he also shows knowledge of the Byzantine rite and the 'Gregorian service', the Latin rite associated with Gregory the Great.[9]

He discusses at some length what he regards as the vital part of the rite as affecting the consecration, firstly in general terms:

Consecration of the elements was made indeed with thanksgiving, not by it; by blessing it was performed, by blessing joined with thanksgiving in one continued form of prayer, or by blessing concomitant with thanksgiving in two distinct forms.[10]

Thus consecration is achieved by blessing of the elements, and he notes this is always joined with thanksgiving; 'blessing' is his translation of $εὐλογια$, which he also translates rather more fully ' "invocation" of His blessing upon them'. He explains his understanding of this more precisely when discussing the institution narrative, which he does not regard as achieving consecration by itself:

The recital of these words pass in common vogue for a consecration; were I Romishly inclined, I should rather impute unto them the power of transubstantiation, for that a bare narrative can be qualified to consecrate is certainly new divinity, unknown to Scripture, and antiquity interpreting it. Therefore I must adhere in judgement to those learned men who derive consecration from the word of God and prayer, the very way by which our Saviour Himself sanctified those elements in His first institution, Mt 26.26 $εὐλογησας$, 'calling upon God for his blessing', and $εὐχαριστησας$, 'giving thanks' . . .[11]

112

He goes on to say of the institution narrative in the thought of the Fathers:

And though the primitive fathers, in the act of consecration, did usually join the narrative of Christ's institution with the words of blessing and thanksgiving, thereby as it were showing their commission; yet were they far from imagining that the elements were sanctified any other way than by prayer . . .

All ancient liturgies affix a prayer of benediction, a εὐλογια, to the institution narrative, something they would not have done were the latter sufficient to achieve consecration by itself. For the Roman Canon he regards this prayer of benediction as the central part of the *Quam oblationem,* 'ut haec oblatio nobis corpus et sanguis fiat dilectissimi filii tui Domini nostri Jesu Christi';[12] for the Eastern the epiclesis prayers, quoting Basil, Chrysostom, and the Clementine, noting this latter as being older than either version of the Byzantine rite.[13] From this standpoint he goes on to draw the logical conclusion about the English rite, which he does in a comment on the tradition of the manual acts:

By the marginal ascription of the first book of Edward VI we may observe from whence the custom is derived for the minister to take the elements into his hands upon his pronouncing of the words of institution. I humbly offer it to better judgements, whether that direction being expunged by our second reformers, it would not be a safe and as proper a cause to begin that action at these words, 'Grant that we receiving these thy creatures . . .', and to continue the rite until the words of institution be past. For as I said before, the words of invocation of God's blessing, jointly with those of Christ's institution, constitute the consecration.[14]

Here he makes himself quite clear and explicit; the institution narrative together with an appropriate prayer of blessing or invocation effect the consecration, and both are necessary for it. It is clear that he regards 'grant that we receiving . . .' as equivalent to the *Quam oblationem* and the epiclesis prayers in this respect. It would also seem fair to regard the above passage as another piece of contemporary evidence for the performance of manual acts in the pre-Restoration Church. He makes no comment on the supplementary consecration rubric of the Scottish book, or on the absence of one in the English, or on the matter at all.

It is in his discussion of the words of administration that he comes nearest to explaining his understanding of the presence in the eucharist. He greatly commends the Elizabethan Reformers for joining together the forms from the two earlier books, for the formulae in the first book, coming straight from the mass-book, might be suspected of being over-serviceable to the doctrine of transubstantiation, as well as excluding commemoration of the death and passion. But the second book goes too far in the other direction:

the commemoration being let in, and the body and blood of Christ shut out, that real presence, which all sound Protestants seem to allow, might possibly be implied to be denied.

The Elizabethan Reformers therefore achieved a perfect balance between the commemoration and the reception of the eucharistic gifts, which two ideas are inseparably linked together.[15] His doctrine of the presence can be summarised by saying that he believed the elements to convey a real presence of the body and blood of Christ to the believer, and that they become capable of this by their liturgical consecration. Thus the spiritual action of the eucharist is really associated with the liturgical action with the elements, as his criticism of the 1552 words of administration demonstrates. In this connection it should also be noted that he approved of the black rubric, and thus firmly rejects anything approaching Roman ideas on this subject, for he regrets its omission from 1559 and wishes he knew the reason for this omission.[16]

He comments on the rubric concerning the disposal of the elements. He cites with approval various patristic references concerned with reverent consumption of the remains by clergy or people, thus indirectly making it plain that he understands the Anglican rubric as implying that this should be done, and concludes with the cautious comment:

As for the order of our Church, it is very circumspect, for, by saying the curate shall have it to his own use, care thereby is taken to prevent the superstitious reservation of this Sacrament, as the papists formerly practised.[17]

He can thus be seen as a forerunner of those commentators on the post-1662 recension of this rubric for whom it was as much a prohibition of superstitious excesses with regard to reservation as a prohibition of irreverence to the consecrated elements. Yet he is quite happy with the 1549 practice of limited reservation for the purpose of communicating the sick, and felt it might have been retained in the second book, were it not for the background of superstition and adoration against which it was written.[18]

These two works present an interesting contrast in their respective doctrines of consecration, Sparrow laying most stress on the place of the institution narrative, and L'Estrange on thanksgiving and blessing for which the institution narrative provides the commission and authority. Their doctrines of the presence would seem to have been less divergent; both at the very least believe in a true reception of the body and blood of Christ through reception of the consecrated elements.

(iii) Lancelot Andrewes

Moving on from specifically liturgical commentaries to the more general writings of the Caroline divines concerned with the eucharist, we find a great deal of space devoted to discussion of the eucharistic presence, and thus, directly and indirectly, to their understanding of eucharistic consecration. Lancelot Andrewes affirms the reality of Christ's presence in the eucharist, together with a firm denial of transubstantiation:

At the coming of the almighty power of the word, the nature is changed, so that what before was the mere element has become a Divine Sacrament, the substance nevertheless remaining what it was before . . .[19]

Consecration he clearly regarded as being achieved by 'the almighty power of the word', though what he equated this with in liturgical usage is less clear. He did leave some notes on his ceremonial practices when celebrating the Prayer Book rite.[20] From these it seems fair to conclude that for him it is the repetition of the action of Christ at the Last Supper, together with prayer referring to these actions, that constitutes the essentials of the consecration.

(iv) Thomas Morton

Thomas Morton, successively bishop of Chester, Coventry and Lichfield, and Durham in the reigns of James I and Charles I, also believed in a real reception through the consecrated elements. The believer was to discern the Lord's body in the sacrament, not only in use, but also in nature, to distinguish the object of faith from the object of sense. Before consecration the bread is merely natural, after it is bread sacramental, by which Christ's own Body,

which is the spiritual and supersubstantial bread truly exhibited by this Sacrament to the nourishment of the souls of the faithful . . .

Coupled with this positive way of looking at things is a definite rejection of Roman practice and teaching.[21]

In connection with his views on this, a most interesting discussion of his own positive theology of consecration occurs in his work *Of the Institution of the Sacrament of the Body and Blood of Christ* . . . (from which the above quotation was taken), an anti-Roman polemical work, first published in 1631. In a second edition in 1635 he repeated his 1631 discussion verbatim, with the addition and insertion of fresh material, and it is in this additional material that a specific discussion of the practice of supplementary consecration occurs, the only one that the author has found in the writings of the pre-Restoration Caroline divines.[22] In the first part of his discussion he is concerned to demonstrate that consecration is achieved by blessing accompanied by prayer, and he points out that Christ at the Last Supper had done this before speaking the dedicatory words 'This is . . .' He demonstrates that this is the viewpoint of the Greek Church, and that the Fathers universally witness to it before the rise of the modern Roman doctrine that consecration is achieved simply by the institution narrative, which he refutes polemically at length, denying that the institution narrative can be an invocation, or a blessing with prayer by itself.[23] He continues by explaining what he does see as the place of the institution narrative in the eucharistic prayer:

Nevertheless, this our Conclusion is not to be so interpreted, as . . . to exclude out of the Words of this Celebration the Repetition and Pronouncement of these words, 'This is my Body', and 'This is my blood of the New Testament'. Far be this from us, because we hold them to be essentially belonging to the Narration of the Institution of Christ, and are used in the Liturgy of our Church: For although they be not Words of Blessing and Consecration, (Because not of Petition but of Repetition) yet are they Words of Direction; and, withal, Signification and Testification of the mystical Effects thereof. For a further Manifestation, hearken you unto that which is written (1 Tim. 4 v 4), Every creature of God is good, if it be sanctified with the Word of God and with Prayer'. Wherein we find a double Acception of Sanctification;

116

the one of Ordination by the Word of God; the other of Benediction, namely by Prayer.[24]

After an example concerned with the eating of swine's flesh, he concludes his general argument:

Both of these are to be found in our sacramental food, wherein we have the Sanctification thereof, both by the Word of Christ in the Tenor of his first Institution, 'He took Bread', etc. adding 'Do this'; as also by public blessing in Prayer, which is more properly called Consecration.

After this general discussion he explains how he understands the supplementary consecration provision of canon 21:

and though in our Domestical Feasts, the second Course is blessed in the Grace, which was said upon the first Service; so the second Supply of Bread and Wine (if it shall inordinately so happen) may not altogether be denied to be consecrated by the Blessing pronounced on the first (even as the Sanctifying of the Sheaf of Corn was the Hallowing of the whole field), notwithstanding our Church has cautelously *(sic)* ordained, that the Words of Institution, 'He took Bread', etc., be applied to every Oblation of new Bread and Wine, for Accommodation-sake, as they are referred to in our Liturgy, wherein they are necessarily joined together with the words of Prayer and Benediction.[25]

Thus Morton's doctrine of consecration and of the place of the institution narrative within it is quite clear. Consecration is achieved by prayer and blessing of the elements, and the reciting of the institution narrative witnesses to the fact that the prayers and blessings said are in accordance with what Christ instituted and thus guarantee that their effect will be what Christ intended. And this is the purpose of an institution narrative at a second consecration, to join the fresh supply of elements on to the rest of the rite, as it were, and to link them to the effect of the whole of the eucharistic prayer already recited, the crucial phrase here being 'wherein they are necessarily joined together with the Words of Prayer and Benediction'. And it follows that, given this rationale of the use of the recital of the institution narrative alone to effect a second consecration, this method is valid *whatever* material the rest of the eucharistic prayer contains. That is, using Morton's reasoning, this method of supplementary consecration would be just as appropriate to a 1637 style of canon as to the 1604 rite as it stood in Morton's day.

(v) John Bramhall

John Bramhall, who ended a varied ecclesiastical career as archbishop of Armagh after the Restoration, in his *Answer to M. de la Millitière,* written in 1653, asserts a definite belief in the real presence:

Christ said, This is My Body; what He said, we do steadfastly believe. He said not, after this or that manner . . . And therefore we place it among the opinion of the schools, not among the Articles of our Faith.[26]

There is a more specific discussion of his doctrine of consecration as such in his *Protestant Bishops Vindicated,* written about 1658, in the context of a defence of the Anglican Ordinal, where he writes as follows:

whether it be done by enunciating the words of Christ, as it is observed in the Western church, or by prayer, as it is practised in the Eastern church; or whether these two be both the same thing in effect, that is, that the forms of the Sacraments be mystical prayers, and implicit invocations. Our church for more abundant caution useth both forms . . . In the Holy Eucharist, our consecration is a repetition of that which was done by Christ, and now done by him that consecrateth in the person of Christ.[27]

Consecration is the repeating of Christ's action so that what happened at the Last Supper may happen again in the celebration of the eucharist as Christ guaranteed, and any form of words that makes this clear and explicit will properly serve as a consecration prayer; a prayer to this end including the institution narrative would seem to be his liturgical ideal, and he clearly understands and interprets the Prayer Book rite in this way.

(vi) John Cosin

Of great importance are the views of John Cosin, one of the leading Laudians in the reign of Charles I, and bishop of Durham under Charles II, not least because of the great influence he exercised on the various projects for revision of the Prayer Book after the Restoration. In 1656 he wrote his *Historia Transubstantiationis Papalis* in which he set out his eucharistic doctrine in relation to that of the Roman Church. Consecration is an objective reality to him while at the same time he denies any change of substance:

Hence it is most evident that the bread and wine . . . are neither changed as to their substance, nor vanished nor reduced to nothing, but are solemnly consecrated by the Words of Christ, that by them His Blessed Body and Blood may be communicated to us.[28]

He sets out his views on consecration again in the context of a description and defence of the Anglican Communion rite:

The priest also blessing, or consecrating, the bread and wine, saith thus: 'Hear us, O merciful Father . . . *(quoted in full to)* . . . in remembrance of Me'.[29]

A further quotation expresses the same doctrine:

Likewise our Blessed Saviour, having sanctified the elements by His words and prayers, gave them to His disciples as seals of the New Testament.[30]

He presumably believed that consecration was effected by the institution narrative set within the context of a suitable prayer to the end of the use and benefit of the communicant:

For the Body and Blood of our Saviour are not only fitly represented by the elements, but also by virtue of his Institution really offered to all by them, and so eaten by the faithful mystically and sacramentally.[31]

By this the faithful 'are fed by the operation of the Holy Ghost', but to the unspiritual man it is a mere nothing.[32] Again in relation to the Roman view he sets out his beliefs:

We own the union betwixt the Body and Blood of Christ and the elements, whose use and office we hold to be changed from what it was before.[33]

He goes on to deny the Roman doctrine of transubstantiation:

But we deny what the Papists affirm, that the substance of bread and wine are quite abolished and changed into the Body and Blood of our Lord . . . And we also deny that the elements still retain the nature of sacraments, when not used according to the divine institution, that is, given by Christ's minister, and received by his people; so that Christ in the consecrated bread ought not, cannot, be kept and preserved to be carried about, because He is present only to the communicants.[34]

He discusses his views on consecration as such at considerably greater length in his notes on the Prayer Book. Many of these are much earlier than the *Historia,* dating from well before the Great Rebellion. Indeed tradition suggests that his first series of notes is largely simply a copy of some made previously by Overall,[35] whose chaplain he had been, but this does not matter. The fact that he copied them means that he accepted the doctrine they contained, and thus they may be regarded as truly reflecting his views. His notes are in part concerned with defending the Prayer Book against Roman attack. He says of the consecration prayer in his first series of notes:

For we have first the recitation of Christ's command to have His Death and Passion remembered; and then we have prayer to perform it as we ought to do. After that we have the words of consecration, as fully and amply as any priest whatsoever can or may use them.[36]

After a lengthy discussion setting out his view that the eucharist is a commemorative sacrifice, there follows a note on the phrase 'creatures of bread and wine' that is illustrative of his doctrine of the presence:

We term them so before consecration: after that we call them so no more, but abstain from that name, because our thoughts might be wholly taken up with the spiritual food of Christ's Body and Blood . . . In the mean while we deny not the bread and wine to remain there still, as God's creatures;[37]

a belief he maintains the Roman Canon also witnesses to, in its doxology.[38] He then goes on to state that it is the institution narrative that is the words of consecration, with patristic references.[39] He denies the validity of puritan eucharists because they 'boldly deny any words of mystical consecration at all'.[40]

In his second series of notes, completed after the *Historia,* though much of it probably dates from the 1640s, and to which he refers his readers in connection with his doctrines of the presence,[41] he comments on the communion rite in some detail. In a note on the institution narrative itself, he comments that there were some manual acts accompanying this in the 1549 rite, which are 'still observed among us',[42] and goes on to express his dislike of and rejection of Roman elevation and adoration.

In his general introduction to the communion rite he has already set down his essential doctrine of consecration. After the prayer of humble access:

deinde surgens celebrans per preces et recitationem verborum Domini quibus Sacram suam Coenam instituerit, panem et vinum coram posita reverenter in sacramentum consecrat.[43]

Later on he describes what he holds to be the overall effect

120

of the prayer containing the institution narrative:

constat ex commemoratione unici Sacrificii per Christum semel in cruce oblati, historia et institutione Sacramenti, una cum oratione ut simul cum benedicto pane et vino de Corpore et Sanguine Christi communicemus.[44]

As in the *Historia,* the essential doctrine here is that it is the institution narrative set within the context of a suitable prayer that consecrates. H.R. Gummey has noted these quotations and those from the *Historia,* but they will not bear the interpretation he wished to put on them, namely,

Bishop Cosin clearly shows that he felt the force and need of the Invocation,[45]

particularly when it is remembered that by 'invocation' Gummey means something having the force of an Eastern epiclesis prayer in its native and authentic meaning.

Comparing the first series of notes with the second series and the *Historia,* one can see there is a change of emphasis perhaps in his later writings towards a more moderate form of expression, but there does not appear to be any really essential change of doctrine, and to this extent the view expressed by C.W. Dugmore and G.J. Cuming that he changed from being a high to a central churchman during his exile in the Commonwealth period[46] does not seem to affect the fundamentals of his eucharistic doctrine. In his belief in the eucharist as a commemorative sacrifice; in the institution narrative set within the context of a suitable prayer being the esentially consecratory part of the rite; and in a true reception of the Body and Blood of Christ through reception of the elements, which remain bread and wine still, he does not seem to have changed, and these remain the characteristics of his eucharist theology throughout.

(vii) Herbert Thorndike

Another theologian of considerable importance for the development of Anglican eucharistic doctrine in this period is Herbert Thorndike (1598-1672). In his *Of Religious Assemblies and the Publick Service of God,* published in 1642 in defence of Anglicanism against the gathering puritan storm, he discusses his doctrine of consecration and of the presence:

The creatures of bread and wine are deputed to the effect of becoming the body and blood of Christ to them that receive them aright by the appointment of our Lord, executed by the Church . . .

He goes on to maintain that consecration is not by thanksgiving alone:

To me it seemeth unquestionable that the thanksgiving wherewith our Lord in the Gospel is said to have celebrated this Sacrament at His last Supper, contained also prayer to God for the effect to which the elements, when they become this Sacrament, are deputed: and that the Church, upon His example, hath always frequented His institution with the like, rehearsing His institution out of the Gospel, and praying for the effect of it at the present, after the thanksgiving hitherto described.[47]

Thus consecration is by prayer for the effects Christ appointed, and the institution narrative is included in the prayer as a recital and pledge that this will be the case. It is important too to note that the end of consecration is inseparable from the form that consecrates; the contrast he claims between his own doctrine of consecration (a deputing to the effect of becoming the body and blood of Christ to them that receive) and the Roman, whose end is transubstantiation, makes this quite clear. Thus his doctrine of consecration and of the presence are inseparably linked, and his ideas about the presence can be summarised as follows. The bread and wine remain the same in substance, and someone disposed with a lively faith actually receives the body and blood of Christ; yet grace in the consecrated elements is tendered to all, worthy and unworthy, because how otherwise would Paul have condemned the unworthy drinkers as being guilty of the body and blood of Christ, and why otherwise would Christ have said, 'This *is* . . .?[48] It is important to note here both what he is saying and what he is not saying. He *is* saying that grace is offered to all who receive the consecrated elements, be they worthy or unworthy; he is not saying that there is any kind of objective presence permanently associated with the consecrated elements in themselves.

It is clear that he has been much influenced by the Clementine rite in his liturgical thinking, regarding it as archetypal of all Eastern liturgies, and indeed as stating the universal faith of the patristic era in these matters.[49] This is an outlook that was to bear very important fruit in the post-Restoration era, and he may well be its originator in Anglicanism. He regards the prayers of the Roman Canon as witnessing to his own ideas,[50] and hints that he thought its prayers were originally nearer to those of the Clementine. He quotes the oblation and epiclesis prayer of the Clementine rite to prove his doctrine and says of them:

Which if we compare with the testimonies of ecclesiastical writers, which divers have produced to prove that the elements are not consecrated by the affirmative words of Christ, as operative, but by the prayers of the Church, it will appear that it is the prayer whereof we now speak, always used in the Church, to obtain of God the promise which the institution of Christ supposeth, that the elements present might be deputed to the effect of becoming visible signs, tendering and exhibiting the invisible grace which they figure. Which is that which in this matter is called consecration, as I suppose.[51]

This passage once again illustrates his doctrine of the presence and of consecration and how they link together; consecration is by prayer that the elements might offer and exhibit grace; it is interesting to note that he translates ἀποφηνῃ in the Clementine epiclesis prayer as 'exhibit'. That the epiclesis prayer prays for the descent of the Spirit upon the bread, proves that consecration is not by the institution narrative, but by this section of the prayers, the institution narrative being used as a profession that what is done is done in obedience to the gospels.[52]

Thorndike, giving his considered opinion about revision of the Prayer Book in his *Just Weights and Measures*, published just after the Restoration, says of the Prayer Book consecration prayer:

The prayer, which we consecrate with, seemeth agreeable to the intent of God's Church; but more agreeable is that form which the first book of Edward VI (revived by the Scottish Liturgy) prescribeth. And that memorial or prayer of oblation, which is there prescribed to follow immediately after the consecration, is certainly more proper there, than after the communion, ending with the Lord's Prayer, and the peace after that.[53]

Thus Thorndike is to be numbered among those who wished the Church of England to return towards the 1549 Prayer Book in its eucharistic practice.

Archsbishop Laud occupied the place of prime importance in English ecclesiastical affairs in the 1630s and early 1640s, and also influenced the course of events in Scotland. His views on eucharistic theology are therefore of considerable importance.

The main source for his eucharistic doctrine comes in his account of his *Troubles and Trial,* particularly in connection with the accusations levelled against him by the Scottish Commissioners for his part in the production of the 1637 Prayer Book. But before studying this in detail, it is worth noting a comment of his on the English book as it stood in his day:

I shall for my part never deny, but that the Liturgy of the Church of England may be made better; but I am sure withal that it may easily be made worse.[54]

As for the new Scottish book, he is prepared to defend everything to be found in it.

I like the book exceeding well, and I hope I shall be able to maintain anything that is in it, and wish with all my heart that it had been entertained there; yet I did ever desire, it might come to them with their own liking and approbation.[55]

He goes on to maintain that it was legally introduced by the Scots according to their own laws, and that the changes from the English book were due to the Scottish bishops.[56] Modern scholarship seems to have demonstrated that Laud was quite truthful in what he said here.[57] Laud meets the charge that 1637 was taken from mass-books and Romish rituals by asserting that his was a reformed church, and that many good prayers are to be found in the Roman book. In any case, the variations in the 1637 rite

were taken, either from the Book of Edward VI, which was not popery; or from some ancient liturgies which savoured not of popery.[58]

The Commissioners' next charge was that the rearrangement of the eucharistic prayers in the 1637 Order was done so that the eucharistic sacrifice might be understood according to the popish meaning. Laud's answer to this is to say, perhaps a little disingenuously, that the alteration of the order of a set of prayers has little overall effect on their compound meaning, unless something obviously stupid is done, such as distributing communion before saying the prayer of consecration.

And though I shall not find fault with the order of the prayers, as they stand in the Communion-book of England, (for, God be thanked, 'tis well); yet, if a comparison must be made, I do think the order of the prayers, as now they stand in the Scottish Liturgy, to be the better, and more agreeable to use in the primitive Church; and I believe, they which are learned will acknowledge it.[59]

He maintains that the offering of the memorial commanded by Christ is not the same thing as the popish oblation, and that both 1637 and 1604 are doing the former, noting with irony that the puritans have to praise the English book in order to damn the Scottish.[60]

Next follows a long argument about the intention of the rubric at the beginning of the 1637 consecration prayer. Laud maintains that its only purpose is that the Minister may consecrate with decency, laying his hands upon the bread and wine as commanded; and the avoidance of possible unseemly disorder at the north end. There is no intention whatever in 1637, he maintains, of a disguised introduction of gestures used in the mass; nor does any English divine use any such gestures.[61] He maintains that neither 1604 nor 1637 intend any elevation or adoration of the elements,[62] nor is any part of the service intended to be said in a low voice;[63] and in both of these points he is wholly justified.

The Scottish Commissioners make the accusation that the doctrine of the corporal presence was contained in the book, and base this charge on two points; firstly, the general sense of the epiclesis; and secondly, the phrase in it 'be unto us'; since this phrase came from the Roman Mass, they say it implies the Roman doctrine of the corporal presence. Laud vigorously denies that the rite signifies this doctrine, and rebuts both charges specifically. He admits that the epiclesis may be taken as implying that 'The change here, is made a work of God's omnipotency' (quoting from the Commissioners' charge), and defends his view as follows:

A work of omnipotency it is, whatever the change be. For less than Omnipotence cannot change these elements, either in nature or in use, to so high a service as they are put in that great Sacrament. And therefore the invocating of God's Almighty Goodness to effect this by them is no proof at all of intending the 'Corporal Presence of Christ in this Sacrament'. 'Tis true, this passage is not in the Prayer of Consecration in the Service-book of England; but I wish with all my heart it were. For though the consecration of the elements may be without it, yet it is much more solemn and full by that invocation.

As for the words 'ut fiant nobis', far from proving the doctrine of the corporal presence in the 1637 rite, they actually tend to eliminate it from the Roman. In his discussion of this latter point he says

the elements after the benediction, or consecration, are, and may be called, the Body and Blood of Christ, without any addition, in that real and true sense in which they are so called in scripture;[64]

and goes on to discuss the meaning of *nobis* in relation to receiving communion, saying:

When they are said to become the Body and Blood of Christ, *nobis,* to us that communicate as we ought; there is by this addition, *fiant nobis,* an allay in the proper significance of the body and blood; and the true sense, so well signified and expressed, that the words cannot be well understood otherwise, than to imply not the corporal presence, but the real, and yet the spiritual use of them. And so the words, *ut fiant nobis,* import quite contrary to that which they are brought to prove.

The accusation is also brought that the omission of the second half of the words of administration as they stand in the English book was also meant to imply a corporal presence. He denies this, saying that in any case the change was due to the Scottish bishops, and quotes from Wedderburn's notes that the phrases from the second Edwardine book

may seem to relish somewhat of the Zwinglian tenet, That the sacrament is a bare sign taken in remembrance of Christ's passion.[65]

Laud seems to agree with this viewpoint of Wedderburn. He concludes his replies on this point by utterly condemning the corporal presence as grossly superstitious.[66]

From this discussion the main outlines of Laud's doctrine of consecration can be deduced. Once again the emphasis is on use; the elements are consecrated not for the corporal presence, but for 'the real, and yet the spiritual use of them'. It is in the reception of the elements that the grace and presence of Christ is received. And consecration is the prayer, invocation, blessing by which God's omnipotence is invoked that the elements may become capable of this use. Laud does not seem to associate this with any one particular form of words; he regards the 1637 form as fuller and better than that of 1604, but both are appropriate and effective. Coupled with this would seem to be a liking for manual acts, as a repetition by the priest of Christ's action as the last supper. Certainly there is no suggestion, either in the Commissioners' accusations or in Laud's replies, that he regarded the institution narrative as the sole and essential consecratory form. This observation leads to the fact that there is no mention of the supplementary consecration rubric.

Now Laud only discusses and justifies those parts of the 1637 rite which the Scottish Commissioners specifically attack, and since the latter make no reference to the supplementary consecration rubric, Laud does not tell us how he understood it, which is a pity. Yet the very silence of the Scottish Commissioners on the point is surely an important piece of evidence in itself. The Scottish Commissioners seized on every conceivable point in the 1637 rite that could possibly be regarded as evidence of Romeward intentions (and added some points that were not in the rite at all), and yet ignored the supplementary consecration rubric, which seems an apparently unambiguous witness to the Roman doctrine that consecration is achieved by the recital of the institution narrative alone. Why? Perhaps because they had overlooked it. But this seems extremely unlikely. However unfair and biased their criticisms were, however much they give the impression of being produced in an almost hysterical climate of anti-papal fear, there is no evidence that their work was done quickly or carelessly; the impression is of a thorough-going attempt to extract every piece of evidence from the 1637 rite that could be adduced to support their case. This leaves only one possible explanation for their not mentioning the rubric, namely that they did *not* regard it as evidence for Roman ideas about consecration. This being the case, they must have understood it in the same way as Bishop Morton, and therefore regarded it as unexceptionable in itself, even if they themselves would probably not have followed its precepts. It also seems fair to conjecture from what he says here in general about consecration that Laud too understood it, and the English canonical practice of which it was an exact adaptation, in a similar way. This seems a piece of evidence that supplementary consecration was not a matter of great controversy between Anglican and Puritan in this period.

Another person whose views are worthy of note is bishop Jeremy Taylor, who both wrote in defence of the Prayer Book, and produced an alternative liturgy for use in the Commonwealth period when the Prayer Book rite itself was forbidden. His doctrine of consecration can be deduced from his technical discussion of the place of the institution narrative, which occurs in his work *The Real Presence and Spiritual of Christ in the Blessed Sacrament proved against the doctrine of Transubstantiation.* Here he maintains that there is no justification for believing that the words 'this is my body' alone consecrate. The words of institution are spoken 'by way of history and narration', being 'declaratory and exegetical, not operative and practical'; otherwise, when the priest said 'Hoc est corpus meum', the bread would turn into his own body and not Christ's. Once again, for Taylor consecration is linked to use:

the words of consecration refer wholly to use, and it is Christ's body only in the 'taking and eating'.[6][7]

Taylor seems to believe that it is the whole of the eucharistic action that achieves this, and that it is therefore by the eucharistic action that the bread becomes the body of Christ to those who use it. It is this as a whole that Taylor means by consecration, the words of institution declaring and articulating what is the effect of the eucharist. These beliefs he put into practice in the liturgy he composed, in some ways a curious and clumsy rite, which he described as being

according to the way of the Apostolical Churches, and the doctrine of the Church of England.[68]

In its composition a great deal of Eastern material has been used, Taylor no doubt believing that in doing this he was following the way of the apostolic church. From the point of view of his doctrine of consecration, the important part is his prayer of consecration, named as such, which follows a fairly long (and apparently invariable) Preface and Sanctus, to which are attached the Lord's Prayer and something Taylor calls an ''Ἐκφώνησις or Denunciation,' which seems merely to repeat the material of the Preface. The first section of his prayer of consecration is an epiclesis prayer:[69]

Have mercy upon us, O Heavenly Father, according to thy glorious mercies and promises, send thy Holy Ghost upon our hearts, and let him also descend upon these gifts, that by his good, his holy, his glorious presence, he may sanctify and enlighten our hearts, and he may bless and sanctify these gifts. That this Bread may become the Holy Body of Christ. Amen. And this Chalice may become the life-giving Blood of Christ. Amen. That it may become unto us all that partake of it this day, a Blessed instrument of Union with Christ, of pardon and peace, of health and blessing, of holiness and life Eternal through . . .

This is followed by some lengthy doxological material, including a couple of acclamations by the people, leading into a recital of the institution narrative which includes rubrics commanding the minister to touch the bread and the wine during the appropriate part of the dominical words. After an Amen, and further acclamations by the people, this is followed by an anamnesis paragraph. After this follows communion of minister and people, the formulae of administration being similar in content to those of 1549. This latter is perhaps slightly curious because in the preface (which More and Cross conjecture was written between 1657 and 1660)[70] to his *An Apology for Authorized and set Forms of Liturgy* he praises the 1559 forms of administration as holding the true balance of positions on the presence, avoiding the errors of both transubstantiation and Zwinglianism.[71] Presumably therefore in his own rite he felt it sufficient to state his beliefs simply and positively.

As to the doctrinal intention of his prayer of consecration, its use of Eastern language, and in particular the apparent plea for a direct conversion in part of the epiclesis prayer, would lead one at first to suppose that he had adopted a fully Eastern theology of both consecration and the presence. This first impression, however, would seem to be quite misleading, for a number of reasons. Firstly, that in terms of structure, though not of content, Taylor's prayer is constructed along the lines of the 1549 Canon. Secondly, the institution narrative, with its manual acts, seems to be as prominent as the epiclesis, which suggests that for him it is just as important in expressing the meaning of the prayer. Thirdly, the apparent conversion phrases in the epiclesis prayer are followed immediately by an 'unto us' prayer; and fourthly, such an interpretation is not in accordance with his eucharistic theology as expounded in the *Real Presence . . .,* as outlined above. The conclusion is that his rite should be interpreted in accordance with this theology, and that in his consecration prayer he has copied Eastern language and forms, understanding them to mean, and intending his prayers to be, a solemn setting-aside for use by which the body and blood were received. In other words, Taylor has copied Eastern language without adopting, probably without really understanding, the underlying meaning of Eastern rites. This is an important point that will be referred to again later on.

(x) Summary

It will thus be seen that there is a great deal of Anglican material concerned with the doctrines of consecration and of the presence coming from this period, the preponderance of it written during the later part of it as apologiae for a tradition of worship under severe pressure or proscribed. The above discussion makes no claim to be exhaustive of all the available material, but it does claim to be a full and representative sample of it, large enough to establish that there was a characteristically Anglican theology of the eucharist in this period, and of what it basically consisted.

To summarise as briefly as possible, it may be said that the Caroline divines believed in the real presence, that it was to be identified with the bread and wine in their use in communion, and that this identification was achieved by the omnipotent power and Word of God in the liturgical action by the recitation of a prayer of consecration, and also in part by the physical repetition of Christ's actions at the Last Supper. But they denied the doctrine of transubstantiation, regarding it as unnecessary and erroneous, and seem to have felt that the only possible end of consecration is use in communion. This combination of ideas leads their view to sound receptionist, and perhaps the term 'Real Receptionist' may fairly be used as a convenient shorthand summary of their position. Thus in a sentence their theology could be summarised as belief in a real presence brought about by liturgical consecration mediated to the faithful communicants in reception of the consecrated elements. As a footnote to this, many of them admitted the legitimacy of a 1549 style of reservation for the sick, though most probably regarded it as unnecessary for their own day.

As to the necessary content of the prayer of consecration, all were agreed that it must contain the institution narrative, and most were agreed that recital of the institution narrative by itself did not consecrate. The institution narrative provided the warrant for celebrating and the guarantee that the effects of the eucharist would be in accordance with the mind of Christ in his institution of the sacrament, and was to be set within the framework of a prayer of thanksgiving containing an invocation or blessing upon the elements, the whole of which complex achieved the consecration. This whole tradition would seem to be very much an elaboration of Hooker's basic idea of 'hallowing with solemn benediction to use'. The above is the majority viewpoint;[72] a few Anglicans of the period adopted a more traditionally Latin outlook, notably Sparrow; but they too hold that the end of consecration is use and not the production of an objective presence, and so this difference in viewpoint as to the essentially consecratory part of the consecration prayer is not as important as it might seem. It is important to remember that by consecration all the Caroline divines seem to have meant the setting apart for the sacred use of communion; this is in sharp contrast to the contemporary Roman view which regarded it as meaning the effecting of an objective change in the substance of the elements. Therefore even with someone like Sparrow who seems to understand the essential consecratory part of the rite to be the institution narrative, it does not seem sensible to say that his doctrine of consecration was the same as the Roman one, because he meant something quite different by the idea of consecration itself. Only bishop Morton specifically discusses the subject of supplementary consecration, but it seems a reasonable conjecture from their general theology of consecration that his understanding of the method ordered by canon 21 would have been the way most Anglicans in this period would have explained it. It is a most important conclusion that this explanation provides a satisfactory rationale for a second consecration using only the institution narrative, whatever the content of the full consecration prayer of the rite.

In parenthesis, one may compare the above conclusions with C.W. Dugmore's comments on Anglican eucharistic theology.[73] It seems that there is less difference in essential basic theology of the eucharist between High and Central churchmen than he maintains; indeed in essentials these two outlooks both seem variations of the basic early seventeenth century position as outlined above, such variations being more concerned with ceremonial and perhaps mental attitude than doctrinal fundamentals. It seems fair too to criticise Dugmore's contention that the High Churchmen failed to provide a satisfactory solution to the problem of eucharistic theology facing them, and took refuge in the idea of a mystery.[74] It can hardly be denied that the action of God in the eucharist is a mystery in the final analysis, but the assertion that the body and blood of Christ are really received by the faithful communicant through the elements set apart for this use in the liturgical action (which is what the early seventeenth century meant by consecration) seems as satisfactory a solution to the problems of eucharistic theology as any produced in the period, and a good deal more so than some.

CHAPTER 6

The Puritan Tradition of Eucharistic Worship

A great deal of the Anglican literature written in this period was produced, in part at any rate, to contain puritan attacks on the Anglican rite. An analysis of the puritan liturgical tradition is therefore of relevance to this subject. And in considering this, the English puritan and Scottish Presbyterian may be considered as part of one and the same developing tradition, just as Anglicans north and south of the border were basically one: indeed the two traditions, Anglican and puritan, interacted with and influenced one another, which is another reason why the latter must be considered in this study.

(i) Knox's Liturgy and subsequent developments

For the sake of completeness, the puritan tradition will be studied in terms of its development from its origins, which for this purpose may safely be taken as the liturgy used by John Knox in the English Church at Geneva during the period 1556-1559. The liturgy of the Lord's Supper[1] begins by the minister reading the commission to celebrate from 1 Corinthians 11. This is followed by an exhortation which contains the following passage:

For the benefit is great, if with a truly penitent heart, and lively faith, we receive the holy sacrament (for then we spiritually eat the flesh of Christ, and drink his blood, then we dwell in Christ, and Christ in us, we being one with Christ, and Christ with us), so is the danger great . . .

Since this is a verbatim quotation from the third exhortation of the 1552 rite, Knox and Cranmer are presumably in agreement here. After this exhortation the minister goes to the table, on which the bread and wine has presumably already been placed, and says a prayer of thanksgiving, which is wholly concerned with thanking God for his salvation, and contains nothing that is in any sense a prayer for the blessing of the elements, or indeed of the people. This is followed by the distribution, a post-communion thanksgiving, and a rubric concerning some singing and the dismissal. The whole is concluded by a rubric expounding the rite's doctrinal content:

If perchance any would marvel why we follow rather this order, than any other in the administration of this sacrament, let him diligently consider, that first of all we utterly renounce the error of the papists; secondly we restore unto the sacraments their own substance; and to Christ his proper place. And as for the words of the Lord's Supper we rehearse them not because they should change the substance of the bread or wine, or that the repetition thereof with the intent of the sacrificer should make the sacrament, as the papists falsely believe: but they are read and pronounced to teach us how to behave ourselves in this action that Christ might witness unto our faith as it were with his own mouth, that he had ordained these signs for our spiritual use and comfort. We do first therefore examine ourselves . . . that we may be worthy partakers of so high mysteries. Then taking bread, we give thanks, break and distribute it, as Christ our Saviour hath taught us. Finally the ministration ended, we give thanks again according to his example. So that without his word, and warrant, there is nothing in this holy action attempted.

Two points seem to call for comment here. Its doctrine of the place of the bread and wine in the rite seems once again very similar to that of Cranmer; in their essential theology of the eucharist, then, perhaps Cranmer and Knox were very similar. The second point is that the use of the institution narrative as a warrant is a feature common to most early seventeenth-century Anglican exegesis of the eucharist, but of course the latter couples this with a prayer for blessing the elements, which was absent in Knox's Geneva rite.

This liturgy was transcribed without significant alteration into the Book of Common Order,[2] first published in Scotland in 1564.[3] The Book of Common Order was the legal liturgy in Scotland until 1645, when it was replaced by the Westminster Directory.[4] This eucharistic liturgy was also the one the English puritans wished to substitute for the Prayer Book during the reign of Elizabeth I from about 1584 onwards,[5] and thus Knox's rite can be considered the original norm for a puritan communion rite, and the basis from which the puritan tradition developed. And it is at this point that one of the basic differences between the Anglican and puritan traditions becomes apparent; there was a much greater degree of freedom in the puritan than in the

Anglican (in theory in the latter there was none at all), and so, if a puritan minister felt the rite he was using inadequate, he amended it accordingly, and the way various people did this supplies additional valuable information about the development of the puritan eucharistic tradition, and a few comments can now be made about this.

G.W. Sprott, W. McMillan and G. Donaldson all comment on this point,[6] showing that by the early seventeenth century the bare thanksgiving form of Knox's rite was felt to be inadequate by itself, and that some kind of blessing or invocation of the elements was commonly added. During the early part of this period most of these expressions were fairly tentative, but by about 1640 Henderson, describing the part of the minister, wrote of the eucharistic action thus:

[He] first readeth and shortly expoundeth the words of institution . . . Next he useth a prayer wherein he both giveth thanks . . . and prayeth earnestly to God for His powerful presence and effectual working to accompany His own Ordinance . . . The elements thus being sanctified by Word and Prayer, the minister, sacramentally breaketh the bread . . .[7]

(ii) Cowper's draft

Another liturgy of interest is that produced by William Cowper, which he probably composed not long before his death in 1619.[8] It is not easy to know whether to class this as a puritan liturgy or an Anglican one. It is puritan in that its roots are undoubtedly in the Scottish tradition of the period, and yet it is the product of an era which saw episcopacy reintroduced into the Scottish Church (Cowper himself was a bishop), and the attempt under James I to assimilate the worship of the Churches in his two kingdoms. It can thus be considered as being on the border between the two traditions, and, though produced in Scotland, may perhaps be taken as expressing a doctrine of the eucharist that both moderate Anglican and moderate puritan might have been happy with, in the absence of other factors exacerbating relations between them. In the event it seems never actually to have been used.[9]

Cowper's draft too was designed to be used after the normal morning service,[10] and a rubric at the beginning directs the bread and wine to be placed on the table, covered, as the minister enters the pulpit at the beginning of the service,

for besides that by the word and prayers they are sanctified to the holy use whereunto God hath appointed them, the doctrine of Christ's death will affect and move the people more easily when they see those holy signs which represent Christ crucified unto us.[11]

At the end of the sermon the minister is directed to go to the table and say the Anglican collect for purity. Then he is to read the Pauline account of the institution, just as in the Book of Common Order. This is followed by the long exhortation from the latter verbatim. After this exhortation Cowper's text departs from that of the Book of Common Order, for it is followed immediately by an invitation to confession that is virtually word for word the 'Ye that do truly and earnestly . . . ' from the Prayer Book. This is followed by the Prayer Book confession, presumably said by the minister alone, which leads without a break (though there is a disjunction in the text as it has survived) into a prayer that can only be described as a kind of prayer of thanksgiving or consecration. This prayer includes a diverse collection of material, including some obviously based on and some actually copied from the Prayer Book, as well as containing echoes of the Book of Common Order. After a memorial of Christ's sacrifice that owes more to the Book of Common Order than to the Book of Common Prayer, there follows:

Him also thou hast vouchsafed to give us this day to be the food of our souls in this sacrament; Merciful Father we beseech thee that we receiving these thy creatures of bread and wine, according to thy Son our Saviour his holy institution, may be made partakers of his most blessed body and blood. Send down O Lord thy blessing upon this Sacrament that it may be unto us the effectual exhibitive instrument of the Lord Jesus.[12]

The rest of the prayer gives thanks, acknowledges the command to remember Christ's death in this way, prays for the benefits of communion, and makes an act of self-oblation; it concludes with the Lord's Prayer. This is followed by the rubric:

The prayer ended the Minister shall repeat the words of the institution for consecrating the elements and say:[13]

The institution narrative follows with rubrics commanding the minister to take the bread and wine into his hands at the appropriate point. A different hand has added an alternative rubric to the above:

Then shall the Minister pray after this manner, and read the words of the Institution,

clearly someone who read Cowper's original rubric as meaning that it is the bare recital of the institution narrative that alone consecrates, and wished to correct this impression. This recital of the institution narrative is followed by an invitation to receive:

Let us lift up our hearts unto the Lord, and by faith lay hold upon Jesus, whom God the father by his spirit offereth to us in this holy Sacrament, that we may draw virtue from the Lord . . .

This is followed by reception of communion, the words of administration used being the current Anglican form.[14] The service concludes with a final prayer of thanksgiving, which clearly owes something to Prayer Book material, the singing of the first two verses of Psalm 106, and a blessing.[15]

The overall doctrinal intention of this rite seems quite clear. It is that the spiritual benefits of the body and blood of Christ are really received in the eating and drinking of the elements that have liturgically been set apart for this sacred use. This setting aside is called 'consecration', and Cowper associates this in particular with the reading of the institution narrative and the manual acts accompanying it. Yet it seems equally certain that he thought more was needed for an effective setting aside of the elements than just this, for the prayer that precedes the institution narrative contains a very clear invocation of God's blessing upon the elements to their use of conveying Christ to the communicant. His doctrine then seems to have been that the prayers of the rite containing such a request for the direct blessing of the elements, and the repetition of Christ's action at the institution narrative, together constitute the consecration, the institution narrative itself perhaps providing a kind of focus on consecration. The whole of the rite, its rubrics and its prayers, witness to this theological outlook. Thus the ideas underlying this liturgy seem almost exactly the same as those of moderate Anglicanism in the same period; again in its essential content, though not in its form or ceremonial, this rite can be seen as a very close anticipation of 1637. And though the rite contains no provision for supplementary consecration, it is perhaps a reasonable conjecture to suppose that Cowper would have been quite happy with the procedure of the English canon 21, and would probably have justified it along similar lines to bishop Morton; his juxtaposition of a description of the institution narrative as being for consecrating the elements with a prayer containing a direct plea for their specific blessing suggests this.

(iii) The Westminster Directory

The next piece of important puritan eucharistic liturgy making is the rite of the Lord's Supper contained in the Westminster Directory of 1644, the rite the puritans designed to replace the Prayer Book. This does not provide a text as such, but detailed instructions to the minister telling him what to do, and what his prayers are to contain.[16] Thus the Directory makes its doctrinal intention just as clear as if it had ·published a full text. After an introductory rubric concerning frequency and previous preparation, the minister is commanded to make a general exhortation concerning penitence and so forth. This is followed by a further instruction concerned with the actual sacramental part of the rite:

After this exhortation, warning and invitation, the table being decently covered, and so conveniently placed that the communicants may orderly sit about it, or at it; the minister is to begin the action, with sanctifying and blessing the elements of bread and wine set before him . . . having first, in a few words, showed that these elements, otherwise common, are now set apart and sanctified to this holy use by the word of institution and prayer. Let the words of institution be read out of the evangelists, or out of 1 Corinthians 11 v.23-27, which the minister may, when he seeth requirement, explain and apply. Let the prayer, thanksgiving, or blessing of the bread and wine, be to this effect:[17]

Instruction on the content of the thanksgiving follows, the first paragraph being a thanksgiving for all the benefits of salvation. It continues:

Earnestly to pray to God, the Father of all mercies, and God of all consolation, to vouchsafe his gracious presence, and the effectual working of his Spirit in us; and so to sanctify these elements of bread and wine, and to bless his own ordinance, that we may receive by faith the body and blood of Jesus Christ crucified for us, and so feed upon him that he may be one with us, and we with him, that he may live in us . . .[18]

Then comes a rubric about the distribution:' . . . The

elements being now sanctified by the word and prayer . . . ', they are to be distributed. The service is to conclude with a final exhortation and thanksgiving.

The essential theology here is very similar to that of Cowper. There is to be a sanctifying and blessing of the elements to the sacred use of communion, in which the body and blood of Christ are received by faith. This setting apart or sanctification is by 'the word of institution and prayer', which is what Anglicans in the period usually meant by 'consecration'. Thus the conclusion is that the essential eucharistic theology of the Westminster Directory's rite is very similar to that of moderate Anglicanism in the same period, and indeed is arguably 'higher' than that of the Prayer Book it replaced.

(iv) Baxter's Liturgy

The final puritan liturgy of significance that must be noted in this study is the rite that Richard Baxter presented to the Savoy Conference as a proposed alternative to the Prayer Book. Unlike the Westminster Directory, a full text is given.[19] It is extremely long. It contains no synaxis, doubtless being intended to follow the sermon. It must be summarised in some detail, for its doctrinal intention can only be properly deduced from its overall structure and content. The rite starts with a long exhortation which includes the following passage:

The Lord's Supper, then, is an Holy Sacrament, instituted by Christ: Wherein bread and wine, being first by consecration made sacramentally, or representatively, the body and blood of Christ, are used by breaking and pouring out to represent and commemorate the sacrifice of Christ's body and blood upon the cross once offered up to God for sin; and are given in the name of Christ unto the Church, to signify and solemnize the renewal of his holy covenant with them, and the giving of himself unto them to expiate their sins by his sacrifice, and sanctify them further by his Spirit, and confirm their right to everlasting life. And they are received, eaten, and drunk by the Church, to profess that they willingly receive Christ himself to the ends aforesaid, (their justification, sanctification, and glorification) and to signify and solemnize the renewal of their covenant with him and with one another.[20]

There is a further long exhortation reminding the worshippers of all that Christ has done and encouraging them to follow him.[21] This includes the phrase 'See here

Christ dying in this holy representation', an idea extremely reminiscent of Langforde's meditations.[22] This exhortation is followed by a long confession of sin, after which comes the actual eucharistic part of the rite. The bread and the wine are to be brought to the minister at the table (though it is noted in parenthesis that they may already be there) and then he is to bless them. After a brief thanksgiving, the prayer set down for this purpose continues:

Sanctify these thy creatures of bread and wine, which, according to thy institution and command, we set apart to this holy use, that they may be sacramentally the body and blood of thy Son Jesus Christ.[23]

Immediately after this prayer, the minister is to read the words of institution, after which he says:

This bread and wine, being set apart, and consecrated to this holy use by God's appointment, are now no common bread and wine, but sacramentally the body and blood of Christ.[24]

A further prayer for forgiveness and for the Spirit follows here. The minister is then to perform the manual acts. He is to break the bread in the sight of the people saying:

The body of Christ which was broken for us, and offered once for all to sanctify us: behold the sacrificed Lamb of God, that taketh away the sins of the world.

After this he takes the cup and pours out the wine in the sight of the congregation saying:

We are redeemed with the precious blood of Christ, as of a Lamb without blemish and without spot.[25]

After a prayer for the blessing of the Spirit upon the worshippers, the distribution follows. There next follow some instructions concerning allowable permissive alternatives in the manner of celebrating. The minister may consecrate and distribute the bread and wine together, or as separate actions, but in the latter case, 'he must use the foregoing prayers and expressions twice accordingly'. The words at the fraction and the pouring are optional. If a shorter order is required, the minister may say one single prayer for consecration, commemoration, and delivery. A form for this is given, consisting of an abbreviated conglomeration of previous material. This contains no institution narrative but does contain the petition 'sanctify these thy creatures . . .'.[26] The rite concludes with a thanksgiving, exhortation, and blessing.

In doctrinal intention this rite is similar to the Westminster Directory. Consecration is setting apart to use, the use of being the sacramental representation of Christ, both for didactic purposes and that the gifts of grace may be received through reception; the great didactic stress on the liturgical action is a new element here. As to where Baxter located the act of consecration itself, it would seem to have been more specifically in the prayer for the sanctification of the elements than in anything else, for the short combined version of his prayer does not contain the institution narrative. However, this is not to be taken as a moment of consecration in any medieval sense; but rather as a focus of consecration where God is asked to validate the rite and make it what he promised it was to be.

(v) Puritan Exceptions to the Prayer Book Prayer of Consecration

With this in mind the puritan exception to the Prayer Book rite concerning the consecration may now be noted. Under a heading 'Prayer at the Consecration'[27] and against that part of the prayer from 'Hear us, O Merciful Father . . . saying, Take, eat, etc. . . .' they say:

We conceive that the manner of the consecration of the elements is not here explicit and distinct enough, and the minister's breaking of the bread is not so much as mentioned.

A number of comments can be made about this. First, it should be noted the puritan complaint was that the consecration was not explicit enough; in other words, by 1662 the puritans had come to regard the 1604 Prayer Book as too 'low' in its doctrine of consecration rather than too 'high'. This is the opposite to what a superficial popular view of puritanism would lead one to expect. Second, that their quotation from the consecration prayer (and it is to be noted that this is how they describe it) starts at 'Hear us . . .' and goes on to include the institution narrative. Their theory of consecration was presumably then that it was achieved by prayer that the effects of the rite might be as Christ promised, coupled with the repetition of what Christ did by reciting the institution narrative with manual acts, a doctrine not significantly different from contemporary Anglican thought.

The bishops met the puritans' point as follows:

That the manner of consecrating the elements may be made more explicit and express, and to that purpose these words be put into the rubric, 'Then shall he put his hand upon the bread and break it', 'then shall he put his hand unto the cup'.[28]

The manual acts, with their physical repetition of what Christ did, make the consecration more explicit, a response with which the puritans, with their stress on the need for breaking the bread, were probably satisfied.

(vi) *Conclusions*

The general conclusion, then, of this study of the puritan eucharistic tradition is that in all basic essentials it was fundamentally the same as the Anglican, both in terms of the presence and of consecration. As for the Anglicans, for the moderate and representative puritans consecration meant the liturgical setting apart of the bread and wine for the sacred use of conveying the spiritual gifts to the faithful believers in communion; this was the sort of theology that had developed in both traditions by the middle of the seventeenth century. This comment leads to the second general conclusion here, namely that as there had been a theological development from Cranmer and the very Protestant attitude of most early Elizabethan Anglicans to the much more positive theology and richer tradition of the middle of the seventeenth century, so there had been an exactly similar and parallel development in puritanism, from Knox to the Westminster Director and Baxter. Thus Knox and Cranmer are theologically equivalent, the rite of the Book of Common Order and 1552; and so a century later are Baxter and the Westminster Directory and the liturgical thinking of the seventeenth century Caroline divines; and between the two equivalents there was a century of approximately similar development. (That Knox and Cranmer were widely seen as equivalent in the early part of the period is partly demonstrated by the fact that both the Book of Common Order and 1552 seem to have been used by Reformed congregations in Scotland during this time.)[29]

This being the case, it will be asked why Anglican and puritan disagreed so violently and vehemently. Why did a puritan tract declaim:

The Communion Booke is an unperfect Booke culled and pyked out of the Popish dunghill, the Portuys and Masse Book, and manye of the contentes therein be suche as are against the Worde of God?[30]

Why was the 1637 Prayer Book whose contents ought to have commended it to the moderate puritans, greeted with a riot?[31] Why did it produce the sort of hysterical reaction evidenced by the Scottish Commissioners' charges against Laud? Why did puritans spend so much of their time and energy during the century between 1560 and 1662 trying to substitute their own liturgy for that of the Prayer Book? And from the other side, why did Anglicans such as Cosin and Thorndike regard puritan celebrations as invalid?

A number of factors seem to contribute towards the answers to these questions. First, secular politics, insofar as these can be separated from ecclesiastical in this period. Anglican so often seemed to be the oppressor of puritan; and from the Anglican side the English authorities felt they had little choice but to be oppressive, for to concede the puritan demands would have been to consent to the overthrow, or at least the drastic modification, of the English State as well as the Church. And in Scotland 1637 was seen as the imposition of an oppressive dictatorial king and a much distrusted English archbishop. The second factor is that much of the controversy between Anglican and puritan centred around matters of ceremonial, particularly kneeling to receive communion and the surplice. Insignificant as these details seem to the modern mind, to a sixteenth- or seventeenth-century one they were of vital importance: to the puritan, the retention of these things in the Anglican tradition was evidence that the Anglican was an imperfectly reformed church, still contaminated with the things of Rome. This leads to the next point, namely the vital question of ecclesiastical polity. Anglicanism had retained episcopacy, and with it the whole medieval system of ecclesiastical administration, in many ways strengthened and developed in the eighty or so years from 1560 onwards, together with the concept of the regular use of liturgical worship, whereas most of the puritans wished to introduce the Presbyterian system of church discipline. These two outlooks were mutually exclusive and caused an enormous amount of strife, and of course at base have deep doctrinal overtones. Added to these basic factors, there was the tendency among some puritans to stay very 'low' in their doctrine of the sacraments and the liturgical forms they used, and the absence of a statutory liturgy increased the risk of imperfect and invalid prayers said by ignorant celebrants. On the other hand, the opposite tendency manifested itself in Anglicanism, with its retention of catholic order and the idea of the liturgy, namely to drift 'higher'. Of this tendency the ceremonial practices of Andrewes and the high Laudian school are an example from this period. Thus, given the differing ecclesiastical politics of Anglican and puritan, the natural tendency of the traditions of the two would be to diverge, as in fact happened in the centuries after 1662. The combination of all these factors produced such an atmosphere of distrust and suspicion between men of the two outlooks that after a century of strife it was finally recognised an impossibility to comprehend them in the same Church. This being the case, it is not surprising that they failed to recognise that their basic essential eucharistic theologies were very similar, and were unable to agree on a common liturgical policy. In the circumstances this failure was inevitable, but it must be judged in retrospect one of the tragedies of English ecclesiastical history.

CHAPTER 7

The Communion Rites of 1637 and 1662

There are two great liturgical monuments to the scholarship and devotion of the Caroline divines, namely the Scottish Prayer Book of 1637 and the English book of 1662, and it is the composition and content of these that must be investigated next.

(i) The 1637 rite

Gordon Donaldson in his *The Making of the Scottish Prayer Book of 1637* traces three separate influences as combining together to produce the book in its final form. Firstly, the influence of the older Scottish bishops and the post-Reformation Scottish liturgical tradition, the puritan tradition whose development was discussed above. Secondly, the position of the English authorities, principally archbishop Laud and king Charles I. Thirdly, bishop James Wedderburn, who became bishop of Dunblane in February 1636.[1]

As noted above, Donaldson points out that in the period 1560-1600 the Prayer Book was quite widely used in Scotland alongside Knox's Book of Common Order, and that there was a much greater degree of doctrinal and liturgical similarity between England and Scotland in that period than there was later on. Throughout the whole of the period between the Reformation in Scotland and the Civil War, church government there fluctuated between presbyterianism and episcopacy, and liturgical practice tended to fluctuate with it. Coupled with this was the sort of liturgical thinking typified by Cowper's draft. Though nothing came of this particular project, the influence of the tradition it represented remained and came to the fore again during the stages of revision that led to the 1637 book.

In the early 1630s the subject was taken up again. Charles I and Laud wanted to achieve liturgical uniformity between the two kingdoms, and to introduce the English book without change. This the Scottish bishops resisted, and started work on a version of their own, revising the English book to suit what they felt to be Scottish requirements; at this stage the leader and spokesman for the Scottish bishops seems to have been Maxwell, who made several journeys to London to consult with the English authorities. This stage in the proceedings takes us to about the middle of 1635. At this stage no substantial changes had been proposed for the Communion service; such verbal changes as had been made were probably due to the Scottish bishops, whereas the English contribution seems to have consisted of rubrical expansion and clarification in a Laudian direction. It is at this stage that Wedderburn's influence becomes crucial, and it seems that the fundamental restructuring of the Canon, both in terms of content and order, are due to him. Thus the book was revised again in 1636, Wedderburn's suggestions being approved by Laud and the king, and then printed.[2]

The first major change in the Canon is the reinsertion of a 1549-style invocation in the 1549 position and obviously derived from it. The result of this is a modified combination of 1549 and 1552 material at this point. The second major change is the placing of the prayer of oblation after the institution narrative, expanded to make quite explicit the making of the memorial 'with these holy gifts'.[3] Rubrical provision for supplementary consecration is provided for by the direction that the appropriate part of the institution narrative be repeated.[4] G. Donaldson regards this as out of harmony with the theology of the 1637 Canon. He comments as follows:

It seems an unaccountable lapse on the part of the compilers of the Scottish Prayer Book that the words of institution alone should have been thought sufficient for additional consecration. This was contrary to the usage of the Book of Common Order, and, although it could claim the precedent of Cowper's draft, was quite at variance with the Scottish liking for an invocation and with the inclusion of an invocation in the new Prayer Book itself.

He continues in a foot-note:

This feature of the Scottish Book is the more surprising in that the English Prayer Book did not as yet contain any directions for additional consecration. Existing practice in England (where the consecration prayer had no epiclesis) was to use the words of institution and the Scots seem to have fallen into unintelligent imitation.[5]

But there would seem to be two different possible ways of

explaining this apparent fault in the book, the first of which derives from Donaldson's own account of how the 1637 book came into being. Donaldson notes that the principal English contribution to the book was the amplification of the rubrics in a Laudian direction.[6] Is it not most probable that this rubric is one such amplification? With current English practice to hand, it would have been logical to suggest such a rubric for the new Scottish book, whereas the new Canon came from the Scottish bishops and Wedderburn in particular. This would be one way of accounting for the apparent disharmony between the theology of the Canon and that of the provision for supplementary consecration. However, this is probably not the correct explanation. A more likely explanation is that there is no disharmony between the two; that far from being 'an unaccountable lapse', the whole of this part of the rite, Canon and supplementary consecration rubric, was put together with deliberation and care. The length of time taken to produce the book, and the number of stages that it went through, makes the existence of a careless blunder in it in so vital a matter as the consecration in the eucharist extremely unlikely. It may well be that the insertion of the supplementary consecration rubric was due to Laud's initiative, but it is strongly suggested that both he and the Scottish bishops understood what they were doing along the same lines as bishop Morton's exposition of supplementary consecration. Thus there is no disharmony between the two, for given early seventeenth-century ideas about consecration and bishop Morton's explanation, the institution narrative method of supplementary consecration is valid whatever the content of the full eucharistic prayer of the rite.

A number of the detailed points in Donaldson's argument also call for criticism. He says the English consecration prayer has no epiclesis, which is perfectly true in that there was no direct invocation of the Holy Spirit to bless the elements in the English prayer. However the early seventeenth-century held consecration to be effected by a prayer for the blessing of the elements that included the institution narrative; and in the English rite the 'Hear us, O merciful Father . . .' was regarded as providing this element in the consecration, and as equivalent to the fuller form provided in 1637. Most of the Carolines would have preferred the latter forms but were quite happy with the former. Therefore, following

Donaldson's argument and applying it to the early seventeenth-century, the supplementary consecration rubric of the 1637 rite would have been just as inappropriate with the 1604 rite. Donaldson has made the mistake of reading into the differing forms of the 1604 and 1637 prayers in this respect a theological distinction not understood as such at the time.

It also seems questionable to state that the 1637 supplementary consecration rubric 'was contrary to the usage of the Book of Common Order. but that it would 'claim the precedent of Cowper's draft'.[7] Presumably in making this comparison he has in mind the final rubric of the Book of Common Order rite that denied to the institution narrative any consecratory force, and the institution narrative paragraph, with its manual acts, of Cowper's draft, which is there described in the preceding rubric as being 'for consecrating the elements'. With regard to the Book of Common Order rite, because of its fundamental theology presumably *any* supplementary consecration provision would be alien to it. And in the case of Cowper's draft, this too contained a direct invocation in the prayer before the institution narrative, so by applying Donaldson's own reasoning, the institution narrative method of supplementary consecration is invalid for this rite too. The fact is that Donaldson, by comparing a rite that contains a supplementary consecration provision with two that do not, has compared like with unlike, and therefore his arguments on this point fail.

The general conclusion about the 1637 rite is that it represents more or less the ideal eucharistic liturgy according to the mind of the Caroline divines of the early seventeenth-century.

(ii) Suggestions for revision in England at the Restoration

The Restoration of Charles II in 1660 provided a fresh opportunity for recasting the Prayer Book liturgy, and a number of the Caroline divines took advantage of this and produced proposals for such a revised liturgy. Among such were Wren and Cosin, who entered their proposals in detail in a 1619 copy of the Prayer Book, which came to be called the *Durham Book*. Their proposals as regards the eucharist are of particular interest in this context, representing as they do, not only their own opinions but in most respects the essence and consensus of Caroline eucharistic theology. Their restructuring of the Canon suggested the reinsertion of a 1549-style epiclesis in the 1549 position, and the placing of the prayer of oblation immediately after the institution narrative. The text of the prayer of oblation was altered in the same way as it had been in 1637 to make it quite clear that the memorial was being made in the holy gifts. A number of other changes were proposed, such as the saying of the Lord's Prayer immediately after the prayer of oblation, and replacing the words 'in these Holy Mysteries' in the Prayer of Humble Access, which itself was to be placed immediately before the reception of communion; but it is the proposal to replace the existing English Canon with, in effect, that of 1637, that is the change of real importance.[8]

A large number of alterations and additions were proposed in the rubrics, all of which illustrate the changed perspective of Caroline eucharistic theology. Wren in his *Advices* suggested the insertion of a formal placing of the bread and wine on the holy table between the Sanctus and the Prayer of Humble Access, which he retained in this position.[9] The *Durham Book* itself proceeds straight from the Sanctus to the Consecration,[10] and in giving the title 'prayer of Consecration' to this prayer in the preliminary rubric is making an addition of considerable importance. There are a variety of drafts of this rubric, all of which command standing as the posture of the priest (as did 1552), but go on to explain the point of this is that the priest may the more readily perform the manual acts.[11] All concerned wanted manual acts at the institution narrative, including a fraction, and this includes the puritans just as much as the bishops at the Savoy Conference, Wren, L'Estrange, and Cosin. Noting that there was a current tradition of performing manual acts, Cosin goes so far as to say:

as in King Edward's service book there was, and in most places is still in use.[12]

Both Wren and Cosin insert rubrics providing for supplementary consecration as necessary by reciting the appropriate part of the institution narrative,[13] the procedure adopted in 1662, which suggests that they saw no disharmony between this and their desire for a much fuller Canon including a more definite invocation. This suggests that their thinking about this matter was along the same lines as that of bishop Morton, and is further evidence for the correctness of the viewpoint adopted about the 1637 rite above. Cosin was fully aware of the English precedents for supplementary consecration, mentioning the 1548 *Ordo* and canon 21 of 1604 in his *Particulars,* and clearly regarded the lack of such rubrical provision in the rite itself as a defect. The final important rubrical change proposed, from the point of view of this study, is that made concerning the rubric 'and if any bread or wine remain the curate shall have it to his own use'. Cosin notes that:

some curates have abused and extended (this rubric) so far, that they suppose they may take all that remains of the Consecrate Bread and Wine itself home to their own houses, and there eat and drink the same with their other common meats . . . whereas the rubric only intends it of such Bread and Wine as remain unconsecrate of that which was provided for the parish, as appeareth by the Articles of Inquiry hereabouts, in the Visitations of divers bishops.[14]

Thus Cosin takes the same line on this point as Sparrow, and it would seem that it was common practice in the early seventeenth-century to interpret this rubric in a sense contrary to its original intention, thus making it conformable to Caroline eucharistic theology. All the proposed changes for this rubric make this quite explicit; only unconsecrated bread and wine may be removed. Any of the consecrated that remains is to be reverently consumed by the celebrant and other communicants in church.

(iii) The 1662 book

In relation to all these proposed changes, the actual changes effected in the 1662 book can be fairly summarised as follows.[15] The 1604 text of the Communion rite was retained practically unaltered, but virtually all the rubrical changes advocated in the *Durham Book,* and certainly all those that can be said to have a bearing on theories of consecration, were adopted in the revised book. Both the Laudian churchmen and the puritans in their different ways desired to see substantial changes in the existing prayer book, and both failed in their aims, partly because they were largely contradictory, but mainly because the Parliament, determined to restore everything as it had been in 'good King Charles's golden days', would not have allowed it. Nevertheless, it can be said that the rubrical changes ensured that all that the Caroline divines regarded as essential to ensure a proper consecration (as they understood it) of all the bread and wine given in communion, and to guarantee due reverence at all points in the service, had been incorporated in the book. Further, it would seem that these rubrical changes made into an official part of the rite the liturgical practice that many of the bishops had been trying to enforce since at least the 1630s.

One other change of importance made was the reinsertion of the 'black rubric'. This was done in response to puritan pressure, but in the form in which it was inserted, denying a 'corporal presence' and not a 'real and essential' one, the Carolines were probably not too unhappy with it. After all, they were concerned to refut the doctrine of transubstantiation almost as much as the puritans.[16]

(iv) Summary: The Caroline liturgical ideal

Nevertheless, the Carolines failed to achieve their theological ideal for a consecration prayer, which ideal is expressed in the 1637 rite. That the 1637 Canon seems actually to have been put together by the Scottish bishop Wedderburn is immaterial; it represents the ideal of the Caroline divines on both sides of the border, influenced by and influencing both. It placed the making of the memorial and of the oblation after the institution narrative, in accordance with the ancient liturgical tradition they had come to know and accept, and it had a full and explicit invocation on the elements, another feature they regarded as extremely desirable. In terms of its essential theology it is to be seen as the expression of, and interpreted according to, the mind of the Caroline divines, as they themselves understood and described the eucharistic action. Thus the insertion of the epiclesis-type prayer should not be seen as evidence that they were adopting an essentially Eastern type of consecration theology; they were not. In this period the 1637-style prayer was seen as expressing the same meaning as that of 1604, but in a 'much more solemn and full' manner, to quote Laud. It is thus an important conclusion of this study that the institution narrative method of supplementary consecration was seen as being wholly congruous with a 1637 style Canon in the period before the Restoration.

In this respect it thus seems necessary to modify E.C. Ratcliff's conclusion that the English usage in respect of eucharistic consecration in the period between the Reformation and the Restoration was 'uniform and "Western" ',[17] consisting of the recitation of the institution narrative, with a variety of doctrinal explanations. The fact is that early seventeenth-century Anglicanism had a doctrine of consecration other than this, that they formed and expressed and interpreted their rites accordingly, and that they had a rationale of supplementary consecration by the institution narrative alone that fitted in with the rest of their theology. This is so different from contemporary, and subsequent, Roman and 'Western' doctrine that it really does not seem sensible to equate the two. And in any case the liturgical resemblance is more superficial than actual, for the Roman 'Western' tradition does not admit of supplementary consecration in this manner for the purposes for which it is used in the Anglican tradition, so the English practice of supplementary consecration cannot properly be used to prove anything about English theories of consecration vis-à-vis Roman ones.

It can be asked what are the theological roots of this early seventeenth-century eucharistic tradition? It seems a reasonable conjecture to suppose that it owes more to a general understanding of the way the three persons of the Godhead operate towards man's salvation in the Church applied to sacramental theology than to any copying or direct adaption of any pre-Reformation liturgical tradition. In other words, it was a piece of more or less original thinking. The 1549 epiclesis prayer provided the source for the wording of that of 1637, though not of course for the puritan prayers very close to it in essential meaning as understood in the early seventeenth-century. (Perhaps Cranmer composed it in the first place in the same sort of way.) And when the epiclesis prayers of Eastern liturgies began to be quite widely known and quoted by Anglicans in this period, they were regarded as patristic evidence for this mode of thinking, which had already evolved, rather than being understood and interpreted according to their own authentic meaning; this did not come until the post-Restoration era.

CHAPTER EIGHT

Developments and Theological Commentaries in England in the period 1662-1764

The Restoration of the monarchy in 1660 paved the way for the restoration of the Prayer Book as the sole official public liturgy of the Church of England. As was noted in the previous chapter, the 1662 eucharistic rite was virtually identical in terms of text with that of 1604, but with substantially altered and, from the point of view of the prevailing Caroline eucharistic theology, improved rubrics. No further changes were made in the Prayer Book during the period under review, and indeed it was to remain unchanged in all essentials for more than three centuries; no changes at all were made in the eucharistic rite during this period.

Though a generalisation, it is probably true to say that in the first half of the seventeenth century, roughly the period from Hooker to the Great Rebellion, the Prayer Book changed slowly and unconsciously from being a government-imposed compromise that few people liked into a genuine religious tradition, valued for its own sake and inspiring a religious ethos of its own. This gave rise to both theological development, much of it moving away from the theology of Cranmer, and to its own devotional literature. The Commonwealth period, during which the Prayer Book was illegal, fostered both these developments, for during it the Prayer Book had changed from being the government-imposed liturgy of compromise into a clandestine and prohibited rite that, if it was to survive at all, could do so only on the basis of its own intrinsic merits and on the courage of those whose devotion to it was sufficient to keep its memory and use alive, despite all the difficulties. That there were many such people is proved by the speed with which it came back into use from 1660 onwards. Thus the latter part of the seventeenth century and the early part of the eighteenth century saw a great flowering of devotional literature and theological commentary on the Prayer Book, including of course its eucharistic rite. It is this abundant source of material that provides the means to understand how the eucharistic doctrine of the 1662 rite was understood during this period, and to trace the development of Anglican eucharistic theology during the 100 years or so under discussion, from the Prayer Book's restoration in 1662 to the publication of the definitive edition of the Scottish rite in 1764.

A comparison of post-Restoration visitation articles with those of the pre-Restoration period shows that very few of the former contain any reference to supplementary consecration. The obvious reason for this is, that since the Prayer Book now dealt with the matter by rubric, there was no need for them to do so.

(i) The 1689 proposals

Before proceeding further it is worth noting briefly the proposals made for prayer book revision in 1689. In the aftermath of the Revolution an attempt was made to encourage as many protestant dissenters as possible to rejoin the Church of England; there seemed to be a real hope at this time that the Presbyterians might be integrated within the church without too many changes of substance, but with some of ceremonial.[1] A commission of 30 was appointed to review the Prayer Book, with very extensive terms of reference, whose composition represented a genuine cross section of all shades of opinion.[2] This commission never officially reported, but its suggestions were entered in a 1686 edition of the Prayer Book that has been preserved in the archiepiscopal archives at Lambeth. These suggestions were reprinted by order of the House of Commons in 1854.[3] The eucharistic section of the catechism was extended from five to six questions, whose general tone is, if anything, slightly more receptionist than those in the 1662 book.[4] The only change of any theological substance in the Communion rite itself in fact concerns supplementary consecration, where the existing rubric was replaced by one which reads as follows:

If the consecrated Bread or Wine be all spent before all have communicated, the Minister shall use this form: 'O merciful Father, hear the Prayers of thy Church that have now been made unto thee in the name of thy Son our Lord Jesus Christ, who the same night that he was betrayed, took bread . . .'[5]

One may also note the very brief account of the Commission's discussion on this point, as contained in Dr Williams' unofficial minutes of the Commission's proceedings:

About the Lord's Supper; Debated the Prayer of Consecration; that it was not the words, but the setting it apart by Prayer, that was the Consecration.

Ordered that when they Consecrate afresh they begin with the Prayer.[6]

The theological intention of this is in harmony with that written into the Prayer Book. The interesting point about this latter quotation is that its general theology of consecration is the standard seventeenth century Anglican one of 'setting apart by prayer'.

The form for supplementary consecration actually written into the 1686 Prayer Book is extremely interesting, for it expresses explicitly the early seventeenth century theology of supplementary consecration that the repetition of the institution narrative links the fresh supply of bread and wine to the prayers of the rite already said – 'the Prayers of thy Church that have now been made unto thee' – while at the same time moving away from it, in that by prefacing the additional material to the institution narrative this latter is turned into a complete petition for consecration in itself, a consecration prayer in miniature in fact. Thus the Commissioners of 1689 still understood and accepted as valid the 1662 method of supplementary consecration in the way that it was understood in the early part of the century, while at the same time no longer regarding it as the best method. Thus they represent an intermediate stage between the thinking of the early part of the seventeenth century in this respect and that of the early eighteenth century; in this later period the early seventeenth century interpretation seems largely to have been forgotten or repudiated. Thus the form for supplementary consecration adopted by the 1689 commission is also an important piece of corroborative evidence that the early seventeenth century viewpoint about this subject has been correctly interpreted.

In general the fact that the 1689 Commission proposed to alter so little in the Communion rite can be regarded as evidence that it was generally acceptable to moderate

Anglicans and puritans in this period, and would seem to argue that in the basic fundamentals of eucharistic theology there was still little difference between them. In particular, their supplementary consecration provision indicates that this too was not a divisive issue in this period.

(ii) 'Oblations' in the Prayer for the Church

One of the comparatively few verbal changes made in the 1662 rite was the insertion of the phrase 'and oblations' after 'our alms' in the prayer for the Church militant. Taken in conjunction with the rubrical direction to place bread and wine on the altar at this point, also newly inserted in 1662, it has often been suggested that 'oblations' was intended to refer to the bread and wine, and that thus the 1662 revisers had deliberately inserted a ritual offertory of bread and wine into their rite, with all that this implies for the doctrine of the eucharistic sacrifice and of their acceptance of it. However J. Dowden seems to have demonstrated quite conclusively that the phrase 'alms and oblations' was intended by the 1662 revisers to mean 'alms and other money offerings for pious purposes', citing a wealth of evidence from pre-Reformation, Reformation, and earlier seventeenth-century sources, including some of the Caroline divines and some of the actual prayer book revisers, that 'oblations' was a word commonly used to denote money given for pious purposes, in particular for the support of the clergy.[7] It would thus seem clear beyond reasonable doubt that this is the sense of 'oblations' intended by the 1662 revisers.

Its meaning however has been variously interpreted ever since. Comber[8] and Nicholls[9] clearly regarded it as a reference to offerings for the support of the clergy. Bishop Patrick in 1667 seems to have been the first to have interpreted the word 'oblations' as referring to the bread and wine.[10] In this interpretation he was followed by the nonjurors and those who thought like them, notably Charles Wheatley,[11] bishop Hickes,[12] and John Johnson.[13] This interpretation should usually be understood as indicating a fairly advanced doctrine of the eucharistic sacrifice on the part of those who advocate it.

(iii) Thomas Comber

The first of the great post-Restoration commentaries on the Prayer Book is Thomas Comber's *Companion to the Temple*, first published in 1675, which is a huge volume of nearly 500 folio pages, packed with small print, clearly the product of an age with more leisure for devotional reading than the present. He starts his discussion of the prayer of consecration by noting the universal custom among pagans and Jews of saying a grace before eating, quoting as an example the Israelites not eating before Samuel had come to the sacrifice. With this precedent in mind he asks whether we ought not all the more to expect the priest to bless the food of communion before we eat of it, and goes on to say:

Jesus himself did not deliver this Bread and Wine until he had Consecrated it by giving thanks.

He then goes on to affirm that some people have thought the apostles themselves used the institution narrative to consecrate the sacrament, notes that it is the most ancient and essential part of all, and that it must never be left out, and continues:

and it is most certain, that no Liturgy in the World hath altered that particular. For in every Church the Priest repeats the words of our Saviour's Institution, and by those words the consecration is made;[14] for it is not the power of the Priest, but the Efficacy of the Author, which makes the Elements to become sacramentally the Body and Blood of Christ.[15]

He continues with a criticism of the Roman rite:

The Roman Church indeed has made large additions to this Primitive Form . . . But these corruptions and innovations being removed, our excellent Reformers have given us the Apostolical and Catholic Form alone, only with a short Prayer to introduce it.

Comber's doctrine of consecration is thus quite explicit and unambiguous; it is achieved by the institution narrative and by that alone; further witness to this belief is contained in his exhortation to the Minister to pronounce it with great deliberation.[16] Also, unlike other writers, he does not link the petition 'Hear us, O merciful Father . . .' with consecration, but regards it simply as a petition for grace.[17]

Like all Anglican writers of this period he explicitly rejects transubstantiation, but some of the reasons he gives for this are interesting from a liturgical point of view. He maintains the view that both the *Quam oblationem* of the Roman Canon and the epiclesis prayers of the Eastern rites witness against the doctrine, the latter because the epiclesis prayers speak of the elements as bread and wine in a section of the prayer coming after the institution narrative: he does not connect the epiclesis with consecration in any way at all, or show any knowledge of the fact that other people do.[18]

On the question of his doctrine of the presence, he believes that the gifts are really received by faith through reception of the elements, and he is thus to be classed as a 'real receptionist'.[19]

He does not discuss the subject of supplementary consecration or comment on any of the other rubrics, such as that concerned with the disposal of the remains, relevant to the doctrine of consecration and of the presence.

His doctrine of the sacrifice in the eucharist is memorialist, as his paraphrase of the relevant part of the prayer of consecration shows.[20] Yet he believes it right to pray for the benefits of Christ's sacrifice in the eucharist, for he regards the first post-communion prayer as:

A supplication to the Father, for the acceptance of our Sacrifice of Praise, for the benefits of the Oblation made by Jesus Christ, . . . and an oblation of ourselves,[21]

but he nowhere goes further than this.

(iv) William Nicholls and Thomas Bennet

Probably typical of the views of many in this period are those of William Nicholls, who published his *A comment on the Book of Common Prayer* in 1710. This is another vast book of many hundred folio pages, in which he prints out the actual text of the Prayer Book, with details of the variant readings contained in 1549, 1637, etc., copious notes, together with a 'paraphrase' which, like Comber's, is an expanded version of the text giving what Nicholls assumes is its sense. It is unpaginated, so detailed references cannot be given in notes; they can, however, be quite easily found by following the Prayer Book text in order throughout the book.

Interesting are the comments he makes in his preface on the historical origins of the first Prayer Books. He attributes both 1548 and 1549 to the traditional list of the 13 divines, that is Cranmer and his twelve associates. He says of the book of 1552:

wherein some Ceremonies and Usages were laid aside, and some New Prayers added, at the Instance of Mr. Calvin of Geneva, and Bucer, a Foreign Divine, who was invited to be a Professor at Cambridge.

The legend that the second Edwardine Prayer Book is largely the result of interference by foreigners in English ecclesiastical affairs goes back a long way, and is widely believed and supported by some of the commentators in the period being considered. It would be interesting to trace this view of the origins of the second Prayer Book, with all its variants, back to the first holder of the theory, if possible, and to see if there are any common denominators in the theological opinions of those who have held to it.

Nicholls has comparatively little to say on the subject of sacrifice. On the subject of consecration he takes up a deliberate 'middle of the road' position, and he regards the prayer of consecration as keeping from all extremes of contending parties and adhering to the ancient practice of the church:

And so again, whereas there was a Contention, what it was that made the change in the Elements; whether, as the Roman church would have it, the bare pronouncing of the words, 'This is my body', or, whether, as some Protestants say, only the Prayer to God to sanctify them for a Spiritual use; Our Church has ordered both a Prayer to God, and also the Words of the Institution to be repeated.

Thus Nicholls believes that consecration is achieved by prayer, and a prayer which ought to include the institution narrative, and this he backs up with patristic quotations; in the English rite he would presumably attribute the consecration in general to the whole of the prayer of consecration, rather than to any specific part of it. He does not comment on the supplementary consecration rubric, so no further light can be shed on his views from his attitude to this. He gives us some idea of his doctrine of the presence in part of his paraphrase of the prayer of consecration:

may be Partakers of his most precious Body and Blood, which are in a spiritual and extraordinary manner conveyed to us therein.

Thus once again the phrase 'real receptionist' can be used to describe his views; and presumably he regarded the elements as becoming capable of this by virtue of the prayer spoken over them.

He says, in connection with the rubric about the disposal of the remains, that it is fitting for the minister to have to his own use anything left over that is unconsecrated, for it is part of the offerings for his support; the command about the consecrated remains he regards as a prohibition of the abuse of reservation.

Another work on a somewhat smaller scale that was published at about the same time (1708) is Thomas Bennet's *A paraphrase with Annotations upon the Book of Common Prayer.* Bennet was rector of St James', Colchester, and sometime fellow of St John's College, Cambridge, and the format of his work is a reprint of the whole Prayer Book with a long series of footnotes, the 'Annotations'. There is really only one comment in the substance of his work that is relevant to his ideas about consecration, namely what he says about the words of institution:

'Tis manifest from the Connection of these words with the former part of this Form, that they are addressed to God, and not to the Congregation. They are therefore a Part of the Prayer of Consecration, and in the Repetition of them the Mind of the Minister must be directed to God, and not to the People.[22]

It would seem then that his views on consecration and what achieves it were very similar to those of Nicholls. He makes no comment on the offertory rubric, the supplementary consecration rubric, the 'remains' rubric, or the communion of the sick.

The views of Nicholls and Bennet are probably typical of many in the Church of England of that time, perhaps the majority. Men of considerable knowledge, yet not really possessing a great deal of liturgical scholarship, the Prayer Book, its 1662 form already established in the church by nearly half a century of use, was in itself becoming the guide, source, and prime influence of their eucharistic doctrine. They believed that consecration was achieved by a prayer containing the institution narrative, which, once strict Roman transubstantiation ideas are eliminated, is really the only view the Prayer Book allows. In this theology they were followers of the majority viewpoint of the early seventeenth century. Again, once Roman views of the presence are eliminated, a kind of vaguely defined real receptionism is the sort of doctrine one would read out of the Prayer Book, the sort of doctrine that would suggest itself to the man who adopted it as his standard of reference. Furthermore, there is very little that is suggestive of sacrifice in the 1662 rite, so this is an aspect of the eucharist that finds very little mention in the writings of men like Bennet and Nicholls. Thus the eucharistic theology of these men represents the sort of theology that might be expected to evolve in a Church committed to the 1662 rite as its standard of use and doctrine, and something of the sort does seem to have happened, among the majority of churchmen who came to believe the Prayer Book as it stood was virtually the perfect liturgy.

(v) Charles Wheatly

But against the background of a general emerging consensus one finds great divergences of detail and sharply differing viewpoints from men who sought their understanding of the eucharist from a wider base than that of merely the Prayer Book. One such is Charles Wheatly, who wrote a commentary on the Prayer Book with a lengthy title typical of the age in which he lived:

"The Church of England Man's Companion; or a Rational Illustration of the Harmony, Excellency, and Usefulness of the Book of Common Prayer etc., wherein all the Rubrics, Prayers, Rites, Ceremonies, etc., are explained, vindicated and compared with the Ancient Liturgies, and the Practices of the Primitive Church".

Wheatly is particularly interesting in that between the publication of the first edition in 1710 and the third in 1720, he evidently changed from a 'central church' viewpoint like that of Bennet and Nicholls to one much more similar to that being evolved by the more liturgically advanced non-jurors, though some of the remarks in the first edition perhaps foreshadow his conversion.

To consider first his edition of 1710; it is interesting to note that in his preface he attributes production of both 1548 and 1549 to the usually-quoted committee of thirteen. In his introduction to his section on the Communion rite he says:

As to the Primitive and Original Form of Administration, since Christ did not institute any one method, it was various in divers Churches, only all agreed in using the Lord's Prayer and reciting the Words of Institution, which, for that reason, some think was all the Apostles used. But afterwards their Successors in their several Churches, added several Forms thereunto . . .[23]

and goes on to mention Basil, Chrysostom, and Ambrose as composing their own liturgies. He then says of the composition of the Prayer Book:

And the Excellent Compilers of Our Common-Prayer used the same Freedom,

and states his opinion of the Prayer Book's qualities:

For we may safely affirm, that it is more primitive in all its parts, and more apt to assist us in worthy receiving than any other Liturgy now used in the Christian World.

He gives evidence in this first edition of a somewhat higher doctrine of sacrifice than found in Nicholls or Bennet. In his comment on the offertory rubric he makes clear his belief in an objective pleading of the sacrifice of Christ in the eucharist. The bread and wine are placed on the holy table

to the intent that we may plead for all the World by the memorial of that Oblation which contained Mercy for all, and by which Christ now intercedes for all in heaven.[24]

And he notes the ancient liturgies had their intercessions in the eucharistic part of the service. In connection with his understanding of the eucharistic sacrifice at this time, it is to be noted that he sees the prayer of oblation wholly as a prayer of self offering. He notes its place in 1637 but attaches no theological significance to this.[25]

His discussion of the consecration and comment on the prayer of consecration is almost verbally identical with that of Comber, with a few omissions that are not of theological importance for this purpose, so much so that it is quite obvious that he has simply copied it, with these few abbreviations; he includes Comber's criticism of the Roman rite.[26] It is therefore quite clear that at this date he must have believed that consecration was achieved by the saying of the institution narrative, and that this was the only essential requirement for it. He does not discuss the supplementary consecration rubric.

His doctrine of the presence is 'real receptionist' and very similar to the prevailing central church viewpoint, as is demonstrated by his wholehearted approval of the words of administration,[27] and his commendation of kneeling to spiritually receive, the believer converses with Christ spiritually present in the sacrament.[28]

By 1720 it is clear that he had changed his mind on many important points; far from thinking the Prayer Book liturgy the best in the world, he had in fact become highly critical of it in many respects. As a loyal Anglican and commentator on the Prayer Book, this of course put him in a difficult position, from which he escapes by adopting the 1549 book as his basic standard and praising it highly, and putting forward the view that the 1552 book was a regrettable development brought about by undesirable foreign influences. Very briefly, the main points in which he has changed his outlook are that his doctrine of sacrifice in the eucharist has become very much more 'advanced', and his doctrine of consecration has undergone a radical change. He also manifests his dislike of things puritan and presbyterian by saying of Baxter's liturgy that it was a 'dull, tedious, crude and indigested Heap of Stuff'.[29]

The third edition is a beautifully produced folio volume of more than 500 pages filled with fairly large and elegant print, and he makes the point in his preface that it is a very much enlarged edition of his former work, so much so that it is almost a new book.[30]

That his doctrine of sacrifice in the eucharist has become considerably more 'advanced' is demonstrated by the following quotations. He says that in the eucharist we are not only to pray

but are also commanded, by visible Signs, to represent and set forth to his Heavenly Father His all-sufficient and meritorious Death and Sacrifice, as a more powerful way of interceding, and obtaining the Divine Acceptance.

And also that we are to

plead the Virtue and Merits of the same Sacrifice, here, which He is continually urging for us there.[31]

Having established his view of the eucharistic sacrifice, he then goes on to discuss in general terms the origins of the primitive liturgies. He makes exactly the same points as he did in the first edition regarding the fact that Christ did not appear to prescribe any one particular method of celebration, and that in due time a number of liturgies grew up; the liturgies of the patriarchal sees came first, and then, because these were not regarded as of divine institution, Basil, Chrysostom, Ambrose, and Gregory composed their own. It is also interesting to note his belief that the Clementine liturgy is the primitive and apostolic ligurgy of the Church of Rome. He then goes on to describe the origins of the first two Prayer Books, and this quotation neatly summarises his approach to this subject:

And so the excellent Compilers of our Common-Prayer, following their Example,[32] no otherwise confined themselves to the Liturgies that were before them, than out of them all to extract an Office for themselves; and which indeed they performed with so exact a Judgement and happy Success, that it is hard to determine whether they more endeavoured the Advancement of Devotion, or the Imitation of pure Antiquity. BUT *Bucer* being called in (as I have observed elsewhere) to give his Opinion of it, this momentous and principal Office of our Liturgy had the Misfortune to suffer great Alterations. Some Amendment in the Method it might possibly have born; But the practice of foreign Churches, and not Primitive Liturgies, being always with him the Standard of Reformation, the most ancient Forms and Primitive Rites were forced to give way to modern Fancies. It is true, some of these were again restored at the last Review: But it is still much lamented by learned Men, that some other Additions were not made at that time, that so everything might have been restored which was proper or decent, as well as everything left out that was superstitious or offensive.[33]

This represents the attitude he now adopts towards the first two Prayer Books throughout. Of course it is true that the foreigners were here and did put forward their views about the first Prayer Book, but the use that Wheatly, and those with similar ideas, made of this fact seems much more illuminative of their own theology than it does of the facts of history: their understanding of history seems, in effect, to have been dictated by their theology.

His comments on the offertory rubric of the 1662 rite are fully in accordance with his more advanced sacrificial doctrine. He notes the 1549 provisions concerning the placing of the bread and wine upon the altar, regrets their omission from 1552, and commends the restoration of the custom in 1637 and 1662,[34] emphasising the 'offering' aspect of the ceremony in both cases.

The first paragraph of his discussion of consecration is verbatim from the first edition, which had in its turn been copied from Comber, and includes here his noting of the universality of the institution narrative. The criticism of the Roman rite, together with its accompanying commendation of the 1662 form of the consecration prayer is omitted, and is replaced by:

But besides this, (the institution narrative) there was always inserted in the Primitive Forms a particular Petition for the Descent of the Holy Ghost upon the Sacramental Elements, which was also continued in the first Liturgy of King Edward VI in very express and open terms.[35]

He proceeds to quote the 1549 epiclesis in full and then continues:

This, upon the Scruples of Bucer (whom I am sorry I have so often occasion to name) was left out of the Review in the 5th of King Edward; and the following Sentence which he was pleased to allow of, inserted in its stead, viz., 'Hear us . . . may be Partakers of his most blessed Body and Blood, who in the same night, etc.' In these Words, it is true, the Sense of the former is still implied, and consequently by these the Elements are now consecrated and changed into the Body and Blood of our Saviour Christ.

Thus, sometime between 1710 and 1720, Wheatly changed his mind from believing that consecration was achieved by the institution narrative, and that alone, to believing that it was essentially effected by the epiclesis. True he regards the petition 'Hear us . . .' as theologically the equivalent of the epiclesis, and thus apparently the essential consecratory part of the 1662 rite; but, since he quite clearly regrets its substitution for the 1549 form, with the theology of consecration he had come to hold, this was the only viewpoint he could adopt without invalidating the rite on which he was commenting. Thus it is fair to conclude that Wheatly had come to the conclusion that the consecration of the elements was achieved by the invoking of the Holy Spirit upon them, and perforce had to regard the petition 'Hear us . . .' as a prayer to this effect.

Having reached this conclusion, the rubric about supplementary consecration is clearly a source of considerable embarrassment to him, and he has to explain it away as best he can; he clearly does not know how it was understood in the early seventeenth century. He says of it:

In the Rubric indeed, after the Form of Administration, the Church seems to suppose that the Consecration is made by the Words of Institution;

He quotes it in full and then continues:

This Rubric was added at the last Review, but to what end, unless to save the Minister some time, does not appear.

One is led to wonder from this remark if he thought that before 1662 a celebrant lacking the consecrated species with which to give communion was supposed to repeat the whole consecration prayer. However, he does not amplify this, but notes the derivation of this 1662 rubric from 1637, which he regards as even odder:

But what is very remarkable is, that it was taken from the Scotch liturgy, which expressly calls the words of Institution the words of Consecration; tho' the Compilers of it had restored the Sentence that had been thrown out of King Edward's Second Common-Prayer, imagining, one would think, that the Elements were not consecrated without them.

From Wheatly's point of view this was a perfectly reasonable criticism for him to make about the 1637 book. Leaving the point unresolved, Wheatly continues:

For though all Churches in the world, through all Ages, used the words of Institution at the time of Consecration; yet none, I believe, except the Church of Rome, ever before attributed the Consecration to the bare prouncing of those Words only: But the Change of the Elements into the Body and Blood of Christ was always attributed by the most Ancient Fathers to the Prayer of the Church.[36]

At this point there is a footnote in the main text in which reference is made to supplementary material at the end of the book, and in this he notes that both Lutherans and Calvinists agree with Papists that consecration 'is made by bare repetition of the words of Institution' because these alone are the words recorded in scripture. But Jesus must have used other words at the Last Supper, which are not recorded, because scripture tells us that he gave thanks and blessed, which can only be done by words addressed to God; this leads him to the conclusion he is to draw from this argument:

Therefore the Words which our Saviour spake to his Disciples, could not be the whole consecration of the Elements, but rather a Declaration of the Effect which was produced by his consecrating or blessing them.[37]

In seeking scriptural backing for the theology of consecration he is now advocating, this is a neatly made point. He returns to his main argument with the rather regretful admission that those who added the supplementary consecration rubric must have thought along different lines from his own about these matter, and continues:

But yet I humbly presume that if the Minister should, at the

Consecration of Fresh Elements after the others are spent, repeat again the whole Form of Consecration, or at least from those words, "Hear us, O merciful Father, etc." he would answer the end of the Rubric, which seems only to require that the latter part of the Form from those words, "Who in the same night, etc." be always used at such consecrations.[38]

But the words of this rubric do not *seem* only to require this; they do only require this. Interpreting the Prayer Book as meaning what it does not say is not confined to post-Oxford Movement Anglicanism.

However, he does not wish to minimise the importance of the institution narrative, for he continues with reference to it:

And this is certainly a very essential part of the Consecration: For during the Repetition of these words, the Priest performs to God the Representative Sacrifice of the Death and Passion of his Son. By taking the Bread into his Hands, and breaking it, he makes a Memorial to him of our Saviour's Body broken upon the Cross; and by exhibiting the Wine, he reminds him of his Blood there shed for the Sins of the World; and by laying his hands upon each of them at the same time that he repeats those words ('Take, eat, this is my Body, etc.' and 'Drink ye all of this, etc.') he signifies and acknowledges that this Commemoration of Christ's Sacrifice so made to God, is a Means instituted by Christ himself to convey to the Communicants the Benefits of his Death and Passion, viz., the Pardon of our Sins, and God's Grace and favour for the time to come.[39]

Thus it would seem that though he regarded the epiclesis or its equivalent as the essential petition for consecration, he did not regard the consecration as complete until the institution narrative, with its accompanying manual acts, was said: his theology of consecration, to summarise it fully, seems to be that the epiclesis invokes the blessing to consecrate, and the narrative completes and seals it. It is interesting to note that this theology depends in detail for its validity on the 1549/1637 order of material in the Canon.

Interesting too is the way he links the institution narrative and the manual acts (which he clearly regards as very important) with the explicit liturgical offering of the sacrifice. Once again, the rite he is commenting on has influenced his theology, for if the breaking of the bread at the institution narrative makes the memorial of Christ's body broken upon the cross, it can only do so in the 1662 rite; neither 1549 nor 1637 have a liturgical fraction at this, or indeed, at any other point. He does however wish that the prayer of oblation was in its proper place after the institution narrative, and regrets its truncated form in the 1662 rite, linking it with the solemn offering to God of the proper sacrifice.[40] This again is a viewpoint he had adopted since 1710, for in his first edition he had attached no such significance to it, even in the 1637 position.

On the other hand his understanding of the eucharistic presence does not seem to have changed since 1710, for his comments on the words of administration are repeated exactly from the 1st edition, and in a comment on the black rubric he says he regards the doctrine of the corporal presence as so ridiculous that he does not need to refute it.[41] He approves of the provisions of the rubric about the remains, both consecrated and unconsecrated.[42]

Thus in Wheatly's third edition we have an unchanged doctrine of the presence coupled with a much stronger doctrine of the sacrifice, and a different theology of consecration. The question arises as to what led to this change of mind. He seems to have been aware of the usages controversy among the non-jurors, but as a substantial public pamphlet warfare was being carried on among the protagonists on both sides of this dispute, information about this would not have been difficult to obtain by someone interested in the subject.[43] More than this, he was certainly in contact with some of the usagers, for some time early in 1719 he had written to Thomas Brett, telling him he liked the liturgy of 1718.[44] He never joined the non-jurors, but held ordinary parochial appointments from 1713, when he left the fellowship of St John's College, Oxford, until his death in 1742. Also he clearly regarded John Johnson's *Unbloody Sacrifice* as an authoritative work, since he refers to it in connection with his discussion of the correct position for the prayer of oblation.[45] It therefore seems fair to say that he derived the ideas that led to his change of mind about some of the fundamentals of eucharistic theology from the school of thought associated with the usagers, and those who held similar opinions and remained within the established church, men such as Johnson. It is possible to trace most of the basic elements of this position in Anglicanism back into the reign of Charles I, even though its synthesis as a detailed theological position was not achieved until the early years of the eighteenth century, in fact probably within the very decade between the publication of Wheatly's first and third editions. To what extent Wheatly was a disciple of this school of thought and to what extent he aided its development, it is not possible to say in detail, without knowing a considerable amount about all the people concerned and about their relationships with each other. But he was much younger than either Johnson or, for example, Brett, being only 24 in 1710 when he published his first edition, in which year Johnson was 48 and Brett 43.[46] The first edition of Johnson's *Unbloody Sacrifice* appeared in 1714,[47] and so it would seem probably that Wheatly was among the influenced rather than the influencing. Having said this, it can also be said that the fairly advanced doctrine of the eucharistic sacrifice he already held in 1710 clearly made him a likely candidate for conversion to views like those of Johnson and Brett.

(vi) John Johnson

This leads naturally to a consideration of the views held by John Johnson. Most of Johnson's work is concerned with his beliefs about the eucharist as a real sacrifice, but he also gives us his views on consecration and of the nature of the eucharistic presence. The following two quotations will neatly summarise his doctrine on the former point, the first of which also illustrates how he linked consecration to his doctrine of sacrifice:

We offer the Bread and Wine, separated from all other oblations of the people; we offer them, as having been solemnly pronounced by the words of institution to be the full representations of Christ's Body and Blood. And we make propitiation with them, after God has first, by the illapse of the Holy Spirit, perfected the consecration of them.[48]

The second quotation is more directly a simple statement of his views on consecration; though embodied in the form of making a point about ancient liturgies, it clearly represents his own viewpoint on the matter:

Now I have already proved, that the Holy Ghost was, by the vote of antiquity, the principal immediate cause of the Bread and Wine's becoming the Body and Blood. It now remains only that I show, that the subordinate or mediate cause of it is, 1. The reciting the words of institution. 2. the oblation of the symbols. 3. the prayer of invocation. All these three did, in the ancient Liturgies, immediately follow each other, in the order that I have mentioned them; and each of them was believed to contribute towards the consecration of the elements into the Body and Blood.[49]

Thus the Holy Spirit is the agent of consecration, and he operates through the threefold liturgical sequence of institution narrative – oblation – epiclesis.

On the question of the presence, Johnson is just as concerned to refute the doctrine of transubstantiation as any other Anglican at this period, high or low. For his positive doctrine he takes his stand on the simple assertion of the catechism that

the Body and Blood of Christ are verily and indeed taken and received by the faithful in the Lord's Supper,

as being a positive and direct statement of scriptural truth;[50] and he criticises both Romans and Lutherans for importing false notions of change of substance into this simple truth. He also criticises Calvinists, saying that, in their zeal to refute Roman error, they have ended up by denying the scriptural truth about the reality of the presence of Christ's body and blood in the eucharist.[51]

He does explain his understanding of the presence in more detail, and this derives from his interpretation of antiquity and his understanding of the Holy Spirit's operation in the eucharistic action. He understood the 'Ancients' to have believed the bread and wine to be the body and blood of Christ, not in substance, but in a spiritual manner, in power and effect, and this they became,

by the inward invisible power of the Spirit; by which the Sacramental Body and Blood are made as powerful and effectual for the ends of religion, as the natural Body Itself could be if It were present . . . Though bread and wine in themselves can be no more than figures, yet when the Holy Ghost has blessed and sanctified them, they are in Power and effect to us the same as the archetypes would be.[52]

Thus his understanding of the presence is wholly in line with his doctrine of consecration; it is important to realise that he is not teaching any kind of receptionist doctrine, but an objective real presence doctrine. This is proved by the fact of his belief that consecration was permanent, something he regards as proved by the ancient practice of reservation. He says of the 'Ancients' in this respect:

For this proves not only that they thought it the Body and Blood, without any respect to the faith of the receiver, but that its consecration was permanent, and remained after the holy action was at an end.[53]

In saying that this is what the ancients believed, here as elsewhere, he is in effect saying that this is what *he* believed about the matter.

Since his work is primarily a theological treatise and not a liturgical commentary, he does not comment in detail upon the Prayer Book rite. Nevertheless, it is difficult to believe that with the views he held about consecration he can have been very happy with it, and indeed he does urge those who believe the Prayer Book rite to be inadequate to supply its defects as best they can by their private devotions.[54] We should probably read this suggestion as the only advice he could give in the circumstances, rather than as witness to any belief that the private prayers of the laity could really play a part in the eucharistic consecration; he had a firm belief in the absolute necessity of the episcopal ministry for this.[55]

In summary, one may say of Johnson that he had a far higher doctrine of sacrifice in the eucharist than had most Anglicans of his day, that he articulated in a coherent theological scheme ideas about consecration in the eucharist that had been germinating and growing among some Anglicans since the Restoration. These ideas derive in part from attaching a fresh interpretation to certain pre-Restoration rites, notably 1549 and 1637, though Johnson was probably not aware that he had done this. On the question of the presence, he would seem to have been in a definite minority in his important assertion of the permanent effect of consecration.

(vii) Robert Nelson

One of the most popular eighteenth-century devotional works was Robert Nelson's *Companion to the Festivals and Fasts of the Church of England,* first published in 1703. Nelson was a layman, educated at Trinity College, Cambridge, well connected and well-to-do. As its title implies, it is primarily a commentary on the Prayer Book feasts and fasts, but under some of them there are discussions of doctrinal points relevant to this discussion.

He has a high doctrine of the eucharistic sacrifice, saying that the purpose of the institution of the sacrament was to be the Christian sacrifice, wherein bread and wine are offered to God, to acknowledge him Lord of the creatures . . .,

which is the reason why the Church of England, as well as the ancient Church, orders them to be placed on the table by the priest. He continues:

Which by consecration being made the symbols of the body and blood of Christ, we thereby represent to God the Father the passion of his Son, to the end he may for his sake, according to the tenour of his covenant in him, be favourable and propitious to us miserable sinners. That as Christ intercedes continually for us in heaven, by presenting his death and satisfaction to his Father; so the church on earth, in like manner, may approach the throne of grace, by representing Christ unto his Father, in these holy mysteries of his death and passion.[56]

Thus Nelson sees the eucharist as a real pleading of the sacrifice of Christ, and the mediation of the benefits of it to believers:

And to communicate to all worthy receivers the benefits of his sacrifice, upon which account it is called the communion of his body and blood.

His answer to the question as to how the consecration was performed in the primitive church not only sets out his doctrine of consecration, but also his understanding of the presence:

The priest that officiated not only rehearsed the evangelical history of the institution of this holy sacrament, and pronounced these words of our Saviour, 'This is my body, this is my blood'; but he offered up a prayer of consecration to God; beseeching him, that he would send down his Holy Spirit upon the bread and wine presented to him on the Altar, and that he would so sanctify them that they might become the body and blood of his son Jesus Christ; not according to the gross *compages* or substance, but as to the spiritual energy and virtue of his holy flesh and blood, communicated to the blessed elements by the power and operation of the Holy Ghost descending on them; whereby the body and blood of Christ is verily and indeed taken by the faithful in the Lord's Supper. This prayer is found in all the ancient liturgies; and some learned men have thought that St Paul alluded to something of this nature, when he speaks of the offering of the Gentiles being acceptable by the sanctification of the Holy Ghost, there being no less than five liturgical words in that text, as hath been observed by learned men.

Thus it would appear that Nelson believed that consecration was effected by the invocation of the Holy

Spirit on the elements, and that the recital of the institution narrative was an essential preliminary to this; he does not comment on the Ordinary of the Prayer Book rite, and so how he reconciled his views with it we do not know. His doctrine of the presence is dictated by his understanding of consecration; by the power of the Holy Spirit the bread and wine acquire the virtue and energy of the Body and Blood. This is remarkably similar to Johnson's doctrine on this point, down to the same quotation from the catechism being used in the same sense, so much so that one is led to postulate a literary relationship between the two; but if this is the case, Johnson must be the one who depended on Nelson, for the latter died in 1715,[57] the year after the publication of Johnson's first edition.

(viii) Daniel Waterland

That the 'high church' theology of Nelson, Johnson, and Wheatly had a considerable following is shown by the circulation of their books: Wheatly's publisher would hardly have undertaken the printing of the much enlarged third edition, had he not been sure that there was a market for it, and Nelson's book achieved many reprints. Naturally this theology called forth a reaction from those who disagreed with it, both from the moderate centre as expressed by Waterland, in his *A Review of the Doctrine of the Eucharist*, and from the extreme left as expressed by Hoadly, who regarded the eucharist as purely memorialist.[58]

Waterland's central views came to be regarded as a typical and indeed authoritative exposition of Anglican views, and were reprinted as such at the request of both archbishops as late as the middle of the nineteenth century.

His work was first published in 1737, consciously as a 'central church' rejoinder to the writings of Nelson, Johnson, Wheatly, and Brett, and the liturgical works of the non-jurors. But even as a central churchman it is clear that he thinks it less dangerous to ascribe too much to the sacrament rather than too little.[59]

In his doctrine of sacrifice in the eucharist he rejects a mere memorialism,[60] and accepts that ἀναμνησις can have the sense of 'memorial before God'[61] as well as before men.[62] Christ's death is a 'vicarious punishment of sin' and a 'proper expiatory sacrifice for the sins of mankind', and is to be remembered as such at the eucharist.[63] Christ intercedes for us in heaven, commemorating there his same sacrifice that we commemorate at the Lord's table.[64] While Waterland uses much the same sort of sacrificial terminology as Johnson, the essential and vital difference between their positions is that, while Waterland allows that we remember with thanksgiving the sacrifice of the cross, and maybe even pray for its benefits, he rejects the idea of the eucharist as an effectual pleading of Christ's sacrifice and the means by which its merits are mediated. Linguistically, the difference between these two positions may seem small; theologically, it is vast.

He argues that consecration involves a real blessing of the elements,[65] and that they are blessed by the priest before he delivers them to the people.[66] He is further quite explicit that, though the blessing is pronounced by the priest, the actual blessing is solely the work of God: the divine word gives effect to the divine warrant and leads to the fulfilment of the divine promise.[67]

The effect of the consecration is that:

the bread and wine being 'sanctified by the word of God and prayer' . . . do thereby contract a relative holiness, a sanctification, in some degree or other,

that is nowhere precisely defined, but which relates to their sacred use.[68] The substances remain unchanged, but their use is changed, and they have come within the sphere of the divine interest, and thus a proper reverence is due to them.[69]

He continues by discussing three further points: the place of Christ and the Holy Spirit as the principal cause of the sacramental action; prayers, thanksgiving, and benedictions as the instrumental cause; and the significance of the institution narrative. His discussion of the first point is principally concerned with the place of the Holy Spirit in the sacramental action, and it is obvious that the background of his remarks here is the theology of Johnson and those who thought like him. It is worth quoting his argument here at some length:

It is observable that the doctrine of the Fathers, with regard to consecration, was much the same in relation to the waters of Baptism, as in relation to the elements of the Eucharist. They supposed a kind of descent of the Holy Ghost, to sanctify the waters in one, and the symbols in the other, to the uses intended; and they seem to have gone upon this general Scripture principle, (besides particular texts relating to each sacrament,) that the Holy Ghost is the immediate fountain of all sanctification. I believe they were right in the main thing, only not always accurate in expression. Had they said, that the Holy Ghost came upon the recipients, in the due use of the sacrament, they had spoken with greater exactness; and perhaps it was all that they really meant.[70]

He attributes what he here assumes to be lack of precision to the lack of a need for it, and quotes with approval Hooker's idea that the real presence of Christ in the sacrament is to be found in the believer and not in the elements; the same is true of the relationship of the Holy Spirit to the sacrament. He rejects the idea of a union of the Holy Spirit with the elements themselves (not, of course, that this is what Johnson and those who thought like him actually believed). Elsewhere there is a specific rejection of Johnson's teaching: some people had supposed that the bread and wine were the body and blood of Christ

in power and effect, or in virtue and energy: which is not much amiss, excepting that it seems to carry in it some obscure conception either of an inherent or infused virtue resting upon the bare elements, and operating as a mean, which is not the truth of the case.[71]

His final point concerns the place of the institution narrative. The reciting of this he seems to see as the pledge and guarantee that the bread and wine are, in the celebration of any particular eucharist, what Christ declared them to be at the Last Supper, whatever the exact sense of this latter may have been; the words of institution do not consecrate in themselves, but they do ratify and seal it.[72]

Thus Waterland's views on consecration may be summarised by saying that he believed it was effected by the prayers of the celebrant and that the institution narrative declares and guarantees the effect of the prayer; thus though the institution narrative is not consecratory by itself, the conclusion would seem to be that he would not have regarded a rite that did not include it as valid. He does not comment on the Prayer Book rite as such, but his ideas about consecration fit in perfectly well with its prayer of consecration. What he thought about the supplementary consecration rubric must remain a matter of conjecture, but perhaps, like bishop Morton, he would have regarded the earlier prayers in the rite as covering it. To explain his understanding of what the consecrated elements are he uses his concept of relative holiness. The elements once consecrated (and consecrated they must be) really are the means by which the believer receives the gifts of the body and blood, and are of sufficient importance that to be irreverent towards them is to be guilty of the body and blood of the Lord. Although they are no longer common bread or wine, he feels bound to add the reservation in parenthesis about the impermanence of this state of affairs, in contrast to Johnson. He rejects Johnson's presence doctrine, and in effect denies Eastern ideas of consecration by postulating that they expressed themselves so carelessly as often to give the impression of saying something they actually did not mean. Thus the presence is really to be found in the worthy receiver, and not in the symbols themselves. So his doctrine too is 'real receptionist'.

Waterland is thus the heir to the eucharistic theology of most Anglicans and moderate puritans of the early seventeenth century, in contrast to Johnson, and others who thought like him, who developed a much more advanced theology from some of the higher elements of seventeenth-century Anglicanism.

CHAPTER 9

The rites of 1718 and 1764 and Related Matters

The authors discussed in the last chapter illustrate Anglican beliefs about the eucharist and the Prayer Book Communion rite in the century or so after the Restoration. All these men, whatever their diverse views, remained within the established Church and thus lacked the freedom to alter the Prayer Book rite, even if they had wanted to. Next to be considered are those Anglicans whose circumstances and ideas led them into the field of liturgical composition. These can be roughly divided into four classes: firstly, those who wished to provide an alternative to the proscribed Prayer Book liturgy during the Commonwealth period. Secondly, those produced by individuals who can only be described as eccentric. Thirdly, the two rites produced by the English non-jurors, namely those of 1718 and 1734, of which the first is much more important than the second. And finally, the liturgical tradition of the Scottish Episcopal Church from the beginning of the eighteenth century, which culminated in the publication of the definitive edition of the Scottish rite in 1764. Before 1700 the worship of Episcopalian congregations in Scotland seems to have been virtually indistinguishable from that of the Presbyterian congregations; it is only after this date that a genuine Anglican liturgical tradition begins to re-form in Scotland. W.J. Grisbrooke[1] has collected together all these liturgies and published them, together with theological and liturgical commentaries of some detail on each of them. H. Broxap[2] nearly half a century ago published a detailed account of all the complexities of the later stages of the non-juring movement, including of course the usages controversy and the rite of 1718, based not only on previous work but also on a large amount of original material not previously examined. J. Dowden's 1922 edition of the *Annotated Scottish Communion Office* provides a definitive account of the Scottish Anglican tradition and the 1764 rite itself. These three works provide a fairly comprehensive account of this subject matter, together with a thorough discussion of raw materials and sources, and so any fresh work must largely take the form of comment upon and assessment of the significance of a story already well told.

From all this, it is quite clear that both the developments leading to the non-jurors rite of 1718 and those leading to 1764 are of prime importance for Anglicanism, and are indeed both products of what was consciously the same theological movement in thinking about the eucharist. Jeremy Taylor's liturgy is in itself of much less importance than these, though his eucharistic theology may well be one of the links in the chain that leads from the earlier Caroline divines to the position of men like Johnson. The liturgies produced by men like Stephens and Henley can largely be left on one side in this study.

It thus becomes quite clear that in the first half of the eighteenth century there emerged within Anglicanism a distinctive eucharistic theological and liturgical tradition that for convenience can be labelled the 1718-1764 tradition, after the two most important liturgies that it produced. It is one of the oddities of history that the non-juring schism, and the official abolition of episcopacy in Scotland, both events originally unconnected with liturgy or eucharistic theology, should have provided the opportunities for giving liturgical expression to what was becoming an important, cohesive, and coherent eucharistic tradition within Anglicanism. The historical fact of the emergence and existence of this tradition in the first quarter of the eighteenth century, and its final formulation by those who advocated it, has been demonstrated in the previous chapter; that 1718 and 1764 were its liturgical products has been sufficiently demonstrated by the works of Broxap, Dowden, and Grisbrooke taken together. Its exact scheme of eucharistic theology, its doctrine of the eucharistic sacrifice, consecration, and the presence, then, are primarily to be derived from the rites of 1718 and 1764, and from the contemporary commentaries of their adherents.

(i) The 1718 rite

The 1718 rite[3] commences with some rubrics which, among other things, order the altar (significantly, this word is used) to be placed at the east end, and direct the priest to take the north-side position.

The service itself starts with an introit psalm, the list from the 1549 book being given, omitting provision for any day not actually commemorated in the 1662 book. Then follows a salutation, threefold Kyrie in its Prayer Book form, Lord's Prayer, Collect for Purity, Summary of the Law, one of the two Prayer Book collects for the king (the personal name of the monarch is omitted from both of these, no doubt to avoid publicly committing celebrant or congregation to either the House of Hanover or the Jacobite cause), Collect of the day, Epistle, Gospel, and Nicene Creed. Then follows the Prayer Book rubric about notices, with the significant alteration of 'Minister' to 'Priest or Deacon', command for a sermon or homily, and a couple of short rubrics about when the exhortations are to be read; these follow next, reprinted from the Prayer Book with very few changes.

Next follows the offertory. Some of the offertory sentences come from the 1662 book, but several from the Old Testament that concern the offering of sacrifice (mostly taken from 1637) are placed before the others, a clear indication of the theological tendencies of the rite. Next follow rubrics concerned with the collection, and the placing of the bread and wine on the altar; the mixed chalice is ordered, and the water is to be added 'in view of the people'. This is followed by a special offertory collect, which gives quite explicit expression to the doctrine of the eucharistic sacrifice as held by the non-jurors, including as it does the phrase:

here may we be worthy to offer unto thee this reasonable and unbloody sacrifice for our sins and the sins of the people.

The last section of this phrase, together with the wording of the rest of the prayer, suggests that those who wrote it regarded the clergy as holding a divine commission to offer this sacrifice for the people, as well as its being a sacrifice for the whole people in itself. This prayer appears to have been originally composed for this rite; it is certainly not taken from the Clementine.[4]

This is followed by salutation, *Sursum corda*, preface, Sanctus and Benedictus verbatim from 1549, which lead immediately to the rest of the anaphora. The first part of this again appears to be an original piece of liturgical composition, and is certainly not a direct quotation from the Clementine rite, nor does it bear any resemblance to 1549, 1637, or 1662 material. It begins with a three-fold ascription of praise to God for his holiness, as Father, Son, and Spirit. This is followed by a brief recital of salvation-history from creation and the fall via the law and the prophets to the incarnation, together with a few phrases describing Christ's ministry. Then follows the sentence:

And when his hour was come to offer the Propitiatory Sacrifice upon the Cross; when he, who had no sin himself, mercifully undertook to suffer death for our sins, in the same night . . .

followed by the 1662 institution narrative, with the manual acts, verbatim; the only alteration being the printing of 'This is my Body' and 'This is my Blood' in capital letters with two small black crosses in the middle of 'Body' and 'Blood' respectively. The recital of the institution narrative plays an important part in the non-jurors' theology, particularly in connection with the sacrifice; perhaps this is the point of this emphasis here. Presumably the crosses are intended to direct the celebrant to make the appropriate liturgical gesture. Interestingly too, the people are directed to respond 'Amen' after each half of the institution narrative.

Then follows anamnesis and epiclesis, both of which are virtually copied from the Clementine versions of these; more manual acts are prescribed at the epiclesis. The second half of the epiclesis is a prayer for the blessing of the communicants, from the Clementine text; a brief Trinitarian doxology and congregational 'Amen' has been added to bring the consecration section of the prayer to an abrupt halt. The way this whole consecration section is set out is further evidence that those who drew up this rite held to Johnson's theory that the whole of the institution-anamnesis-epiclesis sequence as a unit is the consecratory section of the rite.

Next follows the intercession, following the example of the Clementine rite. The actual 1718 intercession is that of 1549, nearly verbatim, but a few changes have been made in the order of some of the petitions.

Then follows the Lord's Prayer, the Peace, the paragraph 'Christ, our Paschal Lamb . . .' from 1549, Invitation, Confession, Absolution, Comfortable Words, Prayer of Humble Access, all worded as in 1662, followed by reception of Communion. The words of Administration are those of 1549, with the command to the communicant to say 'Amen' after reception in each kind, a provision copied from 1637. After communion, the service concludes with salutation,

Collect of Thanksgiving from 1662, Gloria, and Blessing. Thus from after the end of the intercession to the blessing the 1549 order is followed, the Agnus Dei and the post-communion sentences being omitted, and the Gloria included in the 1662 position.

The printed order of 1718 concludes with the six collects provided by the 1662 book for use when there is no communion, followed by a series of rubrics, which contain the following points of interest. The minimum number of communicants is reduced to two; the priest is commanded to celebrate every Sunday and Holy Day, unless prevented by the lack of the necessary two communicants, sickness, or other urgent cause. The priest is to exhort the people to frequent communion, and to urge them not to forbear coming if they can only give a little in the collection. The 1549 method of reservation is commended for the benefit of the sick, and any of the consecrated elements left over that are not required for this purpose are to be reverently consumed after the blessing. No provision is made in the rite for a second consecration, and this was no doubt deliberate in that those who composed this rite seem to have regarded this as something to be avoided at all costs; one of the points of the 1732 reunion agreement was that the necessity for this should always be avoided by consecrating in the first place more than enough for all who wished to communicate.[5] This dislike of a second consecration is an important witness to a belief in the unity of the eucharistic rite as a whole, as well as their belief that the institution-oblation-epiclesis sequence was necessary for consecration; also, it had probably not escaped their notice that none of the Eastern rites makes any provision for supplementary consecration.

Thus to summarise, it may be said that the 1718 rite consists very largely of a blend of the materials and structures of both 1549 and 1662, and owes something to 1637 as well; the only really new material is to be found in the offertory prayer and in the prayer of consecration.

(ii) Thomas Brett's commentary

The fullest and most valuable commentary on the 1718 rite was provided by Thomas Brett, one of its compilers, who wrote his *Dissertation on Liturgies* in 1720. This is in fact a controversial work, written to defend and prove the viewpoint of the usagers and of the compilation and contents of 1718; and most of the Preface is taken up with a defence of the admissibility of tradition as a source of authority. The book is divided into two parts; in the first he reprints (in English translation where necessary) the eucharistic portion of many liturgies, including the Clementine, James, Mark, Chrysostom, fragments of the Mozarabic Missal, the Roman Missal, 1549, and 1718 itself, together with Justin Martyr's description of the eucharist and part of the fifth *Mystagogic Catechesis* of Cyril of Jerusalem. It is in the second half, the *Dissertation*, that the exposition of his eucharistic theology is to be found.

It is quite clear that he regarded the Clementine rite as a true source of apostolic practice:

by examining that Liturgy particularly, we may easily discover whatever the Ancients thought Necessary or Essential to the Ministration of the Holy Eucharist.[6]

His discussion of consecration theology is in fact based on this rite, and he regards a long introduction of thanksgiving to the eucharistic prayer as a primitive practice.[7]

He discusses the institution narrative at some length, and its importance in the consecration:

The next thing in the Clementine liturgy are the Words of Institution . . . both Papists and Protestants agreeing . . . that these Words are essential to the Consecration of the Eucharist, which I shall in no wise dispute; but whether nothing more is essential is the Question.[8]

He goes on to say that Romans, Lutherans, and Calvinists all agree

that the whole of the Consecration was performed by the Recital of these Words. And from the Consecration Prayer and Rubric following it, I have also showed this to be the Opinion of the Church of England.

As an argument to disprove this point of view, he uses the same reasoning as Wheatly, namely that at the Last Supper the words of institution were a declaration of the effect of the unrecorded words which Jesus had shortly before addressed to the Father.[9] In this context he also gives his definition of the meaning of consecration:

for what is the meaning of the word consecrate but to offer or dedicate to God, or to bless and sanctify.

He then goes on to discuss what he does believe necessary for the consecration,[10] and his viewpoint here is exactly that of John Johnson, whom he quotes as his authority in this respect: though there is great force and energy in the pronouncing of the institution narrative, consecration is not complete without the whole of the three-fold sequence of institution-oblation-epiclesis.

Next follows a long discussion of the supplementary consecration rubric, which he starts by quoting from what bishop Morton had had to say on the subject in the 1630s. Brett acknowledged that Morton had proved that consecration is not effected just by the institution narrative, but goes on to say of what Morton had said:

> But though I conceive he has fully and unanswerably refuted this new Romish Doctrine (as he justly calls it) having so plainly proved it not to be the ancient Doctrine of that Church, yet whether he have sufficiently cleared the Church of England from maintaining that very Doctrine, which he has so learnedly refuted, is a Point in which I am not satisfied. The Words in the Rubric of the Communion Service in the Church of England are these . . . I confess, I cannot find this Rubric in the Liturgy of the Church of England before the Restoration of King Charles II, that is a Year or two after Bishop Morton died and near thirty years after the Publication of his Book . . .[11]

Clearly Brett had no knowledge of the canons of 1604 or of the various visitation articles issued after this date on this subject, for he goes on to say:

> However, there seems to have been some Order or Rubrick to the same Purpose, (though I have not yet met with it) since the Bishop so expressly says 'Our Church has cautelously . . . Bread and Wine' (see p.117). But however the Matter stood then, it is certain that there is such a Rubric now, which every Priest of the Church of England is obliged to give his Assent and Consent to, and to practise accordingly. Let us see how the Bishop solves this, and clear the Church of England from maintaining the same Doctrine which he has so learnedly condemned in the Church of Rome.

Brett continues by re-quoting Morton's argument that the consecration of any fresh supplies of bread and wine is really covered by the original recital of the consecration prayer, and says that this line of argument simply cannot apply to the 1662 rubric as it stands:

> Because, according to the Bishop's Argument, the second Supply is consecrated by the Blessing pronounced on the first. But the Rubric

plainly supposes this Supply to be un-consecrated, and therefore orders the Priest to consecrate it. Now I cannot persuade myself, that those who put this Rubric into the Liturgy, or any that subscribe to it, and officiate accordingly, were or are so weak as to think that what is already consecrated, needs a second consecration. The Command therefore for the Priest to consecrate this Supply, evidently demonstrates that the Church of England does not suppose it to have been consecrated by the former blessing. How then is the Priest to consecrate this Supply? The Rubric directs that he shall only recite the Words of Institution. Is not this a demonstrative Argument, that this Church teaches that nothing more is necessary to the Consecration of the Elements, than the pronouncing over them the Words of Institution? I think it is as evident as if she had said so in express Words. What therefore Bishop Morton says to the Romanists on this Occasion, may too justly be applied to the Communion Office of the Church of England.[12]

This long quotation is a good example of the inexorable logic with which Brett makes his point. The supplementary consecration rubric provides for Brett definite proof that the Prayer Book doctrine is that the institution narrative, and this alone, effects the consecration; while this was almost certainly not the intention of those who originally framed this rubric, once the rubric was in the Prayer Book, Brett's position becomes the only one that can in strict logic be fully defended when allowing the 1662 rite as it stands to be self-interpreting, and judging it on the basis of a theology like Brett's.

He refutes Wheatly's defence of this rubric as being an interpretation of it contrary to its plain meaning.[13] He finishes his discussion of this point by quoting Comber and concludes that the Church of England is proved guilty by Morton of Romish error in this respect.

He continues his discussion of consecration by commenting upon the epiclesis. He notes that all the Eastern liturgies have it, as well as the Gallican, Gothick, and Mozarabic. He regards the *Quam oblationem* as its equivalent in the Roman rite;[14] and he notes that in the 1549 adaptation of this a specific invocation of the Spirit has been included. But while he acknowledges Rome and 1549 to be 'full in Substance', he says that their order is not the 'natural' one, which is 'the Holy Spirit by his descent completing and perfecting the Consecration'. When the Church celebrates the liturgy it is right to put the institution narrative at the beginning of the consecration as a

Declaration of the Commission and Authority by which we act in this Ministration.

He continues by illustrating what he regards as the immense importance of the epiclesis:

That the Invocation for the Descent of the Holy Spirit upon the Elements, to make them the Body and Blood of Christ, was the Practice of the Universal Church in all Places, is manifest from these Liturgies; That it was practised at all Times ...[15]

And he quotes at length Johnson's patristic proof of this. He continues:

And therefore they supposed not the Elements to be fully consecrated and made the Body and Blood of Christ in Power and Effect, that Flesh and Blood which communicated eternal Life to the worthy Receivers, till they had prayed that the Holy Ghost might come down upon the Elements, and make them the Body and Blood of Christ; because his Descent upon them, and Operation in them and with them is that alone which can make the Food of eternal Life, since, as our Saviour expressly teaches, It is the Spirit that quickeneth ...[16]

This last phrase provides for Brett scriptural authority for the epiclesis. It is a necessary part of the consecration, and its omission in 1552 made the liturgy of the Church of England seriously defective.[17]

He justifies the translation of ἀποφηνη in the Clementine epiclesis as 'make' rather than 'shew', because he regards 'make' as the true meaning of the word and easy to understand, which 'shew' would not have been.[18]

He also comments on the universality of the oblation following the institution narrative.[19] He thought that the omission of this in 1552 was deliberate, and thus that the Church of England was guilty of a vital omission here.[20] He points out that the Scottish book of 1637 did put the oblation in its proper place, which proved to Brett that at least some people recognised the defect and tried to put it right.

He concludes his discussion of the consecration by re-affirming his starting point, namely that the sequence institution-oblation-epiclesis is a universal uninterrupted tradition coming to us from the Apostles, and that therefore it ought to be followed. Indeed he goes so far as to quote a remark of Johnson's that, if we had the words with which St Peter and St Paul consecrated the eucharist, it would not differ in substance from the Clementine form of this sequence.[21]

Brett gives some account of the controversy surrounding the rite of 1718 as part of his justification for it, and in saying how it was drawn up he always uses the first person plural form 'we' when referring to it, which shows he was one of the authors. Grisbrooke, in his comment upon it, held that Brett, Collier, and Deacon were its joint authors.[22] Brett regretted the theological controversy and the disunity it had caused among the non-jurors, but hoped that, through the public pamphlet discussion of the matter that was carried on, the theological issues involved might be brought before a much wider public than the then very small number of non-jurors, and that the controversy might thus have a beneficial effect on the established Church.[23]

Brett commends the rite on the grounds that it follows the primitive order, and gives an account of the principles its compilers used in drawing it up.[24] Firstly, they made as much use of 1662 material as possible. Secondly, they restored some of the 1549 usages that had been left out to please Calvin, for example the Benedictus and the mention of the Blessed Virgin Mary in the intercession; though not essential, these are certainly very desirable. Thirdly, they put the communion devotions in the 1549 position, thus following 'the general practice of the church'. Fourthly, only where both 1662 and 1549 have deviated from the practice of the Church, have the 'much elder liturgies' been followed, and that is in that part of the eucharistic prayer leading up to the words of institution which is made to follow, as it should, directly after the Sanctus, and in the oblation and epiclesis. From the description of the rite itself given above, it can be seen that these principles were faithfully followed in its composition.

Among other points, Brett found that he had to defend the rite of 1718 against the criticism that it gave support to the doctrine of transubstantiation, and this because the epiclesis contained no qualifying 'unto us'. Brett has to admit there is an 'unto us' in 1549, as there is in the *Quam oblationem*, from which it was taken; indeed he maintains that the whole of the Canon of 1549 differs but little from the Roman Canon, which he plainly regards as the source of 1549, except for the rubrics.[25] But, he continues, none of the ancient liturgies have an 'unto us' in their prayers. In any case the

Romans do not regard the epiclesis as consecratory, and indeed even objected at the Council of Florence to the presence of the epiclesis in the Greek rite as evidence that the Greek Church denied the doctrine of transubstantiation.[26] He goes on to maintain that the epiclesis without the 'unto us' is only praying that the bread and wine may be what Christ declared them to be at the Last Supper and so such a prayer makes for transubstantiation no more than do the dominical words themselves. He continues by pointing out that there is no elevation in the 1718 rite, and next makes a very illuminating comment on the Latin Canon, which demonstrates that he had a considerable knowledge of the history of the Latin rite as well as a good insight into the content of the prayers of the Canon:

The Canon of the Mass, generally speaking, is very innocent and inoffensive as to the Prayers, and does not favour the Superstitions and Corruptions of the Church of Rome, particularly in the Point of Transubstantiation, more than of the Communion-Office of the Church of England, or any other Church that protests against that Doctrine.[27]

The superstitious rubrics about adoration and elevation, Brett points out, were all added later, as was the absurd doctrine itself. The great length he has to go to in defending 1718 against the charge that it taught transubstantiation is evidence both of how sensitive an issue this still was at that time, and that all Anglicans in this period, however 'high' their eucharistic doctrine may have been in other respects, were equally firm in their repudiation of it.

He continues by discussing his understanding of the eucharistic presence, and it is quite clear from this that this is exactly the same as that of Johnson,[28] from whom presumably he had derived it.

From this discussion it can be seen that Brett's eucharistic theology is in all particulars that of John Johnson, and from his frequent mention of Johnson in his *Dissertation* it is clear that he can be regarded as a disciple of Johnson; he has adopted Johnson's theology completely, and has neither added to it nor altered it. The original contribution of Brett and the other composers of the 1718 rite is that in it they gave Johnson's theology exact liturgical expression.

One final point in connection with Brett's defence of 1718 should perhaps be mentioned. It was the four usages that Brett and his fellow compilers regarded as absolutely essential; if these could be agreed upon, the non-juring schism could be ended. Yet in compiling 1718 they had taken the opportunity to produce a liturgy that conformed as nearly as possible to what they regarded as the ancient liturgical norms, and this had led them to make some alterations which they regarded as desirable but not absolutely necessary.[29]

(iii) The 1764 rite

Bishop Dowden has traced out in detail the course of developments that led to the Scottish rite of 1764, so it will be sufficient here to note a few points in the story that are indicative of the rite's theological viewpoint. Dowden comments that its sources were 1549, 1552, 1637, and 1718, together with certain of the early Greek liturgies and liturgical writings,[30] which is in itself an important indication of its theological standpoint. He makes the point that, when liturgical worship began to be recovered in Episcopalian congregations in Scotland in the early part of the eighteenth century, it was the 1662 book that tended to be used,[31] partly because it was available, and partly because there was no definite wish for a 1637-style liturgy in any case.[32] The 1637 rite was reprinted for the first time in 1712 by the earl of Winton,[33] and it seems that in the early period it was used practically unaltered.[34] As in England, so in Scotland, the history of the non-juring Episcopalian clergy, their liturgical ideas and practices, was a complicated business, but as the century wore on, the sort of theology developed by Johnson and the English non-juring school became more influential, and so the Scottish rite became more widely used, as did the practice of altering the order of the prayers into a form approaching that of 1764. Dowden makes the point that the concordat of 1731 distinctly allowed the use of the Scottish Order, and that it does not seem to have been regarded as a breach of this concordat to alter the order in which the prayers were said.[35] Indeed the phrase 'Scottish Office' seems to have been somewhat loosely used to include variations of the Scottish Office as it was carried out in practice.[36] Nor is this at all surprising seeing that there was no such thing as a 'sealed book' in Scotland; the absence of a formal law meant that usages and custom were free to develop. At a later period still:

The Usagers of the early non-juring controversies ceased to be a party; they became the main body of Scottish Churchmen during the second half of the last (i.e. 18th) century.[37]

It is this background that produced the definitive edition of the Scottish rite in 1764, which will now be described.

Dowden states that the synaxis was not printed until 1844, and reconstructed what he considered to have been the most likely usage.[38] The 1764 text starts with an exhortation, whose text is that of the third of the 1662 exhortations with a few unimportant verbal alterations. Then follows the offertory, introduced by the admonition 'Let us present our offerings to the Lord with reverence and Godly fear'; this seems in fact simply to be intended to refer to the collection of money. Then follow the offertory sentences, unchanged from 1637 except that the 1 Chronicles 29 sentence has been omitted from the sequence and turned into a mandatory offertory prayer to be said as the presbyter presents the collection before the Lord and places it upon the Table; it is of interest to note that this money is referred to as 'the oblation'. This is followed by a rubric commanding the presbyter to offer up and place the bread and wine on the Lord's Table. The phrase 'offer up' is in 1637, but, as compared with 1718, there is no special offertory prayer relating to the bread and wine.

As in 1718 the Canon follows the offertory immediately, starting with salutation, *Sursum corda,* proper preface as appropriate (the 1662 selection only), Sanctus and Benedictus, The prayer continues with a brief thanksgiving for our redemption through the Saviour's passion which, except for the additional opening phrase 'All glory be to thee', is virtually identical with the beginning of the 1662 consecration prayer. The section 'Hear us, O merciful Father . . .' is naturally omitted (its place being taken by the epiclesis later in the Canon), and the institution narrative follows immediately in its 1662 form with all the 1662 manual acts. Thus the fraction in 1764 still comes in its unprimitive 1662 position; no doubt this is deliberate, for the manual acts and institution narrative had come to be thought of as an important part of the liturgical expression of the eucharistic sacrifice. This latter point is further emphasised by the printing of 'DO' in capital letters at both the points at which it occurs in the institution narrative, 'do' being interpreted to mean 'offer'.

Next follows the oblation paragraph (and it is labelled as such by the rite), worded exactly as in 1637, with the insertion of the phrase 'WHICH WE NOW OFFER UNTO THEE', printed in capital letters, after 'with these thy holy gifts'. This insertion emphasises the sacrificial doctrine of the authors of the rite and of the rite itself; it first occurs in print in the Scottish tradition in 1735, in an unofficial 'wee bookie' published as a commercial venture.[39] This particular booklet was the first to be published in which the prayers of the 1637 rite were set out in the order in which it was becoming customary to say them; and though Dowden is quite right to say that the insertion of this phrase was a clear breach of the 1731 concordat, its presence in print no doubt indicates that its use was already widespread by 1735. Here the 1764 rite was making 'official' what was obviously Scottish liturgical theory and practice already.

Next follows the epiclesis; again the 1637 wording is followed, with the additional introductory phrase 'And we most humbly beseech thee', and with 'that they may be unto us' changed into 'that they may become'. This latter form is clearly in line with non-juring thought; witness Brett's defence of 1718 in this respect. This change did have the effect of making the epiclesis simply a prayer for the blessing of the elements, and not a prayer for the blessing of both elements and communicants; but this latter aim is well provided for in the material that follows. This part of the prayer concludes with most of the material to be found in the first of the two 1662 post-communion prayers.

Next follows the intercession, introduced by the bidding 'Let us pray for the whole state of Christ's Church'. The phrase 'militant here in earth' is left out; this omission too was an innovation first occurring in print in the 1735 booklet, and thus also doubtless reflects current practice at the time. This is the 1718 position for the intercession; in content it is very largely 1662, with a certain amount of 1549 material woven into it, mainly that connected with the commemoration of the departed and praise for the saints. As in 1549, 1637, and 1718, the congregation assembled 'to celebrate the commemoration' of Christ's precious death is prayed for. The one oddity in the prayer is the retention of the phrase praying for God's acceptance of the 'alms and oblations', which seems entirely out of place here, and its retention has all the appearance of a piece of unintelligent copying.

After the intercession comes the Our Father, followed by the Communion Devotions, Invitation, Confession, Absolution, Comfortable Words, and Prayer of Humble Access, all in their 1662 form. Then follows the communion of the people, the words of administration being as in 1549. There is inserted here a rubric concerned with supplementary consecration; this orders the presbyter to consecrate more in both kinds (by implication, but the implication is unmistakable) and to say the whole of the consecration prayer from 'All glory be to thee . . .' to the end of the epiclesis, which of course means that the whole of the institution narrative, oblation, and epiclesis have to be repeated. This rubric is the clearest possible proof that those who framed this rite intended it to express the developed consecration theology associated with John Johnson.

After the communion, the remains are to be placed on the Lord's Table and covered with a fair linen cloth. Then the presbyter is directed to say a short exhortation, whose material anticipates the prayer of thanksgiving (virtually identical with the second of the two 1662 post-communion prayers) which follows. The service concludes with the Gloria and the Blessing. There are no final rubrics, but doubtless reverent consumption of the remains is to be assumed.

Thus a comparison of 1718 and 1764 shows their similarity of structure and content, and this fact, taken together with the known historical links between the English non-jurors and the Scottish Episcopalians, make it quite clear that the theological intention of the two rites is the same, and moreover that this theology is that expounded by Johnson and Brett. The main difference between the two rites is that the compilers of 1764 limited themselves, with the single exception of the phrase 'which we now offer unto thee', to material already found in the rites of 1549, 1637, and 1662, whereas the compilers of 1718 felt free to use material from the Clementine, and to be original where they felt that the Anglican source materials were not adequate for their purpose. Both rites of course contain all four of the usages; the only qualification that could be added to this is that 1764, by referring to the 'bread and wine prepared for the sacrament', makes the mixed chalice optional.

(iv) Concluding comments

It is now possible to attempt to summarise the results of this chapter and the previous one. During the first half of the seventeenth-century, as Anglican eucharistic theology developed, a distinct tradition of eucharistic theology embracing a fairly wide range of ideas emerged from what might almost be described as the theological vacuum of the Elizabethan Settlement. By the second quarter of the eighteenth-century this general outlook had crystallised into two distinct traditions of eucharistic theology, which may be labelled for convenience as the 1662 tradition and the 1718-1764 tradition. One important difference between them is that the 1662 tradition can almost be considered as arising out of the existence of the 1662 rite, and thus a consequence of the balance of ecclesiastical and political forces that produced the 1662 rite in its present form, whereas 1718 and 1764 were composed to give liturgical expression to a previously developed theological tradition of some sophistication and refinement. It will thus be appreciated that the 1662 tradition cannot be stated with the same degree of precision as the 1718-1764 tradition.

Perhaps the majority of eighteenth-century Anglicans, certainly in England, should be regarded as adherents of the 1662 tradition, and probably a lot of them held to it unconsciously rather than consciously; Waterland can be regarded as typical of those who gave it theological expression. Liturgically, this tradition was satisfied with the 1662 rite as it stood; theologically, its characteristics can be defined as holding to a memorialist doctrine of the eucharistic sacrifice, a real receptionist view of the presence, and a belief that the consecration of the elements was effected by prayer, a prayer that must include the institution narrative. Though what is understood by consecration is not closely defined, it was believed to be a necessary and distinct part of the eucharistic action. It follows from the above argument that though the 1662 rite is the liturgical vehicle, and partly the generator, of this tradition, it cannot be regarded as its definitive liturgical expression. Indeed by the very nature of its history the 1662 rite cannot be said to be the designed liturgical expression of *any* particular eucharistic theology.

However it is to be noted that the theology of the exponents of the '1662 school' in the early eighteenth century follows fairly closely the mainstream outlook of the early seventeenth century.

The 1718-1764 tradition too can be seen as emerging from part of the outlook of the earlier part of the seventeenth century, and finally coming together and receiving definitive expression in the writings of Johnson, Nelson, Brett, and men like them. Though this viewpoint came to be associated very largely with the English non-jurors and the Scottish Episcopalians, and received its liturgical expression there, it is also an important minority viewpoint within the established Church. Theologically, the characteristic beliefs of this school of thought may be summarised as follows. Firstly, a belief in the eucharistic sacrifice as a real, objective, and effectual Godward pleading of Christ's sacrificial offering of himself on Calvary (with which offering some would have wished to link the Last Supper). Secondly, a belief in a permanent and objective real presence, expressed by saying that by the action of the Holy Spirit, the bread and wine become in power, virtue, and effect the body and blood of Christ. Thirdly, a doctrine of consecration that was quite specific in regarding the Holy Spirit as the agent of consecration, combined with a belief that the institution narrative-oblation-epiclesis sequence was the necessary and essential liturgical material by which consecration was effected. Both 1549 and 1637 were important sources of liturgical material for the men of this school, and these two rites were in degrees regarded as expressing the eucharistic theology they themselves believed in, even if in an imperfect form. The 1718 and 1764 rites were drawn up to give liturgical expression to this developed eucharistic theology, and can thus be regarded as authoritative liturgical formulations of it. It is to be noted that the men of this school not only regarded Eastern-style anaphoras as models and sources for their own consecration prayers, but adopted something very like the native theology of these prayers as well. This is in contrast to the pre-Restoration era, which had started to draw on Eastern-type prayer materials but not the theology underlying them. Thus in the early eighteenth century the men of this school regarded the 1549 and 1537 rites as evidence that their own theology was that of the earlier period too, something that on balance is not the case.

CHAPTER TEN

The Latin Rite from Trent to the present time

The point of distinction between pre-Reformation Roman and post-Reformation Roman, Latin may conveniently be taken as the Council of Trent. This resulted in the 1570 Missal of Pius V, which, as successively amended, remained in force until superseded by the 1969 *Ordo Missae*, which now forms part of the 1970 *Missale Romanum*.

(i) The Council of Trent and the Missal of 1570

The Council of Trent recognised both the necessity and the widespread demand for the reform of the Missal. Because the Council was meeting in response to the crisis posed by the Protestant Reformation, one strand of their reforming work was a firm restatement of the tradition of the Latin West as they had understood it and received it. A second strand was the recognition of the need to remove medieval accretions and to correct medieval corruption and abuses, for example, the excessive growth of votive masses. The actual work of reforming the Missal was done by a commission, and the end product of their labours was the Missal promulgated by Pius V in 1570.[1]

A number of important points must be made about this Missal and the theological teaching associated with it. Firstly, the principle that the Missal should be based on the ancient sources of the Christian liturgy was recognised,[2] even though the limited liturgical scholarship available and the prevailing situation rendered this more a hope than an achievement at the time. Secondly, the objective nature of the eucharistic sacrifice was maintained by the Council of Trent itself in its dogmatic definitions,[3] in a refutation of Protestantism. The effect of this was to fasten on to the Pian Missal a doctrine of the eucharistic sacrifice essentially medieval in character. Thirdly, the scholastic doctrine that the specific moment of consecration was located in the institution narrative was maintained. Fourthly, a great many of the worst excesses of medieval liturgy were cleared away, and in this respect post-Tridentine liturgical practice was often a considerable improvement on what had preceded it. Fifthly, liturgical uniformity was imposed in place of the immense variation in detail that had been characteristic of Western liturgy previously; only uses that could demonstrate a history of more than 200 years were permitted to remain.[4] Such uniformity was only made possible by the invention of the printing press; furthermore, this uniformity was intended to be changeless, and the function of the Congregation of Rites, founded in 1588, was not further liturgical reform or continuing development, but the resolution of doubtful questions in accordance with existing standards.[5] Sixthly, and of the greatest importance, the exclusion of the people from participating in the liturgy itself continued. It is true that Trent did encourage frequent lay reception of Communion, but without effect. It was widely held that the mass was a sacred mystery, participation in and knowledge of which was to be withheld from the lay person. Indeed, vernacular translation of the Missal, and in particular the Canon, even for the purposes of private knowledge and devotion, was strictly forbidden.[6] The people were to be occupied at mass by private prayers, devotions, and songs, an inheritance from, and continuance and development of, late medieval practice. Thus the overall effect of the Tridentine Reform and the promulgation of the Pian Missal was to impose on the eucharistic liturgy of the Latin rite with apparent finality what can only be described as 'reformed medievalism'. However, and most important, the ancient prayers of this rite, Canon, collects, secrets, and post-communions, were preserved and continued in use as the core of the liturgy.

This remained the situation until the rise of the modern liturgical movement, whose practical beginnings can be dated to early in this century, given that some of the foundations for it had been laid in the nineteenth century, for example, at Solesmes. One of the most important of the early beginnings was the papal decree encouraging frequent lay communion which appeared in 1905. At first, this giving of communion was a more or less independent act, dissociated from the mass; but in time it was realised that communion was an integral part of the eucharistic action, and so it was restored to its proper place. Increasingly, the laity followed the actual prayers of the rite during the celebration of mass, using translations of the Missal. A further development of this trend was 'dialogue' mass. The work then of the liturgical movement during the first half of this century was to involve the people more and more in the worship of the mass itself, though the actual liturgy and the priest's place within it remained unchanged.[7] These developments prepared the way for the liturgical revolution that was to follow the Second Vatican Council, and for the new Roman Missal of 1970.

(ii) The Second Vatican Council and the Missal of 1970

The first and most important change of all is that mass is now universally celebrated in the vernacular, with the full participation of the people throughout. The liturgy has been recovered as the rite of the people of God. Thus the ritual tradition of centuries has been overturned. Secondly, the rite itself was revised in many ways. In terms of the central and eucharistic part of the liturgy, the most important changes are the very considerable simplification of the offertory, the writing of many new prefaces, and the composition of three new eucharistic prayers. Given these changes, the central core of Secret, Canon, and post-communion was retained, and even restored to a proper prominence.

Given the changes in text and liturgical practice, what of theological teaching concerning the mass? The first important source for this is the foreword to the *General Instruction* to the New Missal.[8] This stresses the continuity of doctrinal tradition, both in respect of the sacrifice of the eucharist, and in terms of consecration and the eucharistic presence. On the former point, the Tridentine definition is referred to, together with the Second Vatican Council's enunciation and reaffirmation of it. The ancient prayer that is now the Secret of the Second Sunday of the year is quoted as an authentic expression of the Church's doctrine, and it is maintained that this is the teaching of the new Canons Two, Three, and Four.[9] Likewise, on the question of the presence and the consecration, what is seen as the traditional doctrine is maintained:

In the celebration of Mass there is proclaimed the wonderful mystery of the real presence of Christ our Lord under the eucharistic species.

196

The Second Vatican Council and other magisterial pronouncements of the Church have confirmed this truth in the same sense and in the same words as those in which the Council of Trent defined it as an article of faith. It is proclaimed not only by the words of consecration whereby Christ becomes present through an essential change in the elements, but also by the meaning of the celebration and the several external manifestations of deep reverence and adoration occurring during the course of the eucharistic liturgy.[10]

Here the reformed medievalism of Trent seems as firmly entrenched as ever. The Preface goes on to note Trent's desire to return to the early sources of the liturgy, and makes the point that this is now much more possible than it was at the time of Trent, both because of advances in liturgical and historical scholarship, and because of the ecclesiastical situation. The 1570 and 1970 missals embody the same tradition in this respect but 'the new Missal is a considerable improvement on the old one'.[11]

Of equal importance to the *General Instruction* are the commentaries of Roman Catholic scholars on the new rite. At first sight it might seem strange to regard these as being of equal importance to an officially promulgated *General Instruction,* but whereas the latter is a statement of the official position, the views of the theologians both reflect and contribute to the Roman Church's developing understanding of her own eucharistic tradition, and a few of these will now be very briefly examined.[12]

Among the important areas explored are the relationship between the New Testament accounts of Christ's institution of the eucharist and the Canon as a whole, the linguistic style of liturgical prayers, and an analysis of the theology of the Gelasian Canon. On the first question the point is made that the purpose of the institution narrative in the Canon is not self-evident; nor can it be regarded as the basis from which the rest of the Canon has grown, because the whole eucharistic action and Canon together express and perform the meaning of the rite whose institution is recorded in the New Testament.[13] The all but universal occurrence of the institution narrative in all anaphoras is noted.[14]

The point is made that the Canon is not intended to be precise theology or dogmatic definition, but a poetic expression of the mystery of redemption that is taking place in the eucharistic action.[15] And in their very interesting discussion about the translation of Canon One, A.M. Roguet and L.C. Sheppard show that they understand it to be this sort of prayer.[16]

Paul Tihon's article on the 'Theology of the Eucharistic Prayer'[17] demonstrates how a modern Roman Catholic theologian approaches this matter. He argues for the necessity of communion:

in no way can it be thought that the memorial instituted by our Lord is fully accomplished merely by the blessing uttered over the offerings, and leave out of account all emphasis on the explicit reference in the institution narrative to the actual sharing of the bread and the cup.[18]

He makes the same point about the nature of the relationship between the institution narrative and the eucharistic performance as was made above:

What Jesus did and what he commands us to do we repeat at each Eucharist in the institution narrative, and we do it at distinct times,[19]

that is, through the sequence of offertory, blessing (the eucharistic prayer), fraction, and communion. The communal nature of the rite is stressed:

The eucharistic prayer is the president's prayer, but at the same time it appears to us as the prayer and action of the whole congregation.[20]

Of the greatest importance to his discussion of the eucharistic sacrifice, he says:

The eucharist is a sacrifice because it is a sacrificial memorial. Only the leaving out of account of the efficacious value of the actual representation of the memorial, turning the latter into a mere recollection, has caused the search elsewhere in a multitude of theories for the proof of the sacrificial character of the Mass.[21]

This represents a return to the classical Thomist position, and adequately safeguards the uniqueness of the cross. The Church can only be said to offer Christ in the eucharist because Christ identifies himself with his Church and subsumes his own offering into it. The eucharist is

a visible and ritual sacrifice (in the form of a memorial rite of blessing and sharing out) but even this rite only has validity because it imparts to us the power of the Spirit of God.[22]

On the question of the consecration, he discusses the varying Eastern and Western traditions in this respect in an irenic spirit, and concludes:

As for wishing to attribute the conversion of the bread and the wine to the formulation of the epiclesis of the Holy Spirit there are as few decisive arguments for this as there are for attributing it to a certain minimum of words within the narrative of the institution. The present tendency of theology is rather to attribute this 'consecratory' power to the words and actions constituting the memorial as a whole, and this includes all the eucharistic prayer.[23]

Thus the whole of Tihon's comments represent a strong move away from medieval eucharistic theology and back towards the sort of theology that, it was argued in the early chapters of this book, is the true and native theology of the Latin rite.

Concerning the prayers of the rite themselves, the Secrets, Canon One, and the post-communions remain more or less as they always have been. This liturgical continuity of the essential eucharistic core of the rite is a very important feature of the Latin liturgy. The offertory has been much simplified and returns to being a setting forth of the eucharistic gifts in preparation for the saying of the eucharistic prayer. Even the removal of the medieval invitatory, the *Orate Fratres,* was apparently considered, but in the event it was retained.[24] A large number of new prefaces have been provided to increase the element of explicit thanksgiving; the variable prefaces are only used with Canons One and Three. In all the Canons the people are brought more fully into the action through the acclamations. In terms of the range of theological ideas contained in the new eucharistic prayers, it may fairly be said that this is the same as that of the ancient prayer, Canon One, with the amount of specific thanksgiving increased, and more explicit reference made to the place of the Holy Spirit in the sacramental action. These are both welcome and unexceptionable changes. The one possible controversial section in these prayers comes in the anamnesis section of Canon Four where occurs the phrase: 'we offer you his body and blood, the acceptable sacrifice which brings salvation to the whole world'. At first sight this seems to go beyond the offering of 'the bread of life and the cup of eternal salvation' of Canon One, and to include in the eucharistic prayers an expression of a theology frequently expressed in the medieval and post-medieval period, but never hitherto contained in the central prayers of the rite themselves. In this respect, it seems a pity that Canon Four does not use the 'bread and cup' language of Canon One at this point, though even here it could doubtless be argued that Canon Four means no more

199

than the subsuming of the church's offering in the one perfect offering of Christ. With this one possible exception, the new Roman eucharistic prayers are seen to be fully in harmony with the ancient prayers of the Latin rite and with the theology of these prayers.

What then may be said in summary of the Latin rite since Trent? After centuries of rigid reformed medievalism, the last decade has witnessed a revolution only slightly anticipated by changes that had occurred in the earlier years of this century. In terms of liturgical practice there has been a return to the celebration of mass as the communal worship of the people of God, with the whole rite said aloud in the vernacular, with all invited to share in the offertory and in reception of communion. Here is the modern equivalent of the praxis of the *Ordo Romanus Primus;* the prayers of the rite have recovered a ceremonial equivalent in spirit to that which originally accompanied them. In terms of theology, official documents still stress continuity with Trent, as is perhaps only to be expected, as well as a return to the 'norms of the Holy Fathers',[24] itself a Tridentine objective. The author would argue that the latter can only be achieved by going behind some of the former, and recognising Trent as in part an alien medieval imposition on the true meaning of the Latin rite. The writings of the theologians, as reviewed above, do seem to indicate that this is happening, in theory as well as in practice. Abandoning scholarly neutrality, the author would expect and hope this to continue, for the recovery of a proper liturgical practice can only lead to a recovery of that balanced, scriptural, and beautifully satisfying formulation of eucharistic doctrine that the prayers of the Latin rite so nobly express.

(iii) The correction of defects and supplementary consecration

In the Pian Missal there is a section dealing with defects in the celebration of mass and their rectification, the section *Defectus in Celebratione Missarum* or *De Defectibus in Celebratione Missarum Occurrentibus.* This first appeared in the missal in 1557, when it was inserted at the beginning of the book; it is of unknown authorship.[25] It became part of the 1570 Missal, and remained there until the latter was superseded by the *Ordo Missae* of 1969 and hence the Missal of 1970.

J. B. O'Connell discusses and describes at length the provisions of *De Defectis,* all of which are designed to remedy defect or accident, to ensure that the rite of the mass as a whole may always be complete, that is, that there may always be an offertory in both kinds, a consecration in both kinds, and a communion in both kinds.[26] When necessary, the relevant portion of the institution narrative is repeated to secure these ends, thus continuing the precedent and practice of the pre-Reformation cautels in this respect. Thus the second recitation of the narrative is being used to complete the liturgical action of the mass, and it is in this context that it is to be regarded. It is not for the benefit of intending communicants. Indeed, such a provision would seem to be explicitly excluded, since

under no circumstances may the words of consecration be said over bread, once they have been pronounced over the host of the Mass.[27]

This is derived from Canon 817 of 1917, which directs that

it is forbidden, even in extreme cases of necessity, to consecrate one species without the other or both outside of Holy Mass.[28]

This is confirmed by a description of current Roman Catholic practice, namely that if hosts run out, the priest stops giving communion, and the rest of the people do not receive.[29]

Of the provisions of *De Defectis,* the General Instruction of 1970 retains one provision only:

If the priest should discover, after the Consecration or when receiving Communion, that water has been poured into the Chalice instead of wine, he should pour that water into some other vessel, put wine and a little water into the Chalice and consecrate it. He says only that part of the consecration narrative which applies to the Chalice, and is not obliged to consecrate bread again.[30]

The point of this is solely to complete the action of the mass.

Thus there can be seen in the post-Tridentine Roman provisions for the correction of defects in the celebration of mass, echoes of two different theologies, one involving a great emphasis on the moment of consecration, and the other a belief that the rite of the eucharist is a totality needing the correct performance of all its parts for its wholeness. The second of these theologies is the ancient and original theology of the Latin rite, and the first is medieval in essence; interestingly, medieval doctrine and practice is used to defend the ancient idea of the integrity of the rite.

It is important to realise that none of these provisions are supplementary consecration in the Anglican sense. This latter practice is not now, and never has been, allowed or provided for anywhere in the Latin rite. The rites make no provision for it, and the theologians do not discuss it. Therefore, to seek a Roman Catholic view of this matter is to ask for what is not to be found; presumably however, their view of the necessary integrity of the rite would lead to their regarding the practice as illegitimate. This is also the viewpoint of the Orthodox Churches.[31] One may note too that Old Catholic service-books make no provision.[32]

CHAPTER 11

Eucharistic Consecration in the Anglican Church after 1764

In contrast to the Church of Rome, which for all practical purposes has had just one rite in use for the last four centuries,[1] the Anglican Communion has developed an almost bewildering variety of eucharistic liturgies in the same period of time. The autonomy of the various parts of the Anglican Communion has perhaps made this an inevitable development.

We have already seen that the Anglican Church possessed two distinct eucharistic traditions at the beginning of this period. Both used basically Cranmerian materials in their rites, with the 1764 tradition departing far more radically from both the shape of Cranmer's rite and his theology than did the service of 1662. Up until about 1960, Anglican eucharistic liturgies evolved quite slowly and remained relatively few in number,[2] and, with few and minor exceptions, used Cranmerian materials as their main ingredient. Since then, growth has been rapid, and in general the newer liturgies have been very much less dependent on use of Prayer Book material, deliberately so, as part of the move to attempt to return to liturgical origins.[3] 1960, then, represents a convenient dividing line in this study.

(i) Developments prior to 1960

The first set of rites in this category is the various recensions of the 1662 rite itself. There are four of these, the 1918 Canadian use, the 1926 Irish rite, the version of 1662 printed in the Scottish book of 1929 and that in the Indian book of 1960. All of these are without significant alteration from the 1662 rite itself,[4] and thus their usage of eucharistic consecration and supplementary consecration is unchanged.

The Scottish rite of 1929 is that of 1764 with comparatively few, and for the most part, very minor alterations. The one point of some substance concerns the epiclesis, where a petition for the sanctification of the worshippers has been added to the prayer for the elements.[5] In this respect the 1929 book follows the text of the earlier 1912 recension.[6] Supplementary consecration may only be performed in both kinds, and the institution narrative and epiclesis paragraphs of the Canon are to be repeated; thus, compared with 1764 and the 1912 recension, the oblation paragraph has been omitted from this form.[7] In this respect alone 1929 weakens the consecration theology of 1764, but in general it may be said that these conservative revisions of the English and Scottish rites preserved into the twentieth century the two characteristic Anglican eucharistic theologies that had developed by the middle of the eighteenth. In addition it is worth noting that both traditions in all the rites and recensions mentioned so far prescribe the traditional 1662-style fivefold manual acts at the institution narrative. But 1929 inserted a fraction after the Lord's Prayer;[8] so this rite now has a double fraction. The 1929 rite also conserves the 1764 tradition of adding the intercession on to the end of the Canon.

The American rite is based on the Scottish rite because Samuel Seabury was consecrated by Scottish bishops. First compiled in 1790, it was revised in 1892, and again in 1928[9]. The intercession has been returned to the English position and is preceded by the offertory. The Canon follows the Scottish order, but the epiclesis has been made less directly a plea for conversion, becoming more of a prayer for sanctification for the purposes of communion.[10] The fivefold sequence of manual acts is retained at the institution narrative, and there is no second fraction. Supplementary consecration is in both kinds and involves repetition of the Canon from the beginning of the institution narrative to the end of the epiclesis.

The English rite of 1928 is very similar in shape to the American rite of the same year.[11] The intercession is in the 1662 position and preceded by the offertory. The central portion of the Canon follows the institution narrative — anamnesis — epiclesis order. The anamnesis does not offer the gifts, but sets them forth before God and makes Christ's memorial in them, which is theologically the same thing. The epiclesis is a prayer for the sanctification of both worshippers and elements, to the end that the elements may profitably be received as the body and blood of Christ. The fivefold sequence of the manual acts is retained at the institution narrative, and there is no second fraction. Supplementary consecration may be in either kind, and the form is the appropriate part of the institution narrative followed by an appropriately modified version of the epiclesis.[12]

The 1929 South African Liturgy[13] (incorporated into the full South African Prayer Book in 1954), the Ceylon Liturgy,[14] the Indian Liturgy of 1960,[15] and the Canadian Liturgy of 1959,[16] have the same 'modified Scottish' structure as has the English 1928 rite; in the Canadian rite the epiclesis is a prayer for the worshippers only. All retain the fivefold sequence of manual acts at the institution narrative; South Africa alone of the four has a second fraction like the Scottish rite. These rites vary in the provisions they make for supplementary consecration.[17]

The Japanese[18] and West Indian[19] liturgies manifest certain similarities. Both have 1549-style Canons, but with offertories preceding the intercessions, which in turn immediately precede their *Sursum corda* dialogues. In the Japanese rite the epiclesis is specifically an invocation of the Word and Holy Spirit, whereas in the West Indian it is simply a prayer to the Father for the sanctification of the elements. The Japanese rite has simplified the manual acts to the two actions of taking the bread and wine into the priest's hands, without fraction, and the West Indian has eliminated manual acts at this point altogether. Both have restored the fraction to a position after the Canon.

The remaining four Anglican liturgies printed by Bernard Wigan, the Korean,[20] those of Nyasaland and Northern Rhodesia,[21] and the Swahili Mass,[22] are all rites produced in what would have been termed 'missionary dioceses', by people of an advanced 'Anglo-Catholic' persuasion. For the most part they were composed in local vernacular languages, and depart from the language and style of the Prayer Book much more than do other liturgies produced in this period. The Korean rite has two epicleses, one for the elements before the institution narrative, and another one for the communicants towards the end of the Canon. There are no manual acts at the institution narrative, but the dominical words are printed out in large type, and numerous ceremonial crossings are indicated throughout the Canon. Of the three African rites only Nyasaland lacks an epiclesis. In Rhodesia it follows closely the brief anamnesis after the institution narrative, and in the Swahili mass it occupies the 1549 position. Nyasaland and Swahili borrow quite heavily from the Roman Canon.

It will be seen that, with the exceptions of the earlier recensions of the American rite, the rites described above were all composed during this century. Thus up until 1900 the only rites officially in use in the Anglican Communion were those of 1662 and the Scottish-American family. Between 1900 and 1960 most of the English-speaking parts of the Anglican Communion revised their liturgies, the 1920s being a particularly prolific period in this respect. The above survey shows that most of these revisions were quite conservative, and resulted in what might be called a 'modified Scottish' type of liturgy becoming the predominant form of eucharistic liturgy in the Anglican Communion in the first half of this century. The exceptions to this are to be found in those areas that retained the 1662 rite in use more or less unchanged. Detailed examination of these 'modified Scottish' liturgies shows that they can be seen as a weaving together of materials and ideas from both the Scottish and English traditions.

All the liturgies described in this chapter are official liturgies, the liturgies produced by the proper legislative processes of the churches concerned. (This is true even of the English 1928 rite, even though it was disallowed by Parliament.) The background to this developing process of liturgical revision is the varied spectrum of Anglican eucharistic theology, in particular as this was evolving and changing during the nineteenth and early twentieth centuries. This is clearly a vast field, and in a brief survey only a few points can be made in an endeavour to illustrate why Anglican eucharistic liturgies developed in the way that they did during the first half of this century. In this discussion attention will be limited as far as possible to the doctrine of consecration as such.

One of the most important factors affecting the development of Anglican thought in the nineteenth century was the Oxford Movement. This had wide reaching devotional, ceremonial, and doctrinal effects, and itself provided much impetus towards official liturgical change. Its main effect in terms of the doctrine of consecration was strongly to reinforce the view that the theology of the 1662 rite located the consecration in the institution narrative; both the consecration prayer itself, and the supplementary consecration rubric were regarded as supporting evidence for this contention. Darwell Stone believed this to be the doctrine of the Prayer Book on this point,[23] and welcomed it. And to men who were seeking to demonstrate that the Prayer Book was essentially 'western' in its eucharistic doctrine, this was a logical thing to do. Further, there was precedent for it; some people had put this interpretation on the teaching of the Prayer Book since about 1700. Though it is to be noted that when men such as Wheatly had done this, they were criticising the Prayer Book, not praising it as the high-churchmen of the nineteenth and twentieth centuries were. Nevertheless, this high-church reinforcement of the view that this is the doctrine of the 1662 Prayer Book was to cause considerable controversy in connection with the revision of Anglican eucharistic rites in the 1920s.

This was particularly the case with the English 1928 consecration prayer, where the post-institution narrative epiclesis caused many to think that the doctrine of the Church of England was being altered; and Anglo-Catholics, in particular, to fear that the Church's doctrine of eucharistic consecration was being compromised.[24] The Anglo-Catholics had no objection to an epiclesis section of the prayer, but they wanted it in the 1549 position before the institution narrative;[25] it can then be regarded as the equivalent of the *Quam oblationem* of the Latin Canon. This attitude is strange, because Anglicans in Scotland and America had been using a prayer structured like 1928 for two centuries or so,[26] and prayers whose epicleses were far stronger petitions for consecration than that of 1928. Presumably then, they were simply not aware of the doctrinal background and liturgical thinking behind a 'Scottish' Canon, though with the appearance of H.A. Wilson's edition of J. Dowden's work on the Scottish liturgy in 1922,[27] this knowledge was certainly available at the time. It was the more liberal-minded school in England who were advocates of a 'modified Scottish' style of Canon.[28] The same controversy was going on in South Africa at the same time, where the Canon for the new South African rite was being composed along very similar lines to the English 1928 one.[29]

All this appears to indicate a certain fluidity and confusion over the doctrine of eucharistic consecration in this period; this is further illustrated by the increasing variety of provisions for supplementary consecration made to accompany these new rites. Even in the 1929 version of the Scottish liturgy the oblation paragraph was omitted from the form, showing the Scottish revisers of the time either no longer understood, or thought it unnecessary to follow, the intrinsic theology of their own rite at this point.[30] In contrast, the American rite retained its integrity in this matter. The South African rite permitted either the 1662 method or the 'authentic Scottish' method, a position which has a certain logic about it, provided the true rationales of both are understood, though it must be regarded as doubtful whether the compilers of the rite did. The English 1928 provisions seem simply to indicate muddled thinking on the subject, and were not liked at the time.[31] The general position for this period seems to be a desire for a wide variety of traditional material in the Canon without wishing to locate or define the consecration too precisely, but to see the whole prayer as contributing to it.

The 1922 Doctrine Commission talked about consecration and the eucharistic presence, but did not discuss how it understood the liturgical act of consecration in the eucharistic prayer to take place.[32]

Throughout this period scholarly liturgical research was being pursued. This both contributed to the liturgical developments of the time, and laid the foundations for the next stages of the process. One of the most distinguished liturgical scholars of the first decades of this century was W.H. Frere, who was both officially involved in practical liturgy making and did much fundamental research. His views on eucharistic consecration are therefore worthy of note. He regarded the 1662 rite as having:

fastened upon the English church . . . an extreme and even exaggerated acceptance of the scholastic view of consecration in its most exclusive form.[33]

He himself was a firm believer in a 'modified Scottish' style of Canon, that is one containing, among other material, an institution narrative, an anamnesis, and an epiclesis, in that order. He held that this was the universal and primitive order for the eucharistic prayer, and wrote his book *The Anaphora* to prove this viewpoint.[34] This book represents the last great attempt to uphold this view in this form, and he is thus the last of a long line of distinguished Anglican scholars who argued for this and influenced Anglican eucharistic liturgies in this way over a period of some 250 years. Within this structure he had no wish to isolate a moment of consecration, and regarded the split between East and West in this respect as unfortunate.[35] Rather he held to the idea that the whole prayer was consecratory, which he regarded as being the primitive view.[36] He did not regard the 1549 position for the epiclesis as satisfactory.[37] In spite of his own convictions on the matter, he recognised the difficulty in persuading the whole Church of England to accept happily a 'modified Scottish' style of Canon and, at least for a time, was an advocate of alternative forms of Canon in any new English prayer book.[38] His views on supplementary consecration are interesting.[39] He thought it highly desirable to avoid the necessity for it at all, but if it was necessary his ideal was that the whole consecration prayer should be repeated. If this was not practical, the irreducible minimum should include the institution narrative – anamnesis – epiclesis sequence. He also tentatively advocated commixture for dealing with a shortage of wine.

Just as Frere's work may be said to have closed, in a sense, one era of Anglican thinking about the eucharist, so Gregory Dix's *The Shape of the Liturgy* began another. Dix argued that there was no universal type of primitive eucharistic prayer; what there was, was a universal fourfold shape to the eucharistic action.[40] Though some of the details of Dix's work have been much criticised, his general theory has stood the test of time and has had a predominant influence in determining the shape of most modern Anglican eucharistic rites.

(ii) Developments since 1960

The Anglican Communion has been exceedingly prolific in the production of new eucharistic liturgies during the last fifteen years, but, despite this, certain common strands can be discerned. The Lambeth Conferences have devoted some attention to liturgy and liturgical reform. At the earlier conferences the stress was on the Prayer Book as the bond of unity, and the development of liturgical change within this framework.[41] By 1958 it was felt that something wider than this was needed, and that Conference sought to establish the basic principles upon which future progress should be possible.[42] In terms of eucharistic consecration their material is exceedingly brief. They desired that the thanksgiving element in the consecration prayer should be widened to include 'all the principal "mighty works of God".'[43] They wished to get behind 'controversies with respect to the moment and formula of consecration' back to a theology of 'consecration through thanksgiving' which they regarded as scriptural and primitive. They stated that the Holy Spirit 'informs and vivifies the whole rite', whether or not a specific liturgical epiclesis is included in the consecration prayer.[44] This conference wanted a central liturgical advisory committee to be set up,[45] and this actually happened in connection with the 1963 Toronto Congress.[46] A considerable amount of pan-Anglican liturgical consultation has taken place in the years since 1958. The whole subject of pan-Anglican co-operation and the development of the liturgies themselves has been very fully described and documented by C.O. Buchanan,[47] and so this discussion will limit itself as far as possible to the consecration as such, and to drawing such conclusions as seem appropriate at this particular point in time.

Within a complex scene a number of trends can be discerned. One point to be noted is the considerable influence of the school of English liturgical scholars in the Dix tradition, such as A.H. Couratin and E.C. Ratcliff. Another is the two pan-Anglican documents produced as a result of the process of inter-Anglican consultation referred to above. The first of these was exceedingly brief on the subject of consecration, suggesting that it should be in the form of 'a thanksgiving for creation and for God's mighty acts in Christ and in sending the Holy Spirit', and should include the institution narrative and a prayer for the communicants.[48] The second document was rather fuller in that it asked for the following items to be included in the prayer in the following order: a thanksgiving series, institution narrative, an anamnesis that should be rich but uncontroversial in its expression, and a prayer that through the sharing of the bread and wine and through the power of the Holy Spirit we may be made one with our Lord . . .

This may be termed the 'modified Scottish' order in that it contains the institution narrative — anamnesis — 'prayer concerned with the Spirit' sequence. The influence that these documents have had is less than might have been expected.[50]

Of the rites themselves, most can be classified as belonging to one of four basic families, 1662, 'Scottish', 'Church of South India — Liturgy for Africa family',[51] and the new English family starting from the English Series 2 rite.[52]

C.O. Buchanan regards the 'Scottish' family influence as 'fading into insignificance',[53] but surely this is not the case, in that the 'South India — Africa' family have a 'modified Scottish' style of Canon embodying the institution narrative — anamnesis — 'prayer about the Spirit' sequence. A very large proportion of the rites in both *Modern* and *Further Anglican Liturgies* do have Canons of this sort. The author would greatly regret the demise of the 'modified Scottish' rites from the Anglican scene, for it is a venerable tradition within Anglicanism, which has been and is the vehicle of eucharistic life for those Anglicans who do not regard the 1662 tradition as adequate.

One of the characteristics of all these families of rites, except that of 1662, is agreement about the structure of the eucharistic part of the service. The fourfold shape, and the unity of the eucharistic prayer from initial greeting to doxology, have been extremely widely adopted. The prevailing theological idea now is that it is the whole prayer that consecrates. This is seen as a return to primitive practice away from the widely, though erroneously, held belief that the 1662 rite witnesses to a seventeenth-century Anglican belief in a moment of consecration. Manual acts in the institution narrative have all but disappeared, for the same reason, namely that they are held to teach a moment of consecration at this point. Had it been realised that their seventeenth-century rationale was quite other than this, namely a repetition of Christ's actions as part of the validation of the whole rite, perhaps they might not have become so unfashionable. It is true that in the twentieth century the fourfold shape is now interpreted in much the same way as manual acts were in the seventeenth, but, nevertheless, it is undoubtedly true that this venerable Anglican tradition is now being discarded because of an all but universal mistake concerning the original significance of the acts; retention in the Scottish family of rites should surely have provided a clue as to what this was.

Nevertheless, all these rites do contain the institution narrative, and no-one has anywhere suggested framing a rite that does not include it; rather the contrary. Both pan-Anglican documents demand it. The institution narrative is now seen as an important, indeed vital, feature of the one eucharistic prayer, informing and interpreting the meaning of the whole,[54] which is in fact how Anglicans had understood it in the seventeenth century. In this respect Anglicanism has been truer to itself than it has in fact realised!

Another characteristic common to most of these modern eucharistic prayers is that they include a petition concerned with the operation of the Holy Spirit in the sacramental act. The place of this petition varies, the 1549 and the 'Scottish' being the commonest; and so does its contents, from being a fairly specific request for the hallowing of the elements[55] to a general prayer for the communicants expressed in fairly vague terms.[56] The prayer in the Series 3 English rite is probably fairly typical here.[57] This recognition of the work of the Holy Spirit in the eucharistic action is very welcome, and provides another link with the Scottish tradition, which has long recognised this, even if most people would now wish to modify the precise form in which it was originally expressed.

The ecumenical setting of modern liturgical scholarship, and the increasing mutual regard and understanding between the various wings of Anglicanism have greatly contributed to the harmonious process of much recent liturgical revision. Nevertheless, points of tension do remain, particularly in connection with the anamnesis, in England and other areas that have hitherto had a mainly 1662 tradition. The English debates on Series 2 demonstrated this very clearly.[58] The final result, could be argued, was the compromise of the Series 3 text; opinions as to how satisfactory these English anamnesis prayers are, differ widely, even among 'catholic' Anglicans.[59] Given the balance within the Church of England, which the author would argue originates from the deliberate ambiguity imported into the 1559 rite (in the joining together of the 1549 and 1552 forms of administration) for political reasons, such an outcome is inevitable. The price of being comprehensive is the inhibition of certain liturgical and other developments, one of these being a fully expressed eucharistic oblation in the anamnesis. This latter has always existed in the Scottish tradition, so this problem does not exist there.

Another area of difficulty is supplementary consecration, about which the Anglican Communion as a whole seems very confused,[60] as the length and indecision of the consultations on the subject and the enormous variety of the actual liturgical provisions made in the various rites[61] both demonstrate. In spite of requests for guidance, the only thing approaching a definitive statement on the subject is to be found in the

English Liturgical Commission Commentary on Series 3.[62] This unfortunately contains a number of serious errors. Their basic principle of bringing extra elements into the eucharistic action and associating them with that already consecrated is satisfactory, given that the legitimacy of the process is admitted in the first place.[63] It is the claim that there is 'good historical precedent' for this that is dubious, either silently or with a form of words. We have seen that there is no historical precedent at all for supplementary consecration in pre-Reformation liturgy, the practices involving consecration by commixture being other than this, and in any case they were more than a 'taking in silence'. Wine only could be consecrated in this way, and definite mixing, physical contact, was involved, the consecratory agent being either already consecrated bread or wine. The only precedent for a 'brief form of words' is the 1662 one (the 1764 form can hardly be described as 'brief'), and this the Commission regarded as a bad precedent, not a good one, because in their view 1662 taught a moment of consecration at the institution narrative; as has already been demonstrated, they have misunderstood the seventeenth century on this point. In actual fact, the reasons by which the Commission justify their form are equivalent to the way in which the seventeenth-century authors of the 1662 procedure understood what they were doing;[64] and happily the form actually authorized in Series 3 (and 1 and 2 Revised) is quite adequate and satisfactory for its purpose. Given the very different rites from which they come, the 1662 and Series 3 forms can really be considered as equivalents. Nevertheless, it is suggested that consideration might be given to the use of consecration by commixture to make good a deficiency in the chalice; if this were adopted, care would have to be taken to frame any rubric devised to give effect to this to ensure that the fresh wine be added while the chalice still contained an adequate quantity of the originally consecrated wine.

(iii) Conclusions

In general it may be said that for the most part Anglican eucharistic development since 1764 has operated within the parameters defined by the 1662 and 1764 traditions, and has consisted to a greater or lesser degree in both their conservation and mingling together. The ideas imported by the Oxford Movement do not seem to have altered this balance in respect of the texts of the rites themselves, except for a few, mainly local vernacular, rites produced by Anglo-Catholics. (This is of course not true in matters of ceremonial.) Even in the modern period, with its much more prolific and varied liturgical development, this seems to be true as far as the range of theological ideas employed and expressed is concerned. Thus the conclusion is that, with few and minor exceptions, Anglican eucharistic theology and liturgical development has been defined by and continues to live within the traditions it has inherited from the eighteenth century.

CHAPTER TWELVE

General Conclusions

It was stated in the introduction that the starting point of this study was an investigation of the practice of supplementary consecration, and that it was discovered very early on that this was something only done by Anglicans. One of the questions that this study has sought to answer therefore is why this should be. The study itself led into an investigation of the developing and changing theologies of eucharistic consecration in the Roman and Anglican traditions from the eighth to the twentieth centuries, and at every point the issue of supplementary consecration has proved exceedingly illuminating to the main theme. The fundamental starting point therefore becomes the Roman rite of the eighth century and its theology.

In the eighth century the rite was seen as an organic corporate whole, all of whose parts cohere in an inseparable unity, whose individual parts are not subject to analysis as such. And when the analytically precise theology of the later Middle Ages, with its extremely closely defined theology of consecration, evolved, it did not displace this earlier theology, but co-existed somewhat uneasily alongside it. As always, the liturgical tradition was more conservative than the theological, and so the viewpoint that the eucharistic action could only be performed in its entirety or not at all prevailed. Hence, even though the consecration theology of the Roman rite in the high Middle Ages and later might suggest that supplementary consecration by institution narrative alone was a logical and natural development, no such development took place; on the contrary it was and has always remained strictly forbidden, proof of the determinative influence of the earlier unitary theological tradition.

The general outlook of the Eastern churches was similar to that of the eighth-century Roman, namely that the eucharistic action was a unitary indivisible whole that could only be performed as such. On the whole, Eastern eucharistic theology has never gone through the analytical highly developed forms that Western eucharistic theology has, and has remained nearer to its original style. Therefore the Eastern churches too do not admit supplementary consecration; instinctively so, rather than explicitly and canonically.

When specific doctrines of consecration began to develop in the West, considerable variation of belief existed as to what could actually consecrate, different people seeming to hold to different points of view at different times. These different beliefs included a variety of verbal forms, various portions of the Canon, and also in some instances the Lord's Prayer, as well as consecration by commixture. With regard to the latter it should be noted that the various forms of commixture practiced did not constitute supplementary consecration, but were a regular and normal way in which wine was consecrated in the rites concerned. (Only wine can be consecrated by commixture, but the consecrating agent can be either consecrated bread or wine.) It is also to be noted that these commixture practices have not been regarded as providing precedents for supplementary consecration in this way anywhere in Anglicanism until very recent years, and certainly no Anglican in the period 1548-1764 seems even to have referred to them; the presumption would seem to be that they had no knowledge of them in any case.

By the high Middle Ages Western theology had linked the actual consecration exclusively to the recitation of the institution narrative. At the same time extreme scrupulosity developed both concerning the detailed performance of the rite and the care with which the consecrated element had to be handled. This led to detailed consideration being given to possible defects that might arise during the course of a celebration, and how to correct them. And the principle evolved that the relevant portion of the institution narrative should be recited over a fresh supply of bread and/or wine as necessary to correct the defect in the celebration. The purpose of this was to preserve the integrity and unity of the rite, to ensure the completeness of each celebration. The older theology that the rite was a unity that must always be performed as such provided the impetus that led to methods being evolved to preserve that unity from possible defects; the newer theology that the essential forms for the consecration were simply and only the appropriate parts of the institution narrative provided the means for correcting these defects. Nevertheless, in the Middle Ages, as in the Roman rite to this day, such a separate second use of part of the institution narrative was limited to the correction of defects. It was, and is, never used to remedy an accidental shortage of elements arising in the giving of communion, something that is wholly forbidden and probably regarded as being quite invalid by most exponents of the Latin rite. Thus supplementary consecration in the Anglican sense has never been part of the Latin liturgical tradition. Theories of eucharistic consecration in general remained essentially medieval at Trent and subsequently, and this still seems to be the official view. But the post-Vatican II revolution in liturgical practice in the Latin rite, and developments in modern Roman Catholic liturgical and sacramental theology, seem in actuality to be leading to very considerable changes in this area.

Returning to Anglican developments, it is thus evident that the 1548 provision for supplementary consecration of the chalice was a radical liturgical innovation, just as was the general communion of the people from the chalice. It was probably the small size of medieval chalices that made this provision a practical necessity. History has left no records as to why the originators of this provision inserted it in the form they did, or how they understood it theologically, and so these things can only be assessed by conjecture. But such conjecture is not difficult. The medieval cautels provided an obvious precedent, and they were simply adapted to the new use of providing for supplementary consecration in the Anglican sense; the medieval definition of the consecratory form provided the justification for the 1548 form of supplementary consecration. This conjecture amounts to no more than guesswork, but in the absence of facts an attempt at an intelligent guess is all that can be made here, and it is submitted that some such reasoning is the most likely source for the supplementary consecration provision of the 1548 Order. If this is the case, it has two important consequences. The first of these is that the older unitary theology of the rite had now been lost sight of or abandoned, and that those who framed this provision saw no theological obstacle to the performance of a small part of the eucharistic rite in isolation. The second consequence is that the existence of this provision is a strong piece of evidence in favour of the view that official English eucharistic theology was going through some kind of undefined but definite 'real presence' phase at the time when this order was being prepared and published.

The supplementary consecration provision was omitted from the 1549 rite. When all the available evidence concerning the theological intentions of this rite from the time at which it was enacted by Parliament and published is balanced together, the most probable conclusion is that its theological intention was a 'reformed' one. The omission of the supplementary consecration provision would thus seem to have been deliberate, and an important piece in the somewhat fragmentary chain of evidence that leads to this conclusion in the first place. Having been left out in 1549, it naturally continued to be omitted in 1552, and its omission from both rites is one of the pieces of evidence in favour of the view that the declared intention of the 1552 Act of Uniformity with regard to the 1552 rite — that it 'made plain' 1549 — is an honest one and factually correct.

The situation in the reign of Elizabeth I is rather more difficult to fathom. No supplementary consecration provision appeared in the 1559 Prayer Book, which made only a few cautious steps away from the very negative theology associated with the Edwardine liturgical revolution. Furthermore, the Johnson case appears to have been an isolated incident, no apparent attempt being made to publicise or enforce its ruling at any time during the rest of the reign of Elizabeth; in view of the severity with which Johnson was dealt, this is very curious. The Commissioners' examination at his trial shows that they were still thinking about consecration in basically medieval terms, whatever their doctrine of the presence might have been; it was the joining of the institution narrative to the bread and wine that made them sacramental, and this has to be done independently of their use in communion. It follows therefore that they had completely lost sight of the older unitary theology of the rite. This case is also evidence that the Commissioners had rejected a fully reformed theology of the eucharist, something Johnson implicitly charged them with by quoting Cranmer in his own defence, which is evidence too as to how Cranmer was understood near his own day. It is interesting that they were still sufficiently close to the medieval period to do this in a wholly medieval way. A distinctively Anglican theology had scarcely begun to emerge at this point. What remains an unsolved puzzle is the dichotomy between the severe sentence on Johnson, and the apparent lack of any attempt to publicise or enforce the decision reached in his case.

There seems no doubt that Bancroft was the man responsible for the insertion of the supplementary consecration provision into the Canons of 1604. It was probably put in as an anti-puritan measure, but beyond this there is no firm evidence as to precisely why it was inserted at this time Still less is there evidence as to how Bancroft or the Convocation of 1604 really understood it theologically. However there is quite definite evidence as to how the provision of canon 21 of 1604 was understood in the half century or so following this date, and how this relates to the prevailing doctrine of consecration in this period.

The keynote of the theology of consecration prevalent in the first half of the seventeenth century is Hooker's idea that consecration is the hallowing by solemn benediction to the sacred use of communion. The hallowing by solemn benediction was achieved by the reciting of a consecration prayer, a prayer that was to include a petition of invocation or blessing upon the elements to this end, together with a recital of the institution narrative which, by the repetition of Christ's action, provided the pledge and guarantee that this might be the case. Within the context of a rite containing such a prayer, a second consecration of a necessary additional supply of bread or wine can be achieved simply by the recitation of the institution narrative, because the latter was seen as transferring the whole of the effect of all the prayers of the rite to the newly-brought supply. Bishop Morton seems to be the only person to have specifically articulated this theology, but assessment of all the other evidence from the period leaves little doubt that his was the generally received viewpoint. It is the only explanation that accounts for all the facts and avoids the need to suppose blunders or inconsistencies in the composition of some early seventeenth-century eucharistic rites, notably that of 1637, for by it supplementary consecration by institution narrative alone is a valid use with any rite, whatever the content of the full consecration prayer of that rite. It is suggested that this was the rationale of supplementary consecration in the minds of the 1662 revisers when they framed the present rubric.

This prevailing viewpoint of consecration seems to have been very widely adhered to in the first half of the seventeenth-century, both among Anglicans and moderate puritans, north and south of the border. Indeed there is a century of approximately parallel development in both countries common to adherents of both ecclesiastical polities, from Cranmer and Knox to the Caroline divines and Baxter.

This basic unity of outlook was obscured by their bitter divisions over the issues of church polity and ceremonial, and these issues contained within themselves the seeds of doctrinal and other developments that in the centuries after the Restoration were to drive Anglican and nonconformist eucharistic theology wide apart.

Within this prevailing unity over the fundamentals of eucharistic theology there were of course considerable differences of detail and emphasis, and also in terms of the actual content of the prayers of their rites. However, all the major rites in the early seventeenth century are to be seen as different expressions of the same basic theology, rather than of different theologies. In particular, and of some importance for later developments, the consecration prayer of 1637 was not seen as the embodiment of a different theology from that of 1604 as interpreted in accordance with the ideas of the early seventeenth century, but as a 'more solemn and full' expression of the same theology. Thus though Anglicans had begun to know about and use some Eastern-type material in this period, they were interpreting this as supporting evidence for their own theological ideas rather than adopting Eastern theology along with Eastern prayers. This did not come until the post -Restoration period.

Thus it cannot be said on the basis of its practice in regard to supplementary consecration that, in spite of differences of doctrinal explanation, English usage of consecration remained uniform and 'Western' during this period. There are two reasons for this. First, that prevailing Anglican doctrines concerning consecration and the presence were so different from current Roman ones that it really does not seem sensible to equate the two. Second, that since the Roman rite does not allow the practice of supplementary consecration at all, any comparison is invalid.

In the century between 1662 and 1764 two distinctive traditions of Anglican eucharistic theology evolved from the broadly based but basically uniform theology of the earlier period. The first of these is associated with the 1662 rite, and it is to a considerable extent the consequence of this rite's existence. Its characteristics are a memorialist view of the eucharistic sacrifice, a real receptionist view of the presence, and the view that consecration is effected by a prayer that must include the institution narrative. It continued to use the 1662 rubric for supplementary consecration apparently without qualm, and in general remained much closer to the eucharistic theology of the pre-Restoration era than did that of the 1718-1764 school.

The characteristics of this latter school are a belief that the eucharist is an objective Godward pleading of Christ's sacrifice, that the essential consecratory part of the eucharistic prayer is the institution narrative-oblation-epiclesis sequence, and that there is an objective and permanent real presence associated with the elements and brought about by the Holy Spirit making the bread and wine to be in power, virtue, and effect the body and blood of Christ. This eucharistic theology became the majority viewpoint among Scottish Episcopalians, and was adhered to by an important minority in the English Church. It was built upon the foundations laid by the 'higher' of the Caroline divines, and was worked out in precision and depth by a comparatively small group of learned liturgists much under the influence of certain Eastern rites, notably the 'Clementine' liturgy, who not only adopted the prayers of this liturgy for their own use, but under its influence evolved something akin to its genuine native theology. They interpreted the 1549 and 1637 rites in accordance with this theology, thus understanding them in a way significantly different from the interpretations attached to them in the pre-Restoration era. The rites of 1718 and 1764 are the designed liturgical expression of this school of Anglican eucharistic theology.

With the emergence of these two schools of eucharistic theology there evolved two different traditions of supplementary consecration. By the early eighteenth century, the theological rationale that the early seventeenth century had used with the institution narrative method had been very largely forgotten, though the 1689 proposals represent an interesting halfway stage between these two eras by demonstrating that the explanation of the earlier period was still understood and accepted, but was no longer regarded as being the best method. In fact the 1689 proposals present a move towards supplementary consecration by a form that is a miniature equivalent of the whole consecration prayer. This was the method advocated by the 1718-1764 school of thought, when it allowed the practice at all. The rite of 1764 made supplementary consecration mandatory in both kinds, and ordered the whole of the institution narrative-oblation-epiclesis sequence to be repeated. So the 1764 method of supplementary consecration in effect consists of repetition of all the essentials of the eucharistic action; almost a complete new eucharist within the original eucharist in fact. Thus by the middle of the eighteenth century two distinct traditions of supplementary consecration had evolved within Anglicanism, respectively associated with the two major traditions of Anglican eucharistic liturgy and theology. The first, associated with the 1662 rite, repeats a small portion only of the consecration prayer, the institution narrative, and regards this as linking the new bread and wine to the whole of the eucharistic prayers of the rite. The second, associated with the 1764 rite, consists in effect of a complete new eucharistic action in miniature; a separate complete consecration is performed over the fresh supply of bread and wine.

Though this analysis seems to be the only one to be true and consistent to the facts, it is not claimed that this is how it was understood at the time; indeed it seems quite certain that the early seventeenth-century rationale of supplementary consecration has been very largely lost sight of from about the year 1700 to the present day. The theologians of the 1718-1764 school were highly critical of the 1662 method of supplementary consecration, maintaining that it proved the Church of England to hold to the same doctrine of consecration as the Roman, an interpretation in which they have been followed from that day to this. Nor is this surprising, since if the 1662 rite is allowed to be self-interpreting, if the theology of the 1662 revisers is not understood, and further if it is not realised that the Roman rite regards such a practice as illegitimate, this is the most obvious conclusion for someone reading the book to draw. Nevertheless, it has been shown above to be a false conclusion, and one that has had highly misleading consequences for Anglican eucharistic theology. Nor is it clear how the followers of the 1662 tradition interpreted this matter in the early eighteenth century, since they do not seem to have felt the need to comment on it. Waterland certainly does not.

And so by 1764 the classical period of Anglican eucharistic development was over. For the next two centuries the only fresh ingredient added to the mixture was an infusion of Roman ideas in the wake of the Oxford Movement. And the 1662 method of supplementary consecration was taken by the followers of the Oxford Movement as valuable evidence that the eucharistic doctrine of the Prayer Book was sound and Western; a natural enough conclusion for them to draw, given that its original rationale had been lost. But it added a further powerful vested interest to an interpretation of it current since about 1700.

In the first sixty years of this century a considerable number of revised Anglican eucharistic rites were produced. Analysis of them demonstrates that their theologies can be seen as a mixture of ideas from the 1662 and 1718-1764 traditions. Roman ideas and material appear to have had very little effect on the actual texts of these rites, except for a few, mainly vernacular, rites produced in missionary dioceses; this is of course not true in matters of ceremonial, where the opposite is the case. Since the mid-1960s Anglican liturgy has increasingly set out upon radically new paths. In terms of the wording and structure of these new rites Cranmerian material has been very largely abandoned, so in this respect 1964 may be taken as the date of the end of an era in Anglican eucharistic liturgy much as 1764 was. The range of theological ideas expressed and operating in these new rites still seems to be very largely defined by the parameters of the two traditions that had evolved by the middle of the eighteenth century.

And just as Anglican liturgies, as they developed as a whole in the century since the mid-1860s, may be analysed largely as a fusion and interplay between the two basic Anglican traditions, so the enormous variety of provisions for supplementary consecration that have been set forth may certainly be so analysed. All in some way or other may be seen as deriving from the 1662 method or the 1764 method, and sometimes partly from both, though this is not to suggest that their various authors consciously derived them in this way; indeed, it would seem quite certain that they did not. The great variety of supplementary consecration provisions in Anglicanism indicates that a great deal of thinking on the subject has been muddled and confused; that the theological problems involved in the concept have not been properly worked out; and that the rationales behind both the 1662 method and the 1764 method have been largely lost to sight.

Finally, the question posed at the beginning of this chapter may now be answered. Supplementary consecration arose in Anglicanism, and practically nowhere else, because it alone among the major traditions of Christendom combines a belief that specific consecration of the bread and wine as such is necessary (implicitly so since 1559, explicitly so since 1604, with a brief anticipation of this outlook in 1548) with a belief that all present at every celebration must be able to communicate if they so wish, and really ought to do so. Given this combination of beliefs, supplementary consecration becomes a necessity, because there can never be an absolute guarantee that the celebrant will not underestimate the quantity of bread and wine he needs.

Can any general conclusion be drawn from this study about the Anglican practice of Supplementary Consecration? The major Catholic traditions of Christendom, West and East, regard the practice as invalid and forbid it; and certainly, when the universal belief in the indivisible unity of the eucharistic rite is recovered, it is seen to be a theologically questionable practice. And yet these two characteristics in Anglicanism that gave rise to it in the first place, together with nearly four centuries of usage within Anglicanism, would make its abandonment quite impossible now. Assuming the practice to be accepted, the method finally evolved for the Series 3 English rite seems quite satisfactory, and is actually in harmony with the way the 1662 method was understood by those who incorporated it in the rites of 1637 and 1662. In addition, perhaps one would wish to argue for commixture as an allowable alternative method for the chalice. It would also be possible to speculate whether the Romans, with increasingly widespread general communion at most masses, together with a decreasing reliance on the tabernacle, could even be led to alter their own rules and adopt it themselves. The question could be posed as to whether communion within the eucharist from the tabernacle also violates the principle of the unity of the eucharistic rite, but that is another problem.

APPENDIX

Liturgical Provision for Supplementary Consecration

Supplementary consecration is a peculiarly Anglican practice, and so this survey is limited to Anglican rites, with the exception of a few rites that have been produced for United Churches with Anglican participation. The information set out below has been compiled from a variety of sources, and so it seems useful to gather it all together in one place for ease of reference.

(i) English rites

The 1548 Order of Communion made provision for supplementary consecration for wine only:

The priest after the first Cup or chalice be emptied, may go again to the altar, and reverently, and devoutly, prepare, and consecrate another, and so the third, or more likewise, beginning at these words, *Simili modo* . . . [1]

The Prayer Books of 1549,[2] 1552,[3] 1559,[4] and 1604[5] made no provision. However, canon 21 of 1604 ordered:

no bread or wine newly brought shall be used; but first the Words of Institution shall be rehearsed, when the said bread and wine be present on the Communion-Table.[6]

The Prayer Book of 1662 embodied the above principle into a rubric printed immediately after the formulae for administration which states:

If the consecrated Bread or Wine be all spent before all have communicated, the Priest is to consecrate more according to the form before prescribed; beginning at 'Our Saviour Christ in the same night, &c.' for the blessing of the bread; and at 'Likewise after Supper, &c.' for the blessing of the Cup.

The non-jurors' rite of 1718 makes no provision.[7]

The Prayer Book of 1928 reprinted the 1662 rite verbatim, and so included the above rubric. The 1928 rite as such also permits supplementary consecration in each kind, and directs that the 1662 quotations from the institution narrative are to be used, following in both cases with a paragraph which is a literal verbatim adaptation of the epiclesis section of the 1928 Canon, only varied as necessary to allow for consecration in one kind alone.[8]

Series 1 makes no provision, but as this was produced to legalise existing practices of deviation from 1662, there is a presumption that the 1662 method is to be used.[9]

In the draft of Series 2 published in the Liturgical Commission Report the following rubric appeared:

If during the delivery the consecrated bread or wine be all spent, and there be none to deliver to the people, the Priest shall place both bread and wine upon the Holy Table and shall read the prayer of consecration, beginning at 'Hear us, O Father . . .' and ending at 'through the same Christ our Lord . . .'[10]

In Series 2 as eventually published, this provision was deleted and no provision was made.[11]

In the draft of Series 1 and 2 Revised published in the Liturgical Commission Report the following rubric appears:

If either or both of the consecrated elements are likely to prove insufficient, the priest returns to the holy table and adds more, with these words: 'Having given thanks to thee, O Father, over the bread and cup according to the institution of thy Son, Jesus Christ, who said, "Take, eat; this is my body", (and/or "Drink this; this is my blood") we pray that this bread (and/or wine) also may be to us his body (and/or blood), and be received in remembrance of him.'[12]

In the draft of Series 3 published in the Liturgical Commission Report the following rubric appears:

If either or both of the consecrated elements are likely to prove insufficient, the president returns to the holy table and adds more, either in silence or with these words: 'Having given thanks to you, Father, over the bread and the cup as your Son our Lord Jesus Christ commanded, we receive this bread/wine also as his body/blood.'[13]

In the service as finally approved the option to add in silence was deleted and the form of words altered to:

'Having given thanks to you, Father, over the bread and the cup according to the institution of your Son, Jesus Christ, who said, "Take, eat; this is my body", (and/or "Drink this; this is my blood") we pray that this bread/wine also may be to us his body/blood, and be received in remembrance of him'[14]

Linguistic style apart, this is virtually identical to the form proposed in Series 1 and 2 Revised, and so clearly this form is intended to be the standard form for supplementary consecration in the Church of England in the future.

(ii) The Scottish rite to 1764

The Scottish rite of 1637 made provision as follows, in a rubric printed at the end of the service:

And to the end that there may be little left, he that officiates is required to consecrate with the least, and then if there be want, the words of consecration may be repeated over again, over more either bread or wine: the Presbyter beginning at these words in the Prayer of Consecration (Our Saviour, in the night that he was betrayed, took, etc.).[15]

This is the '1662 method'.

The Scottish rite of 1764 ordered:

If the consecrated bread or wine be all spent before all have communicated, the Presbyter is to consecrate more, according to the form before prescribed, beginning at the words, 'All glory be to thee, &c.' and ending with the words, 'that they may become the body and blood of thy most dearly beloved Son'.[16]

Thus a second consecration in one kind is not permitted, and the whole of the institution narrative – oblation – epiclesis sequence must be said when the necessity for a second consecration arises.

(iii) Other Anglican rites

At present there are somewhat more than 60 different eucharistic rites officially in use or proposed in the Anglican Communion, and the provisions they make for supplementary consecration differ widely, but there are various sub-divisions and classifications that may be made. In such a complex and rapidly developing field as this, it is difficult to be certain of completeness, but it is hoped and thought that no important Anglican rite extant at the time of writing[17] has been omitted from the following survey.

Two major divisions may be made here. First, there are those rites that are derived from 1662 without significant alteration, 'significant' in this context meaning that there is no change in the basic shape of the service or in the wording and structure of the prayer of consecration. These rites are the 1929 Scottish Recension,[18] the 1926 Irish Liturgy,[19] the 1918 Canadian Liturgy,[20] the 1960 Indian Recension,[21] and the 1966 and 1972 Australian Recensions. All of these print the 1662 rubric without change except the two Australian versions, which both contain a general rubric requiring the observance of all the rubrics of the 1662 rite during their celebration.[22]

Secondly, there are those rites that are significantly different from 1662 both in their structure and in the content of their Canons, and this embraces all the rest of the Anglican rites not already described. Between them six basically different provisions are made for supplementary consecration, and these are set in detail in paragraphs A-F following.

A. Permission for a second consecration in either kind, using the relevant portion of the institution narrative only, as 1662: the 1960 Indian Rite,[23] and the 1966 Welsh Rite.[24] To these may be added the 1929 South African Rite, which permits this as an alternative.[25]

B. Permission for a second consecration in either kind, using the relevant portion of the institution narrative, together with a small amount of supplementary material of no great theological significance. This converts the simple recitation of the institution narrative into a short prayer of thanksgiving containing the same. Rites in this category are the 1967 Irish,[26] the 1959 Canadian,[27] the 1964 Liturgy for Africa,[28] the East African United Liturgy,[29] the 1966 Australian Rite,[30] the 1967 Iran Rite,[31] the 1972 Irish Liturgy,[32] the 1973 Australian Liturgy.[33] The 1971 Iran Liturgy uses this as an alternative.[34]

C. Those which permit supplementary consecration in either kind, but which prescribe forms that contain significantly more than the appropriate part of the institution narrative: the 1957 Hong Kong Rite,[35] the Madagascan Rite,[36] the West Indian Rite,[37] and the Melanesian Rite.[38] All the new American (PECUSA) Rites,[39] and the 1975 South African Rite[40] have this as one of their alternatives. In all cases the material in these forms additional to the institution narrative is a direct adaptation as appropriate of the same material from their main consecration prayer.

D. Those that direct that supplementary consecration must always be in both kinds, and prescribe a form containing more than the institution narrative: the 1929 Scottish Rite,[41] the 1928 American,[42] the 1929 South African Rite as one of its permitted alternatives,[43] the 1938 Ceylon Liturgy,[44] the Japanese Rite,[45] and the 1973 Korean Liturgy.[46] All the

new American (PECUSA) Rites,[39] and the 1975 South African Rite[40] have this as one of their alternatives. In all these cases the forms prescribed derive logically from the main eucharistic prayers of the rites concerned.

E. Those that direct that supplementary consecration may be in either kind, and prescribe a form that does not include the institution narrative. The 1967 American Liturgy,[47] and the Brazilian Liturgies of 1967[48] and 1972[49] all have forms consisting of epiclesis prayers alone, which are much stronger pleas for consecration than the epiclesis sections in their full consecration prayers. C.O. Buchanan called attention to this oddity in respect of the first two of these rites.[50] The Brazilian Church has derived a lot from the American, hence presumably this similarity.

The following liturgies use what may be described as a 'taking and declaring' form: the 1966[51] and 1970[52] New Zealand Rites, the 1969 Australian Rite,[53] and the 1971 Iran Rite as one of its permitted alternatives.[54]

F. The following rites make no explicit provision: the Chile Liturgy of 1967,[55] the United Liturgy of the 'Church of Nigeria' of 1965,[56] the 1966 Scottish Rite,[57] the 1965 Hong Kong Rite,[58] the Nyasaland and Northern Rhodesian Liturgies,[59] the Swahili Mass,[60] the 1939 Korean Liturgy,[61] the 1973/4 Tanzanian Liturgy,[62] the 1972 Welsh Study Liturgy,[63] the 1974 Canadian Rite,[64] the 1969 South African Rite,[65] the 1973 Kuching Liturgy,[66] and the 1970 New Guinea Rite.[67] There is room for speculation in almost every case as to the reason for this lack of provision.[68]

(iv) Ecumenical rites produced for United Churches with Anglican participation

Both the original version[69] and the 1972 version[70] of the South India Rite order either the '1662' or the 'taking and declaring' method. The Church of Pakistan uses the South India rite, but permits only the '1662 method' of supplementary consecration.[71] The Church of North India uses the English Series 3 rubric verbatim.[72]

Notes

INTRODUCTION

1. First published 1901; third corrected edition 1905.
2. First published 1932.
3. Published 1969.
4. Published 1961 to 1970. Unfortunately the second volume in the series, planned to deal with the period 1603-1690, had not appeared at the time of writing (November 1975).
5. Published 1942.
6. Published 1941.
7. Published 1908.
8. Published 1935.
9. Published 1971.

CHAPTER ONE

1. L.C. Mohlberg's edition of the manuscript *Vaticanus Reginensis* 316, the Gelasian Sacramentary, in the series *Rerum Ecclesiasticarum Documenta (Series Maior Fontes IV)*, the prayers numbered 1242-1255. The prayers of the sacramentary are numbered consecutively in this edition, and it is to these numbers that the numbers in the text and the footnotes refer.
2. J.A. Jungmann, *The Mass of the Roman Rite,* Vol.II, 151-152.
3. *Ibid.,* 167.
4. Mohlberg, op. cit., 195.
5. *Ibid.,* 370, 379.
6. Jungmann, op. cit., Vol.II, 185.
7. Jungmann, op. cit., Vol.II 260; ed. L.C. Mohlberg, in the series *Rerum Ecclesiasticarum Documenta (Series Maior Fontes I)*, prayer number 205.
8. Jungmann, op. cit., Vol.II, 261; Mohlberg, op. cit., 381.
9. Lietzmann argued this viewpoint in his *Mass and the Lord's Supper.* See chapter 8, p.97 (Fascicle 2).
10. *Prex Eucharistica,* passim. See also R.C.D. Jasper and G.J. Cuming, *Prayers of the Eucharist; Early and Reformed,* passim.
11. *De Sacramentis,* Book IV, Section V, paragraph 21; ed. H. Chadwick p.34.
12. Ellebracht, *Remarks on the Vocabulary of the Ancient Orations in the Missale Romanum.*
13. *Ibid.,* 163.
14. *Ibid.,* 80.
15. *Ibid.,* 77.
16. *Ibid.,* 75.

17. *Ibid.*, 67f.

18. *Ibid.*, 72.

19. *Ibid.*, 88.

20. *Ibid.*, 81.

21. *Ibid.*, 81.

22. *Ibid.*, 83.

23. *Ibid.*, 139; Sr Ellebracht's book actually reads Ps.115 v.7, but this is certainly a misprint for Ps.115 v.17 (Vulgate numbering, Ps.116 v.17 in English versions). Jerome's Latin translation from the Hebrew Psalter of Ps.115 v.17 reads:

    Tibi immolabo hostiam laudis
    Et in nomine Domini invocabo.

    This version of the Psalter was usually displaced in the Vulgate from the time of Alcuin onwards by Jerome's revised translation which he based on the Hexapla, and which reads 'sacrificabo' in place of 'immolabo', but it is clearly the former version, current in the centuries preceding Alcuin, which influenced the Latin liturgical tradition. Note too the phrase 'hostiam laudis'. The source of this information is a recent critical edition of the Vulgate, editor R. Weber, C.S.B., published 1969, introduction, Vol.I, xxi; Psalm texts, Vol.I, 918-919.

24. E.G.C.F. Atchley, *Ordo Romanus Primus,* 136-137; M. Andrieu, *Ordines Romani,* Vol.II, 95, paragraph 87.

25. Ellebracht, op. cit., 76. Used as the secret for Pentecost 9 in the 1570 Missal and, slightly modified, as that for the second Sunday of the year in the 1970 Missal. The translation for this produced by the (R.C.) National Liturgical Commission of England and Wales reads as follows: 'For whenever the memorial of Christ, our sacrifice, is celebrated, the work of our redemption is accomplished'.

26. *Ibid.*, 74.

27. *Ibid.*, 69.

28. *Ibid.*, 166-167.

29. Jungmann, *The Mass of the Roman Rite,* Vol.II, 104, especially footnotes 15 and 16.

30. Andrieu, *Ordines,* Vol.II, 96, paragraph 89.

31. *Ibid.*, p.82, paragraph 48.

32. *Ibid.*, p.91, paragraphs 71 and 73.

33. *Ibid.*, p.92, paragraphs 79 and 80, p.94, paragraph 84.

34. *Ibid.*, p.102-103, paragraphs 108-112.

35. Andrieu, *Immixtio et Consecratio,* Vol.II, 435; Migne, P.L., Vol.LXXXIX, Col.525.

36. L. Duchesne, *Christian Worship, its Origins and Evolution,* English tr., 5th ed., 187.

37. Jungmann, op. cit., Vol.II, 383.

38. Published in *Revue des Sciences Religieuses,* Vols.II,III,IV; 1922, 1923, 1924 respectively: Vol.II, pp.428-226; Vol.III, pp.24-61, 149-182, 283-384, 433-471; Vol.IV, pp.65-96, 265-295, 454-484.

39. Andrieu, *Ordines,* Vol.II, 249, paragraph 67.

40. Andrieu, *Immixtio et Consecratio,* Vol.III, 42-45.

41. Andrieu, *Ordines,* Vol.II, 233-238.

42. Andrieu, *Ordines,* Vol.II, 440; Migne P.L., Vol.CL, Col.1013-1014.

43. Andrieu, *Immixtio et Consecratio,* Vol.II, 442.

44. F.L. Cross, *Oxford Dictionary of the Christian Church,* 41.

45. Mohlberg, op. cit., 63, number 390; 67, number 418.

46. Andrieu, *Immixtio et Consecratio,* Vol.III, 27.

47. Andrieu, *Ordines,* Vol.III, 152, paragraph 35.

48. *Ibid.,* 189, paragraph 97.

49. *Ibid.,* 294, paragraphs 32, 37, 38.

50. Andrieu, *Immixtio et Consecratio,* Vol.III, 37-41.

51. *Ibid.,* 283-304; for an example from the Sarum Missal see Dickinson's ed. col.332; from Hereford, Henderson, *Missale Ad Usum . . . Herfordensis,* 96; from Exeter, Dalton, *Ordinale Exon,* Vol.I, 321.

52. Andrieu, *Immixtio et Consecratio,* Vol.IV, 65-96, 265-275 passim.

53. *Ibid.,* Vol.III, 433-471, passim.

54. See Chapter 4 Section (ii) below.

CHAPTER TWO

1. Q.78 Art.1, reply; this and succeeding references from *Summa Theologica,* Part III.

2. Q.83 Art.1, reply.

3. Q.83 Art.1, reply.

4. Q.81 Art.4.

5. Q.78 Art.1 and Art.3.

6. Q.78 Art.1, reply obj.4.

7. Q.78 Arts. 5 and 6, replies.

8. Q.76 Art.2, reply obj.2; Q.78 Art.3, reply obj.2; Q.74 Art.1, reply

9. Q.74 Art.1, reply obj.2.

10. Q.77 Art.8, reply.

11. Q.83 Art.4, reply obj.6.

12. Q.80 Art.12.

13. Q.80 Art.11, reply.

14. Q.75 passim.

15. Q.77 Art.3, reply.

16. Q.77 Art.7, reply.

17. Q.76 Art.2, reply.

18. Q.80 Art.12.

19. Q.83 Art.6, reply obj.1.

20. Q.83 Art.6, reply obj.2.

21. Q.83 Art.6, reply obj.3.

22. Q.83 Art.6, reply obj.4.

23. Q.83 Art.6, reply obj.5.

24. Q.83 Art.6, reply obj.6.

25. Q.83 Art.6, reply obj.7.

26. W. Maskell, *The Ancient Liturgy of the Church of England,* pp.164-167, for notes on the cautels; pp.168-176, for a reprint of the same from a French missal of 1529.

27. *Missale Romanum 1474,* Henry Bradshaw Society, Ed., Vol.II, p.369f; especially p.372, for those concerned with the correction of defects.

28. W.E. Scudamore, *Notitia Eucharistia,* 2nd Ed., 760-762.

29. See H.R. Gummey's collection of pre-Reformation Latin rite texts on the celebration of the eucharist in his work *The Consecration of the Eucharist.*

30. Gummey, op. cit., 399.

31. *Ibid.,* 398.

32. Gummey, op. cit., 405, quoted from J. Wickham Legg, *Tracts on the Mass,* 116.

33. Wickham Legg, op. cit., xxiv-xxv.

34. T. Cranmer, *On the Lord's Supper,* Parker Society ed., 6; *The Work of,* Courtenay Library edition, 57.

35. But is the comparatively conservative shape and appearance of 1549 evidence that he had a inkling that the rite as such was not wholly to blame for this situation? Did he only come to believe a fully reformed rite as well as a fully reformed theology necessary when 1549 failed to fulfil his expectations of it?

36. Published in *Tracts on the Mass,* ed. J. Wickham Legg, 17-29; see also xv-xvi for a note about the manuscript he used.

37. Published in *Mirk's Festial,* Early English Text Society Edition, ed. T. Erbe, 168-171.

38. Edition published by the Early English Text Society, ed. T.F. Simmons.

CHAPTER THREE

1. Cranmer, *The Work of*, Courtenay Library ed., 231; the text printed in this edition is a literal reproduction of the 1833 Jenkyns edition, Vol.II, 287-463.
2. See Cranmer, op. cit., 230.
3. *Ibid.*, 215.
4. *Ibid.*, 217.
5. *Ibid.*, 217.
6. *Ibid.*, 221.
7. *Ibid.*, 223.
8. *Ibid.*, 57.
9. Cranmer, *On the Lord's Supper*, Parker Society Ed., 36.
10. *Ibid.*, 54.
11. Cranmer, *The Work of*, op. cit., 181.
12. *Ibid.*, 71-72.
13. *Ibid.*, 106.
14. Cranmer, *On the Lord's Supper*, op. cit., 180.
15. Cranmer, *The Work of*, 140.
16. *Ibid.*, 144-5.
17. *Ibid.*, 145.
18. *Ibid.* 146.
19. *Ibid.*, 166.
20. *Ibid.*, 170.
21. *Ibid.*, 181; This is a definition with which the men of the seventeenth century would have concurred; where they differed from Cranmer was in how they understood 'use'. See chapters 4 and 5 below.
22. *Ibid.*, 190.
23. *Ibid.*, 195.
24. *Ibid.*, 213-214.
25. Cranmer, *On the Lord's Supper*, op.cit., 201.
26. See for example a letter he wrote to Vadian in 1537; *Original Letters*, Parker Society, Vol.I, 13-14.
27. In citing these references, I am indebted to P. Brooks' discussion of the problem in his work, *Thomas Cranmer's Doctrine of the Eucharist*.
28. Brooks, op. cit., 43; Cranmer, *Jonas' Catechism*, ed. Burton, 176-7, 2nd pagination.
29. Brooks, op. cit., 44; Cranmer, *Jonas' Catechism*, ed. Burton, 207-8, 1st pagination.

30. Brooks, op. cit., 44-5.

31. Cranmer, *The Work of,* op. cit., 208-9.

32. Cranmer, *On the Lord's Supper,* op. cit., 227.

33. *Ibid.,* 374.

34. This debate is discussed in detail in chapter 3, section vi below.

35. Cranmer, *The Work of,* op. cit., 344-365; where Burbridge's late 19th-century catalogue of it is produced.

36. *Original Letters,* Parker Society, Vol.I, 73.

37. Cranmer, *On the Lord's Supper,* op. cit., 129; Cranmer is here quoting from 'Theodoret's Dialogues', but the quotation is part of his case and thus he has made the sentiment his own.

38. This is also J. Dowden's assessment of Cranmer; see his *Further Studies in the Prayer Book,* 53;

39. H. Gee and W.J. Hardy, *Documents Illustrative of the History of the English Church,* lxvii, 322-8.

40. Ed. D.C. Douglas, *English Historical Documents,* Vol.V, 840-2; E. Cardwell, *Documentary Annals,* Vol.I, V.35-37.

41. C.W. Dugmore, *The Mass and the English Reformers,* 116.

42. This quotation is taken from an original source by F.A. Gasquet and E. Bishop. For their discussion of this topic, see their work *Edward VI and the Book of Common Prayer,* 1891 ed., 74-7.

43. Cardwell, op. cit., Vol.I, No.xiv, 72.

44. Gasquet and Bishop, op. cit., 94-5; H.A. Wilson, *The Order of the Communion 1548,* Henry Bradshaw Society ed., xxiii; F. Procter and W.H. Frere, *The Book of Common Prayer,* 38.

45. Gee and Hardy, op. cit., lxix, 359.

46. Op. cit., 45-52.

47. Op. cit., 134-147.

48. W. Page, 'The First Book of Common Prayer and the Windsor Commission', *Church Quarterly Review,* Vol.XLVII (1924), 51-64.

49. *Ibid.,* 58.

50. T. Fuller, *Church History of Britain,* 368.

51. Page, op. cit., 58 especially footnote 1.

52. Procter and Frere, op. cit., 60-1.

53. See Procter and Frere, op. cit., 40,46; and Page, op. cit., 52-3, for details of the evidence of this. Important examples of official encouragement are to be found in Somerset's Letter to Cambridge University and in the use of English at Farrar's consecration; see Gasquet and Bishop, op. cit., 147, and Procter and Frere, op. cit., 46, respectively.

54. Tomlinson, *The Great Parliamentary Debate,* 13.

55. Gasquet and Bishop, op. cit., 165.

56. Procter and Frere, op. cit., 48.

57. G.J. Cuming, *A History of Anglican Liturgy*, 67.

58. Tomlinson, op. cit., 21-23.

59. *Ibid.*, 25-56. This work is a pamphlet published by J.J. Shaw in 1895 whose full title is: *The First Prayer Book of Edward VI. The Great Parliamentary Debate in 1548 on the Lord's Supper. From the Original MS, now in the British Museum. With an Introduction and Notes by J.J. Tomlinson;* compare Gasquet and Bishop, op. cit.

60. Bodleian Library, *Catalogue of Books printed before 1920*, Vol. Tol-Tom, p.370.

61. See for example Folios 1a, 5b, 6a and b, 8a, Tomlinson, op. cit., 25, 29, 30, 32 respectively.

62. See Folios 5a, b, and 6a, b: *Ibid.*, 29, 30.

63. Folio 5b; Ibid., 29.

64. Cranmer, *On the Lord's Supper*, op. cit., compare p.79 when he says we do not pray this bread and wine 'may be made . . .', with p.271 where in an almost identical sentence, he simply has 'may be . . .'.

65. For example an edition published by Burns, Oates and Washbourne in 1928 has 'become for us', whereas one published by Laverty and Sons in 1936 has 'made for us'.

66. Folio 3a, b, Tomlinson, op. cit., 27: spelling modernised in direct quotations.

67. Fol. 15a, *Ibid.*, 39.

68. Fol. 16a, *Ibid.*, 40.

69. Fol. 29b, *Ibid.*, 53.

70. Fol. 6a, 6b, *Ibid.*, 30.

71. Fol. 7b, *Ibid.*, 31.

72. *Ibid.*, 13.

73. Further contemporary reference to the development of Cranmer's state of mind can be found in the letters of:

Hooper to Bullinger	27.12.1549	P.S.O.L.	71	Ep.Tig.	47*
Hooper to Bullinger	29.6.1550	,,	86	,,	55
Traheron to Bullinger	28.9.1548	,,	321	,,	212
Traheron to Bullinger	31.12.1548	,,	322	,,	213
J. ab Ulmis to Bullinger	27.11.1548	,,	381	,,	252
J. ab Ulmis to Bullinger	18.8.1548	,,	379	,,	250

J. ab Ulmis to
Bullinger   2.3.1549   „   386   „   255

*The original Latin of which the *Original Letters* print an English translation. The same comments and reservations apply to what is said in these letters as to what is said in similar letters about the 1549 Prayer Book, see Page 3/33.

P.S.O.L. – *Original Letters*, Parker Society.

Ep.Tig. – *Epistolae Tigurinae*, Parker Society.

74. *The First and Second Prayer Books of King Edward VI*, Everyman Ed., 219: spelling modernised.

75. *Liturgies of King Edward VI*, Parker Society Ed., 4.

76. *The First and Second Prayer Books of King Edward VI*, op. cit., 222.

77. Cranmer, *On the Lord's Supper*, op. cit., 79 and 271.

78. Apart from the number of the verb; but this is explained very simply by the fact that *fiat* qualifies *oblationem* in the singular, whereas the English verb qualifies (gifts).

79. F.E. Brightman, *Liturgies Eastern and Western*, lxxxiii – lxxxv.

80. Cranmer, *The Work of*, op. cit., 188.

81. Brightman, op. cit., 329.

82. $ευ'λογαω$ and $'αγιαζεω$ only occur in the same sentence twice in the LXX, namely at Genesis 2.3 and Exodus 20.11, both references being about the Sabbath. The two sentences are very similar; their form and content does not suggest that the wording of the Byzantine Epiclesis prayer is in any sense dependent upon them.

83. *Further Studies in the Prayer Book*, 68-70.

84. In 'The Liturgical Work of Archbishop Cranmer', *Journal of Ecclesiastical History*, Vol.VII (1956), 199; and in his article 'Christian Worship and Liturgy', 454, footnote 3, in *The Study of Theology*, ed. K.E. Kirk.

85. In 'The New Prayer Book Examined', *Church Quarterly Review*, Vol.CIV (1927), 236f.

86. See chapters 6, 8 and 9.

87. F.H. Dickinson, *Missale ad Usum Sarum*, col. 615.

88. C.S. Cobb, *The Rationale of Ceremonial, 1541-3*, 25 and 26.

89. E.C. Ratcliff, 'The English Usage of Eucharistic Consecration, 1548-1662', *Theology*, Vol.LX (1957), 231.

90. See Jungmann, *The Mass of the Roman Rite*, Vol.II, 202, footnote 3, for citation of evidence of this.

91. *The First and Second . . .*, op. cit., 223.

92. C.T. Lewis and C. Short, *A Latin Dictionary*, 1340.

93. *The First and Second . . .*, op. cit., 224.

94. *Ibid.*, 225.

95. *Ibid.*, 225; cf. *Liturgies of King Edward VI*, op. cit., 8, for the 1548 forms.

96. Brightman, *The English Rite*, Vol.II, 700 (1st ed.).

97. *The First and Second . . .*, op. cit., 225, compare *Liturgies of King Edward VI*, op. cit., 8.

98. *The First and Second . . .*, op.cit., 226-227.

99. *Ibid.*, 227.

100. *Ibid.*, 230; cf. *Liturgies of King Edward VI*, op. cit., 8, for the 1548 forms.

101. *The First and Second . . .*, op. cit., 268.

102. However it must be noted that non-communicating attendance was widely regarded as effective as actually receiving communion in the late Middle Ages. See Chapter 2 above.

103. Cranmer, *On the Lord's Supper*, op. cit., 51.

104. *Ibid.*, 79 and 83.

105. *Ibid.*, 229.

106. *Ibid.*, 62.

107. *Ibid.*, 84.

108. *Ibid.*, 51 and 92.

109. Procter and Frere, op. cit., 69.

110. Somerset's letter to Pole dated 4.6.1549; see Procter and Frere, op. cit., 47; Pocock, *Troubles Connected with the Prayer Book of 1549*, x.

111. Hooper to Bullinger, 27.3.1550, P.S.O.L., 79, Ep.Tig. 50.

112. Bucer and Fagius to the Minister of Strasbourg, 26.4.1549, P.S.O.L. 535-6, Ep.Tig. 349.

		P.S.O.L.		Ep.Tig.	
John Butler to Thomas Blaurer	16.2.1550	P.S.O.L.	635	Ep.Tig.	412
Richard Hilles to Bullinger	4.5.1549	„	265	„	174
Francis Dryander to Bullinger	25.3.1549	„	348	„	230
Francis Dryander to Bullinger	5.6.1549	„	350	„	231

See also a sermon preached by Roger Hutchinson, Provost of Eton, *Works*, Parker Society, p.232; cf. Preface vi, vii.

113. *The First and Second . . .*, 385-386.

114. *Ibid.*, 388-389, 255.

115. *Ibid.*, 389, cf. 222-223.

116. *Ibid.*, 389, cf. 225.

117. *Ibid.*, 389.

118. *Ibid.*, 389-390, cf. 223 and 227.

119. *Ibid.*, 392.

120. *Ibid.*, 392-393.

121. *Ibid.*, 423, cf. 268.

122. *Liturgies of King Edward VI*, op. cit., 213-4.

123. See p.84/85 below.

124. Latin original in Strype, *Memorials of Archbishop Cranmer*, appendix LXI, Vol.II, 898 (the 1812 edition); English translation: G.C. Gorham, *Reformation Gleanings*, 227-231.

125. Latin original unpublished. English: Gorham, op. cit., 231.

126. Gorham, op. cit., 229.

127. *Ibid.*, 232.

128. *Ibid.*, 228.

129. Cuming, op. cit., 100; the text of the Censura is now easily available in E.C. Whitaker, *Martin Bucer and the Book of Common Prayer.*

130. Hooper, *Early Writings*, Parker Society ed., 144.

131. *Ibid.*, 535.

132. *Ibid.*, 534.

133. *Ibid.*, 534.

134. *Ibid.*, 479.

135. *Ibid.*, 534.

136. *Ibid.*, 536.

137. Ab Ulmis to Bullinger, 31.12.1550, P.S.O.L., 426; Ep.Tig., 281.

138. Cranmer, *The Work of,* op. cit., xxxix.

139. Hooper, op. cit., 190-2.

140. *Ibid.*, 536.

141. Blunt, *The Annotated Book of Common Prayer,* 1890 ed., 21.

142. *Zurich Letters,* 2nd series, Parker Society ed., 156f.

143. Ed. E. Arber, *A Brief Discourse of the Troubles at Frankfurt,* 75. R.W. Dixon seems to have misread the *Troubles at Frankfurt* in making Bullinger the source of this information, *History of the Church of England,* Vol.IV, 697, especially footnote.

144. *Dictionary of National Biography,* Vol.IX, (1921-2 reprint) 1253f.

145. *Zurich Letters,* 1st series, op. cit., passim.

146. *Zurich Letters,* 2nd series, op. cit., 354f; no date or place of origin in this letter.

CHAPTER FOUR

1. F. Procter and W.H. Frere, *The Book of Common Prayer*, 101, footnote 4; J. Strype, *Annals*, Vol.I, Part 1, chapter 4, 123 (84), (the 1824 edition); E.H. Clay, *Liturgical Services of Queen Elizabeth*, xii-xiv.

2. See G.J. Cuming, *A History of Anglican Liturgy*, 120-123, and Procter and Frere, op. cit., 94-103, for a detailed discussion of this topic with reference to sources.

3. Compare *Liturgies of King Edward VI*, Parker Society Ed., 532-533, with E.J. Bicknell, H.J. Carpenter, *A Theological Introduction to the Thirty Nine Articles of the Church of England*, 351-352.

4. E.C. Ratcliff, 'The English Usage of Eucharistic Consecration', *Theology*, Vol.LX (1957), 276-279.

5. *Ibid.*, 279.

6. E. Cardwell, *Synodalia*, Vol.I, 111-163, passim.

7. In his *Visitation Articles and Injunctions of the Period of the Reformation*, Vol.III, '1559-1575'.

8. In his *Elizabethan Episcopal Administration*, Vols.II and III.

9. The 1868 *Ritual Commission Report,* appendix E, only prints or collates 16 sets of articles or injunctions from the reign of Elizabeth I, all of which are full and important sets; of these 16 sets, 10 were definitely issued after 1573. All 16 sets are contained in the works of Frere and Kennedy, op. cit.

10. *Ritual Commission Report,* op. cit., 421; Kennedy, op. cit., Vol.II, 90.

11. *Ritual Commission Report,* op. cit., 418; Kennedy, op. cit., Vol.II, 48.

12. *Ritual Commission Report,* op. cit., 430; Kennedy, op. cit., Vol.III, 199.

13. *Ritual Commission Report,* op. cit., 436; Kennedy, op. cit., Vol.III, 335; in view of Bancroft's later responsibility in this matter, it is particularly interesting to find no anticipation of the canons of 1604 in these articles.

14. Indeed the prohibition of any addition to the communion rite, which occurs quite frequently in these articles, though no doubt a general one aimed at both popery and puritanism, could be construed as a prohibition of the practice of supplementary consecration, given the text of the 1559 Prayer Book as it stood. However, it is not thought that this was intended to be taken in this way; rather that the authors of these articles simply did not have the matter of supplementary consecration in mind at all.

15. Ratcliff, op. cit., 276.

16. *Ritual Commission Report,* op.cit., 426., Kennedy, op.cit., Vol.III, 146.

17. Jewel, *Works,* Parker Society Ed., Vol.I, 122; quoted by Ratcliff, op. cit., 274.

18. Jewel, *Works,* op. cit., Vol.I, 127; quoted by Ratcliff, op. cit., 275-276.

19. Jewel, *Apology,* J.E. Booty's ed., 33. Booty used as his text Lady Bacon's translation of 1564; see his introduction, xlvi-xlvii.

20. R. Hooker, *Ecclesiastical Polity,* Book V, chapter lvii, section 5; Everyman Ed., p.236-237.

21. *Ibid.,* chapter lxvii, section 1; 319.

22. *Ibid.,* chapter lxvii, section 4; 321-2.

23. *Ibid.,* chapter lxvii, section 5; 322.

24. *Ibid.,* chapter lxvii, section 6; 322-323.

25. *Ibid.,* chapter lxvii, section 12; 330-331.

26. For detailed accounts of the Hampton Court Conference see Procter and Frere, op. cit., 136-143; R.G. Usher, *Reconstruction of the English Church,* Vol.I, 310-333; S.B. Babbage, *Puritanism and Richard Bancroft,* 43-73.

27. Usher, op. cit., Vol.I, 314.

28. *Ibid.,* Vol.I, 343-358, passim; Archbishop's Commission, *The Canon Law of the Church of England* (1947), 73.

29. Babbage, op. cit., 98.

30. Archbishop's Commission, op. cit., 73.

31. Babbage, op. cit., 98, cf. Usher, op. cit., Vol.I, 335.

32. Archbishop's Commission, op. cit., 72-73.

33. *Ibid.,* 227.

34. *Ibid.,* 73.

35. Usher, op. cit., Vol.I, 398.

36. Cardwell, *Synodalia,* Vol.I, 256; cf. *1559 Prayer Book,* pub. Grant (1911), 106.

37. Cardwell, *Synodalia,* Vol.I, 258; Usher, op. cit., Vol.II, 276; Cardwell, *Documentary Annals,* Vol.I, 326.

38. Cardwell, *Synodalia,* Vol.I, 259; Usher, op. cit., Vol.II, 276; Cardwell, *Documentary Annals,* Vol.I, 326; cf. *1559 Prayer Book,* op. cit., 103.

39. Usher, op. cit., Vol.II, 276.

40. Cardwell, *Documentary Annals,* Vol.I, 412.

41. Cardwell, *Documentary Annals,* Vol.II, 34; cf. Usher, op. cit., Vol.II, 291.

42. *1559 Prayer Book,* op. cit., 106.

43. *Ibid.,* 103.

44. *Ibid.*, 104.

45. Babbage, op. cit., 379; spelling modernised.

46. *Ritual Commission Report*, appendix E, 444-601.

47. *Ibid.*, 440f.

48. *Ibid.*, 444f.

49. *Ibid.*, 450f.

50. *Ibid.*, 451f.

51. Particularly canon VII, see Cardwell, *Synodalia,* Vol.I, 404-406.

52. F.L. Cross, *Oxford Dictionary of the Christian Church,* 1466.

53. *Ritual Commission Report,* op. cit., 521.

54. *Ibid.*, 555f.

55. G. Donaldson, *The Making of the Scottish Prayer Book of 1637,* 36, 52, and 59.

56. *Ritual Commission Report,* op. cit., 576f.

57. *Ibid.*, 579f.

58. *Ibid.*, 584.

59. *Ibid.*, 580.

60. J. Cosin, *Works,* Library of Anglo-Catholic Theology ed. (hereafter cited as LACT), Vol.II, 12; these articles are not noted in the *Ritual Commission Report.*

61. D. Wilkins, *Concilia,* Vol.IV, 447-454.

62. In canon 18; *Ibid.*, 500.

63. Printed in Laud, *Works,* LACT, Vol.V, part II, 583-606.

64. *Ibid.*, 594.

65. *Ibid.*, 593-594.

66. C. Wordsworth, *The Coronation of King Charles I,* viii.

67. *Ibid.*, 140.

68. *Ibid.*, viii.

69. *Ibid.*, 49.

70. *Ibid.*, 82 and 128.

71. J. Wickham Legg, *Three Coronation Orders,* 32.

72. *Ibid.*, 155; since this date it has only been used once at a coronation offertory, at that of Edward VII, *Coronation Order of Edward VII,* 49. However, it was sung as an introit at the coronations of George V and George VI: Ratcliff, *The English Coronation Service,* 151 and 79; Eeles, *The Coronation Service,* 68; and as a gradual at that of Elizabeth II.

73. Wordsworth, op. cit., 50.

74. *Ibid.*, 129.

75. Wickham Legg, *op.* cit., 33.

76. *Ibid.*, 156; Ratcliff, op. cit., 101; Eeles, op. cit., 82; *The Coronation of H.M. Queen Elizabeth II* (the approved souvenir programme), 36.

77. Private communication from the Reverend Bernard Wigan.

78. Wickham Legg, op. cit., 63.

79. *Ibid.*, xlii.

CHAPTER FIVE

1. In 1655. There is a copy of the 1655 edition in the Cosin Library at Durham. See G.J. Cuming, *The Durham Book*, xx.

2. *Rationale*, 214; The reference is to an edition published by E. Pawlett, London, 1704.

3. More and Cross, op. cit., 519.

4. L'Estrange, *Alliance of Divine Offices*, edition published by the Library of Anglo-Catholic Theology (hereafter cited as LACT), x, xi.

5. *Ibid.*, 38.

6. *Ibid.*, 44.

7. *Ibid.*, 270-271.

8. *Ibid.*, 312.

9. *Ibid.*, 314.

10. *Ibid.*, 317.

11. *Ibid.*. 315.

12. *Ibid.*, 316-7.

13. *Ibid.*, 317.

14. *Ibid.*, 317.

15. *Ibid.*, 323-4.

16. *Ibid.*, 329.

17. *Ibid.*, 330.

18. *Ibid.*, 351.

19. More and Cross, op. cit., no. 200, p.464.

20. L. Andrewes, *Minor Works*, LACT, 151-158.

21. More and Cross, op. cit., No. 206, p.473.

22. For the text of the 1635 edition Brett's extensive quotation of the same has been relied on, but a comparison of Brett's text with the 1631 edition shows him to have quoted accurately all the material to be found in this edition, and there seems no reason to suppose that Brett's text is unreliable as a source for the material occurring in Morton's 1635 edition alone. T. Morton's 1631 ed., 7-11; cf. T. Brett, *Dissertation on Liturgies*, 75-81.

23. Morton, 1631 ed., op. cit., 7-10; cf. Brett, op. cit., 75-79.

24. Morton, op. cit., 10-11; cf. Brett, op. cit., 79-80. The sentence starting 'for a further manifestation . . .' is one of the 1635 additions.

25. Brett, op. cit., 80-81. These two quotations are to be found only in Morton's 1635 edition.

26. More and Cross, op. cit., no. 207, 475.

27. J. Bramhall, *Works,* LACT, Vol.III, 165.

28. More and Cross, op. cit., No. 203, 467-8; also J. Cosin, *Works,* LACT, Vol.IV, 155 (p.16 for the original Latin).

29. Cosin, op. cit., Vol.IV, 158 (19-20 for the original Latin; quoted by H.R. Gummey, *The Consecration of the Eucharist,* 189.

30. Cosin, op. cit., Vol.IV, 180 (58 for the original Latin); quoted by Gummey, op. cit., 189.

31. More and Cross, op. cit., No. 203, 468; also Cosin, op. cit., Vol.IV, 156 (17 for the original Latin).

32. More and Cross, op. cit., No. 203, 468; also Cosin, op. cit., Vol.IV, 156 (17-18 for the original Latin).

33. More and Cross, op. cit., No. 203, 469; also Cosin, op. cit., Vol.IV, 174 (49 for the original Latin).

34. More and Cross, op. cit., No. 203, 469-70; also Cosin, op. cit., Vol.IV, 174 (49 for the original Latin).

35. G.J. Cuming, *The Durham Book,* xiii; see also C.W. Dugmore, *From Hooker to Waterland,* 109, footnote 3 for detailed comment on the authorship of these notes. Gummey attributed them to Hayward, op. cit., 188. Overall used to recite the prayer of oblation immediately after the prayer of consecration, see *Durham Book,* op. cit., 171 for Cosin's comments on this, which come from this same 1st series of notes; see also Cosin, *Works,* LACT, Vol.IV, 114-5.

36. J. Cosin, *Works,* LACT, Vol.V. 106.

37. *Ibid.,* 109.

38. *Ibid.,* 109.

39. *Ibid.,* 109-10.

40. *Ibid.,* 110.

41. *Ibid.,* 345.

42. *Ibid.,* 340.

43. *Ibid.,* 304; cf. Gummey, op. cit., 189.

44. Cosin, op. cit., Vol.V, 332; cf. Gummey, op. cit., 189.

45. Gummey, op. cit., 189.

46. Dugmore, op. cit., 104-5; Cuming, op. cit., xv.

47. H. Thorndike, *Works,* LACT, Vol.I, Part 1, 342.

48. *Ibid.,* 343.

49. *Ibid.*, 346.

50. *Ibid.*, 348-9.

51. *Ibid.*, 346.

52. *Ibid.*, 347-8.

53. *Ibid.*, Vol.V, 245-6.

54. W. Laud, *Works,* LACT, Vol.IV, 29.

55. *Ibid.*, Vol.III, 335.

56. *Ibid.*, 342-3.

57. See Chapter 7, section (i).

58. Laud, *Works,* LACT, Vol.III, 341.
59. *Ibid.*, 344.

60. *Ibid.*, 345.

61. *Ibid.*, 345-7.

62. *Ibid.*, 347-8.

63. *Ibid.*, 348-9.

64. *Ibid.*, 353-5, see also More and Cross, op. cit., No. 226, 509-10.

65. Laud, op. cit., Vol.III, 355-7.

66. *Ibid.*, 357.

67. J. Taylor, *Works,* ed. Heber, Vol.IX, 457f.

68. W.J. Grisbrooke, *Anglican Liturgies of the Seventeenth and Eighteenth Centuries,* 185.

69. *Ibid.*, 193f.

70. More and Cross, op. cit., 169.

71. *Ibid.*, No. 79, 175-6.

72. The difference between this outlook and that of Cranmer is that here the 'use' is to convey the gifts, whereas for Cranmer the 'use' is to remind the people of what the gifts are. This is the contrast between 'real receptionist' and 'virtual receptionist'.

73. Dugmore, op. cit., 30f.

74. *Ibid.*, 50-1.

CHAPTER SIX

1. W.D. Maxwell, *Genevan Service Book,* 121-128; spelling modernised in quotations.

2. G.W. Sprott, *The Book of Common Order,* 120-127.

3. *Ibid.*, 195.

4. *Ibid.*, xxi.

5. P. Hall, *Reliquiae Liturgicae,* Vol.I, viii-xii, 51-61; Bard Thompson, *Liturgies of the Western Church,* X, 311-321, 334-341.

6. Sprott, op. cit., xxxvii-xli; W. McMillan, *The Worship of the Scottish Reformed Church, 1530-1638*, 170-174; G. Donaldson, *The Making of the Scottish Prayer Book of 1637*, 67-68.

7. McMillan, op. cit., 173.

8. Donaldson, op. cit., 36.

9. McMillan, op. cit., 174.

10. G.W. Sprott, *Scottish Liturgies of James VI*, 1871 edition, 65-75.

11. *Ibid.*, 66.

12. *Ibid.*, 72.

13. *Ibid.*, 73.

14. *Ibid.*, 74.

15. *Ibid.*, 75.

16. R.C.D. Jasper and G.J. Cuming, *Prayers of the Eucharist*, 173-178; Hall, op. cit., Vol.III, 52-58; Bard Thompson, op. cit., 345-71.

17. Hall, op. cit., 54-55; Jasper and Cuming, op. cit., 176; Bard Thompson, op. cit., 370.

18. Hall, op. cit., 56; Jasper and Cuming, op. cit., 177; Bard Thompson, op. cit., 370.

19. Hall, op. cit., Vol.IV, 55-79; Jasper and Cuming, op. cit., 179-183; Bard Thompson, op. cit., 375-408.

20. Hall, op. cit., 58-59; Bard Thompson, op. cit., 394-395.

21. Hall, op. cit., 60-64; Bard Thompson, op. cit., 396-398.

22. Dix maintained, on the basis of this kind of evidence, that one of the products of the Reformation was to make medieval Catholic devotional accompaniments to the Eucharist the actual substance of the Reformed rites, *The Shape of the Liturgy*, 609.

23. Hall, op. cit., Vol.IV, 68; Jasper and Cuming, op. cit., 181; Bard Thompson, op. cit., 399-400.

24. Hall, op. cit., 69; Jasper and Cuming, op. cit., 181; Bard Thompson, op. cit., 400.

25. Hall, op. cit., 70; Jasper and Cuming, op. cit., 182; Bard Thompson, op. cit., 400.

26. Hall, op. cit., 73-74; Jasper and Cuming, op. cit., 183; Bard Thompson, op. cit., 402.

27. E. Cardwell, *Conferences*, 321.

28. *Ibid.*, 363.

29. Donaldson, op. cit., 363.

30. A. Peel, *Tracts ascribed to Richard Bancroft*, 25; See also W.H. Frere and C.E. Douglas, *Puritan Manifestoes*, 21, for another very similar quotation.

31. Donaldson, op. cit., 83.

CHAPTER SEVEN

1. G. Donaldson, *The Making of the Scottish Prayer Book of 1637,* 41-59.

2. This short account of the origins and development of the 1637 book is based on Donaldson's detailed account of and discussion of these matters.

3. Donaldson, op. cit., 198-199.

4. *Ibid.,* 204.

5. *Ibid.,* 77.

6. *Ibid.,* 55.

7. The way he has phrased this sentence is misleading, for at first sight it suggests that both of these rites do contain supplementary consecration provisions, and that it is with these that he is comparing the 1637 rubric. However, this is not the case, for neither of these rites contain any such provision.

8. G.J. Cuming, *Durham Book,* 164-178, passim.

9. *Ibid.,* 163.

10. *Ibid.,* 162.

11. *Ibid.,* 162 and 164.

12. *Ibid.,* 167.

13. *Ibid.,* 169.

14. *Ibid.,* 187; English and spelling modernized in this quotation.

15. For a detailed account of the stages whereby the 1662 Book came into existence, see F. Procter and W.H. Frere, *The Book of Common Prayer,* 163-201; E. Cardwell, *Conferences,* 244-392; G.J. Cuming, *A History of Anglican Liturgy,* 149-167.

16. See Cardwell, op. cit., 322 and 354.

17. E.C. Ratcliff, 'The English Usage of Eucharistic Consecration, 1548-1662'. *Theology,* Vol.LX (1957), 280.

CHAPTER EIGHT

1. G. Every, *The High Church Party, 1688-1718,* 23f; F. Procter and W.H. Frere, *The Book of Common Prayer.* 207f.

2. Every, op. cit., 43-46; Procter and Frere, op. cit., 207-208; E. Cardwell, *Conferences,* 411-414.

3. See T.J. Fawcett, *The Liturgy of Comprehension 1689,* for a thorough discussion of this subject, and a complete reprint of the 1686 book with all the alterations proposed.

4. Every, op. cit., 51.

5. Fawcett, op. cit., 111; spelling modernised.

6. *Ibid.,* 167, 244.

7.   J. Dowden, ' "Our Alms and Oblations"; An Historical Study', *Journal of Theological Studies,* Vol.I (1900), 321-346.

8.   T. Comber, *Companion to the Temple,* 3rd ed. (1688), 2nd pagination, 46.

9.   W. Nicholls, *A Comment on the Book of Common Prayer;* see his comments on the offertory sentences.

10.   Dowden, op. cit., 345.

11.   His commentary on the prayer book, 3rd ed. (1720), 276.

12.   G. Hickes, *Treatises,* Library of Anglo-Catholic Theology ed. (hereafter cited as LACT) Vol.II, 186.

13.   J. Johnson, *Works,* LACT, Vol.I, 50-51; Vol.II 385-386.

14.   He refers here in a marginal note to Ambrose, *De Sacramentis.*

15.   Comber, op. cit., 2nd pagination, 119.

16.   *Ibid.,* 122.

17.   *Ibid.,* 126.

18.   *Ibid.,* 126.

19.   *Ibid.,* 123 and 127.

20.   *Ibid.,* 130.

21.   *Ibid.,* 142.

22.   Page 182.

23.   Wheatly, 1st ed., 104.

24.   *Ibid.,* 111.

25.   *Ibid.,* 123-124.

26.   *Ibid.,* 119.

27.   *Ibid.,* 122.

28.   *Ibid.,* 121.

29.   His 3rd ed., (28).

30.   *Ibid.,* xi f.

31.   *Ibid.,* 255.

32.   i.e. that of Basil, etc., who wrote their own liturgies.

33.   His 3rd ed., 256.

34.   *Ibid.,* 276.

35.   *Ibid.,* 289.

36.   *Ibid.,* this and the previous 3 quotations from p.290.

37.   *Ibid.,* 539.

38.   *Ibid.,* 290.

39.   *Ibid.,* 290-291 (misprinted in the text as 391).

40.   *Ibid.,* 540 and 291 (misprinted 391).

41.   *Ibid.,* 312.

42.   *Ibid.,* 309-310.

43. H. Broxap, *The Later Non-Jurors*, 63-65, gives a list of these pamphlets.

44. *Ibid.*, 70.

45. Wheatly, 3rd ed., 291 (misprinted 391).

46. F.L. Cross, *The Oxford Dictionary of the Christian Church*, 1st ed., 1453, 741 and 196 respectively.

47. J. Johnson, *Works*, LACT, Vol.I.,

48. *Ibid.*, 304.

49. *Ibid.*, 329-330.

50. *Ibid.*, 261.

51. *Ibid.*, 305-307.

52. *Ibid.*, 266.

53. *Ibid.*, 342.

54. See T. Brett, *Dissertation on Liturgies*, 358.

55. J. Johnson, *Works*, LACT, Vol.I., 418.

56. R. Nelson, *Companion* . . . 340-341, where all of this series of quotations on consecration and the presence are to be found; the edition used is one published in London in 1811.

57. Cross, op. cit., 943; cf. Nelson, op. cit., 4.

58. Cross, op. cit., 642.

59. All quotations from Waterland being taken from an 1896 reprint of Van Mildert's 1856 edition; this quotation p.10.

60. Waterland, op.cit., 55f.

61. *Ibid.*, 66-68.

62. *Ibid*, 69.

63. *Ibid.*, 71.

64. *Ibid.*, 77.

65. *Ibid.*, 85.

66. *Ibid.*, 88.

67. *Ibid.*, 89.

68. *Ibid.*, 90.

69. *Ibid.*, 91 and 92.

70. *Ibid.*, 93-94.

71. *Ibid.*, 148.

72. *Ibid.*, 98.

CHAPTER NINE

1. In his *Anglican Liturgies of the Seventeenth and Eighteenth Centuries.*

2. In The *Later Non-Jurors.*

3. Grisbrooke, op. cit., prints the complete text of this rite. p.275-296; no further individual page references to it are given here.

4. A convenient English edition of the Clementine rite may be found in J.M. Neale and R.F. Littledale, *The Liturgies of S.S. Mark . . . Clement . . . translated,* 65-91; R.C.D. Jasper and G.J. Cuming, *Prayers of the Eucharist,* 66-73, give the complete text of the Clementine Anaphora in translation.

5. Grisbrooke, op. cit., 113.

6. T. Brett, *Dissertation on Liturgies,* an edition published in London in 1720, p.25.

7. *Ibid.,* 55.

8. *Ibid.,* 69.

9. *Ibid.,* 70.

10. *Ibid.,* 74.

11. *Ibid.,* 81.

12. *Ibid.,* 82-83.

13. *Ibid.,* 83-85.

14. *Ibid.,* 126-127.

15. *Ibid.,* 127-128.

16. *Ibid.,* 132.

17. *Ibid.,* 133-134.

18. *Ibid.,* 387.

19. *Ibid.,* 104.

20. *Ibid.,* 119-122.

21. *Ibid.,* 183-184 and 382-383.

22. Grisbrooke, op. cit., 95.

23. Brett, op. cit., 362.

24. *Ibid.,* 380-382.

25. *Ibid.,* 160-161.

26. *Ibid.,* 383.

27. *Ibid.,* 167.

28. *Ibid.,* 169-170.

29. *Ibid.,* 395-396.

30. J. Dowden, *Annotated Scottish Communion Office,* 1922 ed., p.23.

31. *Ibid.*, 42.

32. *Ibid.*, 48.

33. *Ibid.*, 47.

34. *Ibid.*, 33.

35. *Ibid.*, 64.

36. *Ibid.*, 68.

37. *Ibid.*, 225.

38. *Ibid.*, 117-132, for the full text of the 1764 rite, including Dowden's reconstruction of the synaxis: Grisbrooke, op. cit., reprints the whole rite, 335-348; no further individual page references to this are given here.

39. Dowden, op. cit., 65; see also P.A. Lemprière, *The Scottish Communion Offices of 1637, 1735, 1755, 1764 and 1889,* 38-39. Lemprière sets out the various versions of the Scottish Communion Office in parallel columns.

CHAPTER TEN

1. A detailed account of this subject may be found in J.A. Jungmann, *The Mass of the Roman Rite,* Vol.I, 133-141.

2. *Ibid.*, 136.

3. *Ibid.*, 133.

4. *Ibid.*, 138.

5. *Ibid.*, 139.

6. *Ibid.*, 143.

7. *Ibid.*, 159-167.

8. Published in easily accessible form in English Translation by the Catholic Truth Society, from which quotations in the text are taken.

9. *General Instruction on the Roman Missal,* edition cited, 7 and 8.

10. *Ibid.*, 8. That the concept that the moment of consecration occurs at the institution narrative is unchanged is indicated by the rubric 'a little before the Consecration the server may alert the people by ringing the bell'. Paragraph 109, p.41.

11. *Ibid.*, 9-11.

12. From some of the articles in *The New Liturgy, a Comprehensive Introduction* ed. Lancelot Sheppard, whose contributors include, besides Sheppard himself, Bernard Botte, Louis Bouyer, and Joseph Gelineau.

13. *Ibid.*, 113-115.

14. *Ibid.*, 126.

15. *Ibid.*, 156.

16. *Ibid.*, 161-173, passim.

17. *Ibid.*, 174-193.

18. *Ibid.*, 175.

19. *Ibid.*, 181.

20. *Ibid.*, 183.

21. *Ibid.*, 188.

22. *Ibid.*, 189.

23. *Ibid.*, 191-192.

24. *Ibid.*, 34.

25. J.B. O'Connell, *The Celebration of Mass*, 1956 ed., 10. It is an expanded version of the contents of the 1474 Missal.

26. *Ibid.*, 188-211.

27. *Ibid.*, 199.

28. S. Woywood, *The New Canon Law*, 165.

29. Private conversation with the Reverend G. Hay, Roman Catholic chaplain to Exeter University.

30. *General Instruction*, op. cit., paragraph 286, p.70.

31. Private communication with the Very Reverend Dr. K.T. Ware, who said: 'The normal Orthodox view is that the *anaphora* as a whole — and, indeed, the entire liturgy — constitute an essential unity: it would therefore be contrary to Orthodox liturgical 'ethos' to single out a part of this essential unity — e.g. the epiclesis — and to perform a supplementary consecration of this part alone. The liturgical books nowhere allow for this. If, during the communion of the people, there is insufficient of the consecrated species, I have sometimes known Greek priests pour some additional wine into the chalice (in which, of course, there is both bread and wine). I myself have never done this, and there certainly exists no rubric permitting this. Other Greek clergy disapprove of this practice . . .'
As with Romans, the theological textbooks simply do not discuss the matter.

32. Private communication with the Reverend H.R.T. Brandreth, associate chaplain, the archbishop of Canterbury's Counsellors on Foreign Relations.

CHAPTER ELEVEN

1. This is still the case of course. All the various vernacular versions of the Roman Missal of 1970 are but translations of the one rite.

2. Conveniently collected together in B.J. Wigan's *The Liturgy in English.*

3. These newer liturgies are collected together in C.O. Buchanan's two volumes, *Modern Anglican Liturgies, 1958-1968,* and

Further Anglican Liturgies, 1968-1975, (hereafter cited simply as MAL and FAL respectively).

4. Wigan, op. cit., 26-37.

5. Wigan, op. cit., 44-45, cf. W.J. Grisbrooke, *Anglican Liturgies of the Seventeenth and Eighteenth Centuries,* 343-344.

6. 1912 Version of the Scottish Prayer Book.

7. J. Dowden, *Scottish Communion Office,* 1922 ed., 260.

8. Wigan, op. cit., 47; 1912 has no fraction at this point.

9. Wigan, op. cit., 52-61.

10. Wigan, op. cit., cf. p.58-59 with p.44-45.

11. Wigan, op. cit., 62-72; text also easily available in any published copy of the 1928 Prayer Book.

12. Rubric at end of 1928 Communion Service. Wigan, op. cit., 249, has described this incorrectly, as Buchanan, in FAL, has noted, p.420.

13. Wigan, op. cit., 73-81.

14. *Ibid.,* 82-93.

15. *Ibid.,* 114-126.

16. *Ibid.,* 136-144.

17. See appendix for details.

18. Wigan, op. cit., 127-135. Originally written in Japanese.

19. *Ibid.,* 175-182.

20. *Ibid.,* 166-174.

21. *Ibid.,* 145-161. Wigan regards these as variants of the same rite.

22. *Ibid.,* 162-165.

23. Darwell Stone, *The Holy Communion,* 229.

24. See *Eucharistic Theology Then and Now,* 92-93; Lowther Clarke, *The Prayer Book of 1928 Reconsidered,* 45-47; *Prayer Book Revision in the Church of England,* 10-12.

25. See the proposed Canon in the *'Green Book',* 349.

26. *Prayer Book Revision in the Church of England,* 11.

27. *The Scottish Communion Office of 1764,* published by O.U.P. in 1922.

28. See the proposed Canon in the *'Grey Book',* Part I, I, 15.

29. P. Hinchliff, *The South African Rite and the 1928 Prayer Book,* 9.

30. Compare the relevant rubrics in the 1912 and 1929 recensions of the Scottish Rite.

31. Lowther Clarke, op. cit., 83.

32. The Report, *Doctrine in the Church of England,* 65-171.

33. W.H. Frere, *The Anaphora,* 201; see also *Walter Howard Frere, Correspondence on Liturgical Revision and Construction,* 56, 60, 64.

34. Frere, *The Anaphora*, 204.

35. *Walter Howard Frere, A Collection of his Papers on Liturgical and Historical Subjects*, 175.

36. *Ibid.*, 131.

37. *Ibid.*, 176.

38. *Correspondence on Liturgical Revision and Construction*, op. cit., 115, 117-118.

39. *Papers on Liturgical and Historical Subjects*, 127-128.

40. *The Shape of the Liturgy*, passim.

41. All the resolutions and sections of the reports of the Lambeth Conferences from 1867 to 1948 are conveniently grouped together in *Prayer Book Revision in the Church of England*, op. cit., 42-55, cf. MAL, 8-9.

42. The Lambeth Conference 1958, 1.47-48, 2.78-85.

43. *Ibid.*, 2.81.

44. *Ibid.*, 2.85.

45. *Ibid.*, 1.48.

46. MAL, 23-24.

47. See particularly MAL, 3-32 and FAL, 3-34.

48. MAL, 32.

49. FAL, 30.

50. See MAL, 26-31, and FAL, 6.

51. FAL, 416.

52. FAL, 417f.

53. FAL, 15.

54. See for example *The Eucharist Today*, op. cit., 108-110.

55. e.g. the 1974 Canadian rite; see FAL, 117.

56. e.g. the 1970 New Zealand rite; see FAL, 374.

57. For the record, FAL, 57.

58. MAL, 118-121.

59. Compare the views of R.J. Halliburton, who regards the Series 3 text as good and satisfactory, *The Eucharist Today*, op. cit., 110-116, with those of M.J. Moreton, who does not, *Made Fully Perfect*, 19-23.

60. See MAL, 17-19, and FAL, 31-34.

61. See Appendix for details.

62. *A Commentary on Holy Communion Series 3*, 26-27, quoted fairly extensively in FAL, 32-33.

63. It must be noted that the Latin and Greek churches do not practise it at all and would in all probability deny its legitimacy.

64. In contrast to the Liturgical Commission, R.J. Halliburton does seem to understand this in this light: see his footnote 70, p.127 in *The Eucharist Today*, op. cit.

APPENDIX

1. *Liturgies of King Edward VI.* Parker Society Edition, 8.
2. *The first and Second Prayer Books of King Edward VI.* Everyman Edition, 225. Note: the reference given for a rite that makes no provision is to the place equivalent to the position of the 1662 rubric.
3. *Ibid.,* 389.
4. *The Prayer Book of Queen Elizabeth, 1559,* published Grant, Edinburgh in 1911, 103.
5. F. Procter and W.H. Frere, *The Book of Common Prayer,* 139-140.
6. E. Cardwell, *Synodalia,* Vol I, 257.
7. W.J. Grisbrooke, *Anglican Liturgies of the Seventeenth and Eighteenth Centuries.* 293.
8. *1928 Prayer Book,* an edition published by the Cambridge University Press, 375-376.
9. *Series 1 Holy Communion Booklet,* AS 120, 20.
10. *Alternative Services, Second Series,* Liturgical Commission Report, 160, paragraph 39.
11. *Series 2 Holy Communion Booklet,* AS 220, 10.
12. *Alternative Services Series 1 and 2 revised,* Liturgical Commission Report, GS 217, 24, paragraph 40.
13. *Series 3 Holy Communion,* Liturgical Commission Report, 32, paragraph 35.
14. *Series 3 Holy Communion Booklet,* AS 320, 25, paragraph 35.
15. Grisbrooke, op. cit., 182; also G. Donaldson, *The Making of The Scottish Prayer Book of 1637, 204.*
16. Grisbrooke, op. cit., 347.
17. October 1975; C.O. Buchanan discusses the present state of affairs in this subject, and the reasons for it, in *Further Anglican Liturgies, 1968-1975* (hereafter cited simply as FAL), 31-34.
18. *Scottish Prayer Book 1929,* an edition published by the Cambridge University Press, 202; B. Wigan, *The Liturgy in English,* 248.
19. *Irish Prayer Book, 1926,* an edition published in Dublin in 1960, 151; Wigan, op. cit., 248.
20. Wigan, op. cit., 248.
21. *Indian Prayer Book 1960,* an edition published by the I.S.P.C.K. in 1961, 388-389; Wigan, op. cit., 248.
22. C.O. Buchanan, *Modern Anglican Liturgies, 1958-1968* (hereafter cited simply as MAL), 309-310, and FAL, 332.
23. *Indian Prayer Book,* op.cit., 347; Wigan, op. cit., 248.

24. *An Order for the Celebration of the Holy Eucharist* . . . The Church in Wales, 1966, (14), MAL, 171.

25. *South African Prayer Book,*1954, an edition published by O.U.P. and S.P.C.K., 250; Wigan, op. cit., 249.

26. MAL, 186.

27. *Canadian Prayer Book, 1959,* an edition published in Toronto, 84-85; Wigan, op. cit., 249.

28. MAL, 69.

29. MAL, 89; though ecumenically produced with a united church in mind, no such church yet exists. But it has been authorized for use by Anglican authorities in East Africa, and so may be regarded as an Anglican liturgy. For the present status of this rite, see FAL, 234.

30. MAL, 319.

31. MAL, 249; Buchanan erroneously states in his introduction that this rite makes no provision, 17-18, a mistake corrected in FAL, 251 and 421.

32. FAL, 103.

33. FAL, 352.

34. FAL, 259.

35. MAL, 277.

36. MAL, 109; taken literally the relevant rubric of this rite seems to direct consecration in *both* kinds if there is a deficiency of bread, but of *wine only* if there is a deficiency of wine, but it surely cannot actually mean this.

37. Wigan, op. cit., 249.

38. FAL, 387.

39. FAL, 171 (PECUSA) *Services for Trial Use,* 128; (PECUSA) *Authorized Services 1973,* 119.

40. FAL, 227.

41. *Scottish Prayer Book,* op. cit., 190; Wigan, op. cit., 245.

42. *American Prayer Book 1928,* an edition published in New York in 1945, 83; cit. H.R. Gummey, *The Consecration of the Eucharist,* XXV, concerning the 1892 book which made similar provision.

43. *South African Prayer Book,* op. cit., 250; Wigan, op. cit., 249.

44. Wigan, op. cit., 88 and 249.

45. Wigan, op. cit., 133 and 249.

46. FAL, 303.

47. (PECUSA) *Prayer Book Studies XVII.* Liturgy section.
p. 20 for the supplementary consecration form,
cf. page 15 for the epiclesis section of the Canon;
cf. MAL, pages 215 and 212.

48. MAL, 221 for the supplementary consecration form, 227 for the epiclesis section of the Canon.

49. FAL, 181 for note concerning supplementary consecration form, 179 for the epiclesis section of the Canon.

50. MAL, 17, footnote 3.

51. MAL, 339.

52. FAL, 377.

53. FAL, 340.

54. FAL, 259.

55. MAL, 243; However the 1973 Chilean rite does make provision, FAL, 183, using in fact the 1662 method; private communication from the Revd C.O. Buchanan.

56. MAL, 100; included as Anglican for the same reasons as the East African United Liturgy, MAL, 91. This liturgy is now defunct, FAL, 247.

57. MAL, 158.

58. MAL, 284.

59. Wigan, op. cit., 159.

60. Wigan, op. cit., 165.

61. Wigan, op. cit., 173.

62. FAL, 246.

63. FAL, 88.

64. FAL, 117.

65. FAL, 210.

66. FAL, 296.

67. FAL, 360.

68. See for example, MAL, 17.

69. CSI, *Book of Common Worship,* as authorized by Synod 1962, an edition published by O.U.P. in 1963, 20; Wigan, op. cit., 250.

70. FAL, 288.

71. FAL, 263.

72. FAL, 277.

Bibliography

A. Books and Articles.

B. Editions and Versions of Liturgical Texts.

A. *Books and Articles.*

Addleshaw, G.W.O., *The High Church Tradition,* London, 1941.

Ambrose, St, *On the Sacraments,* Latin text ed. Chadwick, H., London, 1960.

        On the Sacraments and on the Mysteries, trans. Thompson, T., ed. Srawley, J.H., London, 1950.

Andrewes, Lancelot, *Sermons,* Library of Anglo-Catholic Theology Edition (cited hereafter as LACT), Vol. V. Oxford 1843.

        Minor Works, LACT, Oxford, 1854.

Andrieu, M., 'Immixtio et Consecration', *Revue des Sciences Religieuses* Vol. 2, p.428-446; Vol. 3, p.24-61; 149-182, 283-304, 443-471; Vol. 4, p.65-96, 265-295, 454-484; Paris, 1922, 1923, 1924, respectively.

        Les Ordines Romani du haut Moyen Age, 5 Vols., Louvain, 1931-1961.

Aquinas, T., *Summa Theologiae,* Latin text (Leonine) ed. De Rubeis, Billuart and Faucher, P., Pars IIIa et Supplementum, Rome, 1948.

        Summa Theologica, literally translated by Fathers of the English Dominican Province, Vol. XVII, London, 1914.

        Summa Theologiae, Latin text with English translation; General Editors, Gilby, T. and O'Brien, T.C.; Vol. LVIII, ed. Barden W., London, 1965.

ed. Arber, E., *A Brief Discourse of the Troubles at Frankfurt, 1554-1558 A.D.,* London, 1907.

Archbishop's Commission, *Doctrine in the Church of England,* London, 1938.

Archbishop's Commission, *The Canon Law of the Church of England, Being the Report of the Archbishop's Commission on Canon Law, together with Proposals for a Revised Body of Canons; ...* London, 1947.

Atchley, E.G.C.F., *Ordo Romanus Primus,* (Vol. VI of the Library of Liturgiology and Ecclesiology for English Readers), London, 1905.

        On the Epiclesis of the Eucharistic Liturgy and in the Consecration of the Font, Alcuin Club Collections, XXXI, London, 1935.

Babbage, S.B., *Puritanism and Richard Bancroft,* London, 1962.

Barzun, J. and Graff, H.F., *The Modern Researcher,* New York, 1962.

Bennet, T., *A Paraphrase with Annotations upon the Book of Common Prayer*, London, 1708.

Bicknell, E.J., *A Theological Introduction to the Thirty-Nine Articles of the Church of England*, 3rd ed. revised by Carpenter, H.J., London, 1955.

Bishop, E., *Liturgica Historica*, Oxford, 1918.

Blunt, J.H., *The Annotated Book of Common Prayer*, London 1890.

Bodleian Library, *Catalogue of Books printed before 1920*. Vol. Tol-Tom, Oxford.

Booty, J.E., *John Jewel as Apologist of the Church of England*. London, 1963.

Bradshaw, P.F., *The Anglican Ordinal*, Alcuin Club Collections 53, London, 1971.

Bramhall, J., *Works*, LACT, Vol. III, Oxford, 1844.

Brett, T., *A Collection of the Principal Liturgies, used by the Christian Church in the Celebration of the Holy Eucharist . . . With a Dissertation upon them . . .*, London, 1720.

Brightman, F.E., *Liturgies Eastern and Western*, Oxford, 1896.

    The English Rite, 2 Vols., 1st. ed., London, 1915.

    'The New Prayer Book examined', *Church Quarterly Review*, Vol. CIV (1927), 219-252.

Brilioth, Y., *Eucharistic Faith and Practice*, trans. Hebert, A.G., London, 1956 (original first published 1930).

British Museum, *Catalogue of an Exhibition Commemorating the Four Hundredth Anniversary of the Introduction of the Book of Common Prayer*, London, 1949.

Brook, S., *The Language of the Book of Common Prayer*, London, 1965.

Brooks, P., *Thomas Cranmer's Doctrine of the Eucharist*, London, 1965.

Broxap, H., *The Later Non-Jurors*, Cambridge, 1924.

ed. Buchahan, C.O., *Modern Anglican Liturgies, 1958-1968*, London, 1968.

ed. Buchanan, C.O., *Further Anglican Liturgies, 1968-2975*, Nottingham, 1975.

Burnet, G., *History of the Reformation*, edition used published in 6 Vols., Oxford, 1829 (originally published between 1679 and 1714).

Cardwell, E., *A History of Conferences and other Proceedings connected with the Revision of the Book of Common Prayer; from the year 1558 to the year 1690*, 2nd ed., Oxford, 1841.

    Synodalia, 2 Vols., Oxford, 1842.

   Documentary Annals of the Reformed Church of England. 2nd ed., 2 Vols., Oxford, 1844.

Clark, F., *The Eucharistic Sacrifice and the Reformation,* 1st ed., London, 1960.

Clarke, W.K. Lowther, *The Prayer Book of 1928 Reconsidered,* London, 1943.

   (ed.)   *Liturgy and Worship,* London, 1932.

Clay, W.K., *The Book of Common Prayer Illustrated,* London, 1841.

Clements, R.E., et al, *Eucharistic Theology Then and Now,* London, 1968.

Cobb, C.S., *The Rationale of Ceremonial 1541-43,* Alcuin Club Collections XVIII, London, 1910.

Collier, J., *An Ecclesiastical History of Great Britain,* edition ed. Lathbury, T., London, 1852.

Comber, T., *A Companion to the Temple,* 3rd ed. Corrected, London, 1688.

Cosin, J., *Works,* LACT Vol. IV, Oxford, 1851; Vol. V, Oxford, 1855.

Couratin A.H., 'The Holy Communion of 1549', *Church Quarterly Review,* Vol. CLXIV (1963), 148-159.

   'The Holy Communion 1552-1662', *Church Quarterly Review,* Vol., CLXIII (1962), 431-442.

Cranmer, T., *A Short Instruction into Christian Religion being a Catechism set forth by Archbishop Cranmer in MDXLVIII: together with the same in Latin, Translated from the German by Justus Jonas in MDXXXIX,* ed. Burton E., Oxford, 1829.

   Remains, ed. Jenkyns, H., 4 Vols. Oxford, 1833.

   Writings and Disputations of Thomas Cranmer, Archbishop of Canterbury, Martyr, 1556, relative to the Sacrament of the Lord's Supper, ed. Cox, J.E., Parker Society, Cambridge, 1844.

   Miscellaneous Writings and Letters of Thomas Cranmer. Archbishop of Canterbury, Martyr, 1556, ed. Cox, J.E. Parker Society, Cambridge.

   The Work of, introduced by Packer, J.I., The Courtenay Library of Reformation Classics, ed. Duffield, G.E., Appleford, Berkshire, 1964.

ed. Cross, F.L., *The Oxford Dictionary of the Christian Church,* London, 1957.

Cuming, G.J., *The Durham Book,* Oxford, 1961.

   A History of Anglican Liturgy, London, 1969.

ed. Dalton, J.N., *Ordinale Exon,* Vol.I, Henry Bradshaw Society, Vol. XXXVII, London, 1909.

Daniel, E., *The Prayer Book, Its History, Language and Content,* 20th ed., London, 1901.

Davies, H., *Worship and Theology in England*, Vol. I, 'From Cranmer to Hooker, 1534-1603', Oxford, 1971.

Dijk, S.J.P. van, and Walker, J.H., *The Origins of the Modern Roman Liturgy*, London, 1960.

Dix, G., *The Shape of the Liturgy*, London, 1945.

'Dixit Cranmer et non Timuit', *Church Quarterly Review*, Vol. CXLV (1947/8), 148-176; Vol. CXLVI (1948), 44-60.

Dixon, R.W., *History of the Church of England*, 6 Vols, London and Oxford, 1878-1902.

Donaldson, G., *The Making of the Scottish Prayer Book of 1637*, Edinburgh, 1954.

ed. Douglas, D.C., *English Historical Documents*, Vol. V, 1485-1558, London, 1967.

Dowden, J.   *The Workmanship of the Prayer Book*, London, 1899.

Further Studies in the Prayer Book, London, 1908.

The Scottish Communion Office of 1764, Oxford, 1922. This is a revised and enlarged version of his work of 1884, ed., Wilson, H.A.

Duchesne, L., *Christian Worship, its Origins and Evolutions*, English trans., 5th ed., London, 1919.

Dugmore, C.W., *Eucharistic Doctrine in England from Hooker to Waterland*, London, 1942.

The Mass and the English Reformers, London, 1958.

Eeles, F.C.,   *Traditional Customs connected with the Scottish Liturgy*, Alcuin Club Collections XVIII, London, 1910.

The Coronation Service, London, 1952.

Ellebracht, Sr M.P., *Remarks on the Vocabulary of the Ancient Orations in the Missale Romanum*, Utrecht, 1966.

ed. Erbe, T., *Mirk's Festial*, Early English Text Society Edition, Extra Series XCVI, London, 1905.

Every, G., *The High Church Party, 1688-1718*, London, 1956.

Fawcett T.J., *The Liturgy of Comprehension 1689*, Alcuin Club Collections 54, Southend-on-Sea, 1973.

Fortescue, A., *Ceremonies of the Roman Rite Described*, London, 1917. (2nd ed. 1919; impression of 1920 used).

Frere, W.H. and Douglas, C.E. *Puritan Manifestoes. A Study of the Origin of the Puritan Revolt. With a Reprint of the Admonition to Parliament and kindred documents, 1572*, London, 1907.

Frere, W.H., *Visitation Articles and Injunctions of the period of the Reformation*, 3 Vols., Alcuin Club Collections XIV, XV, and XVI respectively, London, 1910; Vol. 1 — Historical Introduction and Index; Vol. II — 1536-1558 (assisted by Kennedy, W.P.M.); Vol. III — 1559-1575.

The Anaphora, London, 1938.

    A Collection of his Papers on Liturgical and Historical Subjects, ed. Arnold, J.H. and Wyatt, E.G.P., Alcuin Club Collections XXXV, London, 1940.

Fuller, T., *Church History of Britain,* London, 1655.

Gasquet, F.A., and Bishop, E., *Edward VI and the Book of Common Prayer,* 2nd ed., London, 1891.

Gee, H., and Hardy, W.J., *Documents Illustrative of the History of the English Church,* London, 1896.

Gee, H., *The Elizabethan Prayer Book and Ornaments,* London, 1902.

Gorham, G.C., *Reformation Gleanings,* London, 1857.

ed. Gould, G., *Documents Relating to the Settlement of the Church of England by the Act of Uniformity of 1662,* London, 1862.

Grisbrooke, W.J. *Anglican Liturgies of the Seventeenth and Eighteenth Centuries,* Alcuin Club Collections XL, London, 1958.

Gummey, H.R., *The Consecration of the Eucharist,* Philadelphia, U.S.A., 1908.

Hall, P.,   *Reliquiae Liturgicae,* 5 Vols. Bath, 1847.

    Fragmenta Liturgica, 7 Vols. Bath, 1848.

ed. Hamilton, W.D., *A Chronicle of England during the Reigns of the Tudors, from A.D. 1485 to 1559, by Charles Wriothesley, Windsor Herald;* Camden Society, New Series XL, London, 1875; Vol. II, Camden Society, New Series XX, London 1877.

Hammond, C.E., *Liturgies Eastern and Western,* Oxford, 1878.

Hänggi, A. and Pahl, I., *Prex Eucharistica,* Fribourg, Switzerland, 1968.

Hapgood, I.F., *Service Book,* New York, 1921. This is a comprehensive translation of Orthodox Service Books.

ed. Harford, G., Stevenson, H., and Tyrer, J.W., *The Prayer Book Dictionary,* London, no date.

Hatch, E., and Redpath, H.A., *Concordance to the Septuagint.* reprinted Graz, Austria, 1954.

Henderson, W.G., *Missale ad Usum Percelebris Ecclesiae Herfordensis,* Leeds, 1874.

Hickes, G., *Treatises,* LACT, Vols. I and II, Oxford, 1847.

Hinchcliff, P., *The South African Rite and the 1928 Prayer Book,* Alcuin Club Pamphlets XVII, Oxford, 1960.

Hooker, R., *Ecclesiastical Polity,* Book V, Everyman Edition, London, 1907.

Hooper, J., *Early Writings,* ed., Carr, S., Parker Society, Cambridge, 1843.

Hope, D., *The Leonine Sacramentary,* Oxford, 1970.

Hughes, J.J.,   *Absolutely Null and Utterly Void,* London, 1968.

    Steward of the Lord, London, 1970.

Hughes, P., *The Reformation in England*, 5th revised ed., 3 Vols. in 1, London, 1963.

Hutchinson, R., *Works*, ed. Bruce, J., Parker Society, Cambridge, 1842.

ed. Jacobson, W., *Fragmentary Illustrations of the Book of Common Prayer*, London, 1874.

ed. Jasper, R.C.D., *Walter Howard Frere, His correspondence on Liturgical Revision and Construction*, Alcuin Club Collections XXXIX, London, 1954.

    The Eucharist Today, Studies on Series 3, London 1974.

    and Cuming, G.J., *Prayers of the Eucharist: Early and Reformed*, London, 1975.

Jewel, J., *Works*, ed. Ayre, J., Parker Society, 4 Vols, Cambridge, 1845-1850.

    An Apology of the Church of England, ed. Booty, J.E., New York, 1963.

Johnson, John, *Works*, LACT, 2 Vols., Oxford, 1847.

Jungmann, J.A., *The Mass of the Roman Rite: Its Origins and Development (Missarum Sollemnia)*, trans. Brunner, F.A., 2 Vols., New York, 1950.

    The Early Liturgy: To the Time of Gregory the Great. trans. Brunner, F.A., London, 1960.

Kennedy, W.P.M., *Elizabethan Episcopal Administration*, 3 Vols. Alcuin Club Collections XXV, XXVI, and XXVII respectively, London, 1924.

King, A.A., *The Liturgy of the Roman Church*, London, 1957.

ed. Kirk, K.E., *The Study of Theology*, London, 1939.

Laud, W., *Works*, LACT, Vol. II, Oxford, 1849; Vol. III, Oxford, 1853; Vol. IV, Oxford, 1854.

ed. Legg, J. Wickham, *Three Coronation Orders*, Henry Bradshaw Society, Vol. XIX, London, 1900.

    Tracts on the Mass, Henry Bradshaw Society Vol. XXVII, London, 1904.

    English Church Life from the Restoration to the Tractarian Movement, London, 1914.

Legg, L.G. Wickham, *English Coronation Records*, Westminster, 1901.

L'Estrange, H., *The Alliance of Divine Offices*, LACT, ed. Oxford, 1846.

Lewis, C.T., and Short, C., *A Latin Dictionary*, Oxford, 1879 (Impression of 1969).

Lietzmann, H., *The Mass of the Lord's Supper*, trans. Reeve, D.H.G., Fascicles 1-5, Leiden, no date.

Liturgical Commission, Church of England, *Prayer Book Revision in the Church of England*, London, 1958.

Liturgical Commission, Church of England, *Alternative Services: Second Series*, London, 1965.

Liturgical Commission, Church of England, *Alternative Services: Series 3, An Order for Holy Communion* London, 1971.

Liturgical Commission, Church of England, *A Commentary on Holy Communion Series 3.* London, 1971.

Liturgical Commission, Church of England, *Alternative Services: Series 1 and 2 revised. Holy Communion*, GS 217, London, 1975.

Marshall, J.S., *Hooker and the Anglican Tradition*, London, 1963.

Maskell, W., *The Ancient Liturgy of the Church of England*, London, 1846.

Maxwell, W.D., *The Liturgical Portions of the Genevan Service Book*, (John Knox's Genevan Service Book, 1556), London and Edinburgh, 1931.

Mede, J., *Works*, ed. Worthington, J., London, 1677.

Michell, G.A., *Landmarks in Liturgy*, London, 1961.

Migne, J.P., *Patrologiae Cursus Completus, (patrologia Latina)*, Vol. LXXXIX, Paris, 1850; CL, Paris, 1854.

More, P.E., and Cross, F.L., *Anglicanism*, London, 1935.

Moreton, M.J., *Made Fully Perfect, A Critique of an Order for Holy Communion Series 3*, London, 1974.

Mortimer, R.C., *Western Canon Law*, London, 1953.

Morton, T.L., *Of the Institution of the Sacrament of the Blessed Body and Blood of Christ*, etc., 1st ed., London, 1631.

McMillan, W., *The Worship of the Scottish Reformed Church, 1550-1638*, Glasgow, 1931.

Neale, J.M., and Littledale, R.F., *The Liturgies of SS. Mark, James, Clement, Chrysostom and Basil, and the Church of Malabar translated*, 2nd ed., London, 1869.

Nelson, R., *A Companion for the Festivals and Fasts of the Church of England;* first published 1704; edition used, pub. London, 1811.

Nicholls, W., *A Comment on the Book of Common Prayer, etc.* London, 1710.

ed. Nichols, J.G., *Chronicle of the Grey Friars of London*, Camden Society, Old Series LIII, London, 1852.

Oberman, H.A., *Forerunners of the Reformation*, London, 1967.

O'Connell, J.B., *The Celebration of the Mass*, Edition revised to 1956, Milwaukee, U.S.A., 1956.

Overton, J.H., *The Non-Jurors*, London, 1902.

Page, W., 'The First Book of Common Prayer and the Windsor Commission', *Church Quarterly Review,* Vol. XCVIII (1924), 51-64.

Paget, F., *Introduction to the Fifth Book of Hooker's Treatise of the Laws of Ecclesiastical Polity,* Oxford, 1899.

Peel, A., *Tracts ascribed to Richard Bancroft,* Cambridge, 1953.

Pocknee, C.E., 'The Invocation of the Holy Spirit in the Eucharistic Prayer', *Church Quarterly Review,* Vol. CLXIX (1968), 216-219.

ed. Pocock, N., *Troubles Connected with the Prayer Book of 1549,* Camden Society, New Series XXXVII, London, 1884.

Procter, F., and Frere, W.H., *A New History of the Book of Common Prayer,* 3rd impression, London, 1905.

Ramsey, A.M., and others, *The English Prayer Book 1549-1662,* Alcuin Club, London, 1963.

Ratcliff, E.C., *The English Coronation Service,* London, 1936.

The Book of Common Prayer, Alcuin Club Collections XXXVII, London, 1949.

'The Liturgical Work of Archbishop Cranmer', *Journal of Ecclesiastical History,* Vol. VII (1956), 189-203.

'The English Usage of Eucharistic Consecration, 1548-1662', *Theology,* Vol. LX (1957), 229-236, 273-280.

Ridley, J., *Thomas Cranmer,* Oxford, 1962.

ed. Robinson, H., *Original Letters Relative to the English Reformation* Parker Society, 2 Vols, with continuous pagination; 1st Portion, Cambridge, 1846; 2nd Portion, Cambridge, 1847.

Epistolae Tigurinae de Rebus Potissimum ad Ecclesiae Anglicanae Reformationem, Parker Society, Cambridge, 1848, (the Latin originals of the *Original Letters).*

Zurich Letters, Parker Society, Cambridge, 1842, (1st Series).

Zurich Letters, (Second Series), Parker Society, Cambridge, 1845.

Royal Commission, *Second Report of the Commissioners appointed to inquire into the Rubrics, Orders and Directions for regulating the Course and Conduct of Public Worship, etc., according to the use of the United Church of England and Ireland: with Minutes of Evidence and Appendices* (cited as 'Ritual Commission Report'), London, 1868.

Schillebeeckx, E., *The Eucharist,* trans. Smith, N.D., London, 1968.

Scudamore, W.E., *Notitia Eucharistica,* 1st ed., London, 1872; 2nd ed., London 1876.

ed. Sheppard, L., *The New Liturgy,* London, 1970.

Shirley, T.F., *Thomas Thirlby, Tudor Bishop,* London, 1964.

ed. Simmons, T.F., *Lay Folk's Mass Book*, Early English Text Society Edition, Original Series, 71, London, 1879.

Smyth, C.H.E., *Cranmer and the Reformation under Edward VI*, Cambridge, 1926.

Sparrow, A., *A Rationale upon the Book of Common Prayer of the Church of England;* edition used published by E. Pawlet, London, 1704.

Sprott, G.W. *Scottish Liturgies of James VI*, 1st ed., Edinburgh, 1871; 2nd ed., Edinburgh, 1901.

Worship and Offices of the Church of Scotland, Edinburgh, 1882.

The Book of Common Order, Edinburgh, 1901.

Standing Liturgical Commission of the Protestant Episcopal Church in the United States of America, Prayer Book Studies XVII, *The Liturgy of the Lord's Supper*, New York, 1966.

ed. Stephen, L., and Lee, S., *The Dictionary of National Biography*, Vol. IX, Oxford, 1921-22 (reprint).

Stephenson, A.A., 'The Views of the Mass: Medieval Linguistic Ambiguities', *Reunion*, Vol. VI (1962), 223-239; (Reprinted from *Theological Studies*, Vol. 22 (1961), U.S.A.).

Stone, Darwell, *The Holy Communion*, London, 1904.

Symonds, H.E., 'Cranmer and the Edwardine Prayer Books', *Theology*, Vol. XLIX (1946), 171-176, 200-204.

Taylor, Jeremy, *Works, ed.*, Heber, R., Vol. IX (of an edition of 15 Vols.), London 1839.

Thorndike, H., *Works*, LACT, Vol. I, pt. I, Oxford, 1844; Vol. I, pt. II, Oxford, 1844; Vol. IV. pt. I, Oxford, 1852; Vol. IV. pt. II, Oxford, 1853; Vol. V, Oxford, 1854.

Timms G.B., 'Dixit Cranmer', *Church Quarterly Review*, Vol. CXLIII (1946/7) 217-234; Vol. CXLIV (1947), 33-51.

Tomlinson, J.T., *The Great Parliamentary Debate in 1548 on the Lord's Supper*, London, no date.

Thompson, Bard, *Liturgies of the Western Church*, New York, 1962.

Usher, R.G., *The Reconstruction of the English Church*, 2 Vols., London, 1910.

Vogel, C., *Introduction aux Sources de l'Histoire du Culte Chrétien au moyen age*, Spoleto, Italy, 1966.

Waterland, D., *A Review of the Doctrine of the Eucharist*, ed. Van Mildert (in 1856), Oxford, 1896.

ed. Weber, R., *Bibla Sacra Iuxta Vulgatum Versionem*, 2 Vols., Stuttgart, 1969.

Wheatly, C., *The Church of England Man's Companion, or a Rational Illustration of the Harmony, Excellency, and Usefulness of the Book of Common Prayer, etc.*, Oxford, 1710.

A *Rational Illustration of the Book of Common Prayer,
etc.* 3rd ed., (the item immediately above this one is the 1st),
London, 1720.

Whitaker, E.C., *Martin Bucer and the Book of Common Prayer,* Alcuin
Club Collections 55, Southend-on-Sea, 1974.

ed. Wigan, B., *The Liturgy in English,* London, 1962.

Wilkins, D., *Concilia Magnae Britanniae et Hiberniae,* Vol. 4, *ab Anno
MDXLVI ad Annum MDCCXVII,* London, 1737.

Willis, G.G., *Immixtio et Consecratio,* unpublished MS notes, no date
or place.

ed. Wordsworth, C., *The Manner of the Coronation of King Charles the
First of England,* Henry Bradshaw Society, Vol. II, London, 1892.

Woywood, S., *The New Canon Law,* 7th Ed., New York, 1929.

B. *Editions and Versions of Liturgical Texts.*

Sacramentarium Veronense (Ver. 85), ed. Mohlberg, L.C., (Rerum
Ecclesiasticarum Documenta, Series Maior, Fontes I), Rome, 1956.

Liber Sacramentorum Romanae Aecclesiae Ordinis Anni Circuli (Vat.
Reg. 316), ed. Mohlberg, L.C., (Rerum Ecclesiasticarum Documenta,
Series Maior, Fontes IV), Rome, 1960.

Missale Romanum, Mediolani, 1474, Henry Bradshaw Society, ed.
Lippe, R.; Vol. I (Henry Bradshaw Society Vol. XVII), London,
1899; Vol. II (Henry Bradshaw Society Vol. XXXIII), London,
1907.

Missale ad Usum Sarum, ed. Dickinson, F.H., Burntisland, 1861-1883.

The Sarum Missal, edited from Three Early Manuscripts, ed. Legg,
J. Wickham, Oxford, 1916.

The Sarum Missal in English, London, 1868.

The Daily Missal and Liturgical Manual, compiled from the Missale
Romanum, revised Kuergens, S.P., Laverty and Sons, Leeds, 1936.

*The Missal, Compiled by lawful authority from the Missale Romanum.
A new edition agreeable with the Vatican Typical Edition,* Burns,
Oates and Washbourne, London, 1928.

Missale Romanum of 1970, Editio Typica, The Vatican, 1970, and
various English Versions.

General Instruction on the Roman Missal (Principles and Rubrics),
English Translation, London, 1973.

The Order of Communion, 1548, ed. Wilson, H.A., Henry Bradshaw
Society, Vol. XXXIV, London, 1908.

Liturgies of King Edward VI, Parker Society Edition, ed. Ketley, J.,
Cambridge, 1844.

The First and Second Prayer Books of Edward VI, (with an
introduction by E.C.S. Gibson), Everyman ed., London, 1910.

Liturgies and Occasional Forms of Prayer set forth in the Reign of Queen Elizabeth, Parker Society Edition, ed., Clay, E.H., Cambridge, 1847.

The Prayer Book of Queen Elizabeth, 1559, (with an introduction by W. Bonham), Edinburgh, 1911.

The Book of Common Prayer of 1662, various printings.

The Book of Common Prayer, with the Additions and Deviations proposed in 1928, edition published by the Cambridge University Press, London, no date.

Holy Communion, Alternative Services, First Series, AS 120, London, 1967.

An Order for Holy Communion, Alternative Services, Second Series, AS 220, London, 1967.

An Order for Holy Communion, Alternative Services Series 3, AS 320, London, 1973.

The Scottish Book of Common Prayer, 1912, an edition published in Edinburgh, no date.

The Scottish Book of Common Prayer, 1929, an edition published in Cambridge and Edinburgh, no date.

The Scottish Communion Offices of 1637, 1735, 1755, 1764 and 1889, together with the English Liturgy of 1549, arranged to show their variations, P.A. Lempriere, Edinburgh, 1909.

The Book of Common Prayer . . . According to the Use of the Church of Ireland, 1926, an edition published in Dublin, 1960.

The Book of Common Prayer . . . According to the Use of the Church of India, Pakistan, Burma and Ceylon, 1960, an edition published in Madras, 1961.

An Order for the Celebration of the Holy Eucharist . . ., The Church in Wales, Church in Wales Publications, Penarth, 1966.

A Book of Common Prayer . . . for Use in the Church of the Province of South Africa, 1954, an edition published in London, 1961.

The Book of Common Prayer . . . According to the Use of the Anglican Church of Canada, 1959, an edition published in Toronto, no date.

The Book of Common Prayer . . . According to the Use of the Protestant Episcopal Church in the United States of America, 1928, an edition published in New York, no date.

(PECUSA). *Services for Trial Use,* New York, 1971.

(PECUSA), *Authorized Services 1973.* New York, 1973.

This Form and Order of the Service . . . Ceremonies . . . in The Coronation of their Majesties King Edward VII and Queen Alexandra, London, 1902.

The Coronation of Her Majesty Queen Elizabeth II, Approved Souvenir
Programme, (contains the complete text of the Coronation Rite used
in 1953), London, 1953.

The Church of South India, *The Book of Common Worship,* as
authorised by the Synod 1962, an edition published in London,
1963.

Index

Administration, Words of 74, 80,
     88, 89, 113, 114, 126, 129,
     137, 162, 168, 180, 191, 212
Alcuin 16, 35, 107
Amalarius 35-39
Ambrose 21, 56, 111, 162, 163
Anamnesis 129, 173, 180, 204,
     208, 210-212
Andrewes, L. 115, 144
Andrieu, M. 34, 35
Anglican, -ism 11-13, 34, 35, 40,
     41, 72, 88, 93, 96, 97, 100,
     102, 106, 108-111, 119, 121,
     123, 127, 130, 131, 133, 134,
     139, 141-144, 152, 156, 163,
     167, 168, 170, 171, 176-178,
     187, 192, 202, 203, 209-216,
     218, 220, 222, 223
Anglican Orders, Ordinal 13, 118
Aquinas, Thomas 41-44, 46, 47,
     49
Articles, 39 89, 105
       42 89
       Irish 105
       Visitation   91, 98,
             100-105, 154, 183
Ascension 20, 62
       Day 17

Babbage, S.B. 97, 100
Bancroft, R.   91, 96-98, 101,
             108, 218
Baptism 55, 56, 174
Basil, Liturgy of 21, 71, 72, 162,
             163
Baxter, R. 139-142, 219
Baxter's Liturgy 139-141, 163
Benedictus   70, 179, 186, 189
Bennet, T. 160-162
Biel, G. 49, 50
Boniface 33
Book of Common Order 134, 142,
             145, 146, 148
Bramhall, J. 118
Brett, T. 168, 169, 173, 181-188,
             190, 191, 193

Brooks, P. N. 58, 59
Broxap, H. 177, 178
Bucer, M.   82-84, 159, 164, 165
Buchanan, C. O.   210, 211, 229

Calvary   20, 21, 24, 26, 27, 30,
             42, 49, 193
Calvin, J. 159, 186
Canon, Roman, Latin, Gelasian
     15, 17-22, 26, 27, 30-33, 35,
     39, 42, 43, 45-49, 67, 70, 71,
          113, 120, 123, 186, 187,
          195-197, 199, 207, 216
     1549 70, 76, 77, 129, 167,
             186
     1637   146, 147, 151, 167,
             220
     1662 164
     1764 189
Canons, of 1604   95-100, 105,
             150, 183, 219, 225
       of 1640 102
       Irish 105
       Scottish 105
Canon Law   91, 95, 97, 101
Caroline Divines   12, 116, 130,
     131, 142, 145, 147, 148, 151,
             156, 178, 219, 221
Catechism 96, 154, 170
Cautels   47, 48, 63, 201, 217
Celebrare 25
Censura, of M. Bucer 83
Ceremonial   15, 33-35, 45, 49,
     132, 143, 154, 200, 206, 214
Charles I, King   106, 107, 115,
             118, 145, 150, 168
Cheke, Sir John 58, 59, 82
Christ   18, 21, 22, 26-29, 33,
     41-44, 49, 51, 53-57, 61, 67,
     68, 71, 73, 75, 76, 81, 93, 95,
     100, 111, 113-120, 122, 123,
     125, 130-132, 138, 139, 141,
     162, 163, 172, 173, 193, 198,
             211, 221
Christmas 17

Clementine liturgy, that of
Apostolic Constitutions Bk
VIII   112, 113, 122, 123, 164,
178, 180, 182, 185, 186,
191, 221
Comber, T.   156-158, 162, 164,
184
Commemoracio   27
Commixture   32-40, 43, 209, 213,
216, 224
Communicantes   17, 70
Communion   congregational
28, 33
of laity   28, 43,
45, 95
of sick   34, 38, 76,
81, 114, 160
Commonwealth period   121, 128,
153, 177
Concomitance   38, 42, 44
Consecrare   35, 36, 38
Consecration   11, 13, 21, 22, 31,
39, 41-44, 46-49, 69, 70, 83,
90, 93-96, 98, 100, 102-105,
108, 110, 112-123, 126-132,
136, 137, 139-142, 147,
149-152, 155, 157-176 passim,
180, 182, 183, 192-194, 196,
198, 201, 203-211, 213, 215,
216, 218, 229
by contact   32, 33, 34-40
supplementary   11, 34, 35,
40, 63, 69, 76, 82, 83, 91, 92,
96, 97, 99, 101-106, 113,
115-117, 127, 131, 137
146-152, 154, 155, 157-176
passim, 181, 183, 184, 191,
200-209, 212, 213, 215-229
Convocation   61-63, 97, 219
Irish   105
Coronation   106-109
Cosin, J.   104, 118-121, 142,
148, 149
Counter Reformation   73
Cowper, W.   135-139, 145, 146,
148
Cranmer, T.   25, 50, 52-63, 65-78,
80, 82-86, 89, 90, 93, 95, 106,
133, 134, 142, 152, 153, 159,
203, 218, 219
Cranmer's *Defence*   52-59, 61, 63,
68, 74, 76, 77, 79, 80, 81, 85, 89
Cuming, G. J.   66, 121

Day, bishop of Chichester   65-68
Defects in celebration   46-49,
200-202, 216
Deferre   25
Dix, G.   209, 210, 246
Doctrine Commission, 1922   208
Donaldson, G.   135, 145-148
Donum   16, 19, 20, 27, 28
Dowden, J.   72, 156, 177, 178,
188-190, 207
Doxology   18, 31, 180
Duchesne, L.   34
Dugmore, C. W.   121, 131
Duppa, B   103

Easter   16, 17, 99
Edward VI, King   82, 85, 89, 98,
106
Elements   22, 122, 126, 130-132,
138, 158, 159, 166, 173-175,
185, 192, 204, 212
Elevation   31, 45, 73, 120, 125
Elizabeth I, Queen   88, 89, 91,
98, 100, 106, 134, 218
Elizabethan Church   90-92, 96
Settlement 88, 92, 96,
98, 110, 192
Ellebracht, M. P.   22, 25, 27
Epiclesis   12, 71, 72, 79, 113,
123, 125, 128, 129, 146, 147,
151, 152, 158, 167, 170, 180,
181, 183-187, 189-191, 193,
203-210, 221, 222
1549   71, 72, 149, 152,
165, 184
Epiphany   17
Eucharistic action   18, 23-31, 33,
35, 93, 128, 197, 209,
213, 215
gifts   19, 24, 25,
28-30, 71, 199
prayers   34, 124, 186,
199, 211, 222
presence   13, 21, 22,
29, 30, 41, 44, 49, 55, 62, 63,
69, 76, 77, 86, 93-95, 108, 110,
112, 114, 118, 122, 123, 126,
130, 131, 142, 157-176 passim,
187, 192, 196, 208, 217

Eucharistic sacrifice   17-21, 23,
    25-27, 30, 41, 47, 49, 50, 53,
    54, 69-71, 73, 74, 77, 112,
    120, 124, 156, 157-176 passim,
    180, 189, 192-194, 196, 198,
                            220, 221
            theology   12, 28, 30,
    41, 49-51, 79, 124, 129, 132,
    168, 178, 182, 187, 192, 204,
        206, 214, 215, 217, 220

Florence, Council of   187
Fraction   44, 73, 135, 149, 189,
                            198, 204
Frere, W. H.   12, 46, 66, 91,
                            208, 209
Fuller, T.   65, 66

Gardiner, S. 52, 57-59, 69, 71, 74,
                            75, 77
Gasquet, F. A. and Bishop, E.
                63, 64, 66, 67
Gelasian Sacramentary,
    Gelasianum   15-19, 36
Genuflection   31, 45
Ghost, Holy see Holy Spirit
Good Friday   34-38
Great Parliamentary Debate on
    the Lord's Supper   59, 66-69
Great Rebellion   119, 153
Gregorian Sacramentary   16
Gregory II, Pope   33
Grisbrooke, W. J.   177, 178, 186

Hanc Igitur   16-19, 48, 70
Hadrianum   107
Hampton Court Conference   96,
                            98
Holy Spirit   55, 71, 72, 119, 123,
    138-140, 147, 165, 169, 170,
    172-175, 180, 193, 198, 199,
                    210, 212, 221
Hooker, R.   92, 94-95, 108, 110,
        111, 131, 153, 175, 219
Hooper, J.   82, 84
Horne, R.   85
Hostia   20, 23-25

Immolare   25, 41
Injunctions   98, 100-105

Institution Narrative   17, 20, 22,
    31, 39, 42, 43, 45, 48, 49, 64,
    70, 73, 80, 83, 89, 90, 92, 98,
    99, 100, 102-105, 111-113,
    115-117, 119-123, 127-131,
    134, 136-138, 140, 141, 146,
        148, 149, 151, 152, 155,
    157-176 passim, 180, 182-185,
    189-191, 193, 194, 197, 198,
    201, 203, 204, 207-211, 213,
    215, 216, 218, 219, 221, 222
Intercession(s)   43, 70, 77, 79,
                    186, 190, 204
Ireland   97
Irish Church   105

James I, King   96, 97, 106-108,
                        115, 135
Jewel, J.   92-94
Johnson, John   156, 168-171,
    173-176, 178, 180, 183, 185,
            187, 188, 191, 193
Johnson, Robert   40, 89-92, 96,
                            218
Jungmann, J. A.   31, 34
Justus Jonas, catechism of   58

Knox, J.   133, 142, 145, 219
Knox's liturgy   133-135

Lambeth Conference(s)   209
Langforde's Meditations   51, 140
Last Supper   33, 116, 118, 130,
                175, 182, 187, 193
Lateran Definition of 1215   49
Latin (language)   23, 24, 31, 67,
                        106-108
Latin liturgical tradition   33, 34,
                            47
Latin Rite: see Rite, Roman
Laud, W.   102, 106, 124-127, 142,
                    145, 147, 151
Laudian   101-104, 118, 144, 146
                    147, 150
Legg, J. Wickham   48, 107
Leonine Sacramentary   16, 18
Lent   17
L'Estrange, H.   110, 111-115, 149
Libera nos   36, 74
Liturgical Commission, English
                            213

Lord's Prayer   36, 39, 74, 128,
    136, 149, 161, 178, 191,
        204, 216
Lutheran, -ism   58-61, 74, 77, 87
    94, 166, 170, 182

Manual acts 73, 92, 113, 120, 127,
    129, 137, 140-142, 148, 149,
    167, 180, 189, 204, 205, 211
Mary I, Queen   73
Maskell, W.   47
Mass of the pre-sanctified   34, 36,
        39
Maundy Thursday   17, 18, 34,
        36-38
Memento Domine   16, 17, 19, 70
Middle Ages   13, 39, 43, 45, 46,
        215, 216
Missal, Roman, 1474   48
        1570   16-18, 38,
    67, 107, 182, 194-196,
        197, 200
        1970 194, 196-200
Montague, R.   103, 104
Morton, T.   115-117, 127, 138,
    147, 150, 175, 183, 184, 219
Munus   16, 19, 23, 27, 107
Mysterium   23, 24, 27

Nelson, R.   171-173, 193
New Testament   50, 56, 94, 197
Nicholls, W.   156, 158-162
Nobis quoque   18
Nominalism   50, 51
Non-jurors   161, 168, 173, 177,
    178, 180, 186, 190, 191, 193
North End or Side   125, 178

Oblatio   19, 23, 25
Oblation   123, 136, 146, 149,
    151, 156, 158, 162, 168-170,
    181, 183, 185, 186, 189, 190,
    191, 193, 207, 212, 221, 222
Offering verbs   25
Offerre   25
Offertory   32, 33, 45, 69, 70,
    106, 110, 112, 156, 160, 162,
    164, 178, 189, 196, 198-201,
        204
Old Catholics   202

Orate fratres   199
Order of Communion, 1548
    52, 58, 60-65, 70, 74-76, 90,
        150, 158, 159, 217, 225
Ordo Romanus Primus   15, 26,
    31-35, 39, 45, 49, 200
    VI   34, 35, 39
Orthodox (Eastern)   13, 202, 215
Oxford Movement   167, 206, 214,
        223

Packer, J. I.   84
Page, W.   64, 65
Pan Anglican Documents   210
Parker, M.   85, 89, 98
Parliament   61, 83, 84, 85, 89,
        150, 206, 218
Passion   20, 43, 51, 114, 120,
        172, 189
Pentecost   17
Pius V, Pope   194
Post-communion prayer(s) (Latin
    rite)   15, 22, 24, 27-31, 195,
        196, 199
Prayer Book,
    1549   64-68, 72, 76-79, 82,
        87, 89, 113, 123, 158,
        161, 163, 164, 225
    1552   78, 83, 88, 89, 126,
        159, 163, 164, 225
    1559   88, 89, 91, 218, 225
    1604   97, 110, 141, 148, 225
    1637   96, 105, 124, 143,
        145, 158
    1662   96, 150, 151, 157-176
    passim, 188, 207, 209, 225
Prayer of Humble Access   74, 77,
        79, 120, 149, 180, 191
Presbyterian   133, 143, 145, 154,
        177
Propitiare   25
Protestant   71, 76, 78, 105, 142,
        154, 159, 182, 194
Puritan 96-99, 101, 102, 121, 127,
    134-145, 149-152, 156, 176,
        219

Quam oblationem   16-19, 21, 71,
    113, 158, 184, 186, 207

Ratcliff, E. C.   90, 92, 152, 210
Receptionism, real   95, 96, 108,
        111, 115, 121, 130,
        158-160, 162, 176,
        192, 220
    virtual   61, 70
Reformation   49, 94, 88, 89, 111,
        145, 152, 156, 194
Reformers   25, 50, 51
Requiem   45
Reservation   31, 34, 36, 57, 83,
        111, 114, 130, 160, 181
Restoration   101, 111, 118, 123,
        148, 152, 153, 171, 177, 193,
        220, 221
Resurrection   20
Ridley, N.   59, 64, 78, 84
Rite,
    Byzantine   112, 113
    Roman, Latin, Western   13, 25,
        41, 50, 69, 74, 75, 106,
        112, 157, 162, 164,
        184, 187, 194-202,
        215-217, 220
    American 1928   204, 228
    English 1549   44, 52, 53,
        58-61, 66, 68-77, 79-82,
        85-87, 89, 123, 164, 171,
        179-182, 186, 188, 190, 191,
        193, 218, 221
        1552   52, 61, 68, 73,
        79-82, 84-87, 149, 164,
        185, 188, 218
        1559   90, 98, 212
        1662   79, 150, 151,
        153, 164, 171, 173, 175, 177,
        179-181, 184, 186, 189-191,
        193, 203, 206, 211, 212,
        220, 222, 224
        Series 2   210, 212, 226
        Series 1 and 2 Revised
        213, 226
        Series 3   212, 213, 226
    Non-Jurors 1718   177-182,
        188-191, 193, 221, 225
        1734   177
    Scottish 1637   106, 137,
        145-148, 150, 151, 162,
        164, 166, 171, 179-181,
        185, 188-191, 193, 219,
        221, 224, 227
        1764   154, 177, 178,
        188-193, 204, 221,
        222, 227
        1912   203
        1929   203, 204, 207,
        228
    South African 1929   205, 207,
        208, 228
Ritual Commission Report of
    1868   101
Rubric, 'black'   81, 82, 85, 88,
        114, 151
Rubric, concerning the remains
    80, 105, 111, 114, 150, 160

Sacramentaries   35, 42
Sacramentum   23, 24, 27
Sacrifice: see Eucharistic Sacrifice
Sacrificium   16, 19, 23, 24, 27
Sanctificare   35, 36, 38
Sanctus   15, 16, 70, 128, 149,
        186, 189
Sarum   37, 47, 48, 69, 73, 74,
        76, 78
Savoy Conference   149
Scholasticism   37, 39, 41, 44, 48
Scottish Church   105, 135, 177
Scotland   97, 124, 134, 135, 142,
        145, 178, 188
Second Vatican Council   196, 217
Secret Prayers   15, 19, 22-27, 30,
        70, 106-108, 195, 196, 199
Sparrow, A.   65, 110, 131, 150
Spirit, Holy: see Holy Spirit
Stone, Darwell   206
Supplices te   18, 19, 21
Supra quae   18
Supplementary consecration: see
    Consecration, supplementary
Suscipere   25

Taylor, J.   128-130, 178
Te igitur   16, 18, 19, 48, 70
Thirlby, T.   64, 66, 67, 68
Thomism, Thomist   198
Thorndike, H.   121, 123, 142
Tomlinson, J.   66
Toronto Congress   210
Transubstantiation   42, 44, 49, 50,
        54, 114, 119, 122, 129, 130,
        151, 157, 160, 170, 186, 187
Trent, Council of   194, 195, 197,
        200, 217

Unde et memores   18-21, 49, 73
Uniformity, Act of,
    1549   68, 86
    1552   81, 82, 86, 218
    1559   88
Usages   187, 188, 191
Usher, R. G.   97-99

Vere Dignum section(s)   15, 16
Vernacular   45, 70, 78, 200, 205,
                      214, 223
Vestments, Ecclesiastical vesture
                      84, 88
Viaticum   34, 38
Votive masses   16, 45

Waterland, D.   173-176, 192, 222
Wedderburn, J.   145-147, 151
Westminster Directory   134, 138,
                  139, 141, 142
Wheatly, C.   156, 161-169, 173,
                  182, 184, 207
Whitgift, J.   96, 99, 108, 111
Williams, J.,   bishop of Lincoln
   and archbishop of York
                  101, 102
Windsor Commission   65-69
Wren, M.   103, 148, 149

Zwinglianism   126, 129